WOMEN IN GOD'S PRESENCE

Women in God's Presence

A Daily Devotional Compiled by

Delores Taylor

CHRISTIAN PUBLICATIONS
Camp Hill, Pennsylvania

Christian Publications
3825 Hartzdale Drive, Camp Hill, Pa 17011

Faithful, biblical publishing since 1883

Trade Paper ISBN: 0-87509-631-X
©1988 by Christian Publications
All rights reserved
Printed in the United States of America

95 96 97 98 99 5 4 3 2 1

Scripture quotations are from the HOLY BIBLE: NEW INTERNATIONAL VERSION. Copyright © 1973, 1978, 1984 by the International Bible Society. Used by permission of Zondervan Bible Publishers.

"Found in the Field" from *Make Warm Noises*, by Gloria Gaither. Used by permission.

My special thanks to Anita Bailey, Bernice Verbyla, Gil Moore and Sue Stephens for the many hours of editing and proofreading that went into this project. I also wish to express my sincere appreciation to Helen Crimm, my special friend, secretary, advisor and prayer partner.

To Mary Bailey, who with her dear husband, Dr. Nathan Bailey, was involved in a tragic automobile accident and was unable to make her contribution.

To Elizabeth Jackson, who soon after completing her contribution passed into the presence of her Lord.

And to Anne Meloon, whose deepest desire was to be able to write her contribution, but due to her sudden illness and death, was unable to fulfill this desire.

FOREWORD

The title of Dee Taylor's devotional book, *Women in God's Presence*, reminds me of her life. Varied and colorful ministries have surrounded her. She is a motivator and an encourager. Perhaps her most notable contribution is the ministry of music God has given to her. Singing in many different cities across America, she is an outstanding witness for Christ!

As a member of the Portsmouth Christian and Missionary Alliance Church, she has been active in every aspect of ministry: teaching in the Sunday school, working in the church office, giving volunteer time in the Christian school, singing in the choir, providing special music. These are just a few of the activities to which she gives herself untiringly. In addition, Dee is a devoted wife and mother, deeply involved in the lives of her husband and children. Now she has the happy privilege of being a grandmother as well. In all of her many and varied activities, she has never lost sight of the primary goal of her life — knowing God and making Him known.

Here is a book that will make women thirsty to know more about God. Women from many walks of life have been selected to speak through the printed page, sharing their life experiences. Each day's meditation is full of helpful insights from the Word of God.

I heartily recommend this devotional book to all women as a practical guidebook for daily meditation.

MARTHA H. MANGHAM
GENERAL WOMEN'S MISSIONARY
PRAYER FELLOWSHIP PRESIDENT
THE CHRISTIAN AND MISSIONARY ALLIANCE
8/12/87

His Strength

Come to me, all you who are weary and burdened, and I will give you rest. Take my yoke upon you and learn from me, for I am gentle and humble in heart, and you will find rest for your souls. For my yoke is easy and my burden is light (MATTHEW 11:28–30).

These familiar verses from Matthew's Gospel have often been used to point weary, sin-sick sinners to the Savior — and rightly so. They also hold a world of meaning for the child of God, for in these verses can be found rest and refreshing, encouragement and instruction and abundance of resource for life and service.

God's children often expend a great amount of time and effort to complete a task for the Lord only to find physical, mental and, yes, even spiritual weariness resulting. When the burden of it all weighs heavily, when problems seemingly have no answers, is it not sweet to hear those comforting words: "Come to me . . . I will give you rest. . . . my yoke is easy and my burden is light"?

Struggling Christian, determined to be all that God wants you to be, are you striving in your own strength? Stop the self-effort and get into the yoke with Jesus, your Savior. His yoke is *easy*, His burden is *light*. If what you are carrying is *hard* and *heavy*, then it must not be of His making.

Everything the child of God needs to live the Christian life is in Jesus. He is the reservoir of life and power. Without Him we can do nothing!

Come . . . learn from Him . . . find rest in Him every day. Do His work in His strength. ESTHER KING

JANUARY 2

Freedom from Offenses

Great peace have they who love your law, and nothing can make them stumble (PSALM 119:165).

Do I really have peace of heart? Do I daily enjoy the experience of peace, or am I as easily disturbed as the worldling over things that happen minute by minute in the daily routine of living?

What a tremendous promise is contained in this verse! If we delight in God's Word, we may have freedom from agitation and unrest. Just think: nothing, but nothing will offend us or make us stumble in our walk in the Spirit.

How easily we are offended by little things. Someone takes the parking space we were headed for and we are offended — little things rob us of the peace Jesus wants us to experience.

It is not enough to want peace. Peter says that we must seek peace and pursue it (1 Peter 3:11). He also tells us that love "covers over a multitude of sins" (4:8). I once heard a man of God say, "I laid down my critical spirit and picked up a bundle of covers." Love will cover the potential offender and offense and put out the fire.

This is not done by our simply deciding to change our ways. The power comes when we receive His Word. The Holy Spirit then reveals the Father's desire for us — death to self, conformity to the image of Jesus and total abandonment to the Spirit to work all of this in us.

What a lovely fragrance of Christ will then arise from our lives to bring blessing into our homes and to those whom we touch in our daily lives.   JEAN HOTALEN

Maidservants for the Lord

"I am the Lord's servant," Mary answered. "May it be to me as you have said" (LUKE 1:38).

There are three people living in each of us: the one we think we are, the one other people think we are and the one God knows we are. Millions of dollars are spent annually at beauty salons and women's dress shops trying to alter the woman we think we are. But the woman I really am is the woman God knows me to be.

God has proven our value by spilling the priceless blood of His Son. He loves us and cares about us. But only when we as women are completely surrendered to God will we know real peace. Mary, the mother of Jesus, was a beautiful example of this kind of woman.

When the angel told Mary she would conceive and bring forth a Son named Jesus, there was an immediate surrender of herself to the will of God. In her I see a person who had a proper idea of herself and was at peace with God. It was not, "I thought you would choose me," or even "I'm not worthy." She allowed God to be God in her life.

Do you know who you are? Or are you still trying to be what others think you are? Have you acknowledged that God really knows who you are anyway? Do you know He loves you? Love Him in return and your life will be what God wants it to be. Surrender fully to His love and you will find peace.   MERLYN BARKMAN

Keep Shining

In the same way, let your light shine before men, that they may see your good deeds and praise your Father in heaven (MATTHEW 5:16).

This verse was dramatically illustrated when we were missionaries in Vietnam during the war. While our husbands were away from home, a missionary friend and I were invited by a Korean general to an important military ceremony. The only women amidst thousands of Korean, Vietnamese and American troops, we sat on the reviewing stand with the three-nation generals to watch the elaborate ceremonies and observe the presentation of medals to individuals and units. Later, after hors d'oeuvres, we were among the guests selected to receive lovely gifts.

Still thoroughly mystified as to why we had been invited, we were conducted to the general's mess where we ate a sumptuous meal on crested china and gold-plated flatware.

Finally, at the end of the meal, the Korean general called for his interpreter and, after polite opening conversation on both sides, said to me, "I am sure you are wondering why I invited you here today!" He continued with this remarkable comment: "When I was a small boy in Korea, an American lady missionary led me to Jesus Christ, and I never had an opportunity to thank her. So wherever I go, I look up the missionaries and honor them!"

Someone had faithfully let her light shine, and a little boy, one day to be a leader of his nation, came into its light-path.

There are no doubt many who have illuminated our paths through this life. As we are obedient to His command there will be those whose lives we may brighten. Let your light so shine!   CHARLOTTE STEMPLE

What Kind of People Are We?

"The day of the Lord will come like a thief. . . . Since everything will be destroyed . . . what kind of [person] ought you to be?" (2 PETER 3:10–11).

Washing windows is not one of my favorite household tasks, so I had someone wash them for me. After each washing, I noticed there were still streaks and spots on them. This continued for several months until I decided to wash them myself. I washed each window three times. They were so clean and shiny—no more spots!

The next morning I went into the den just as the sun was coming up. What a beautiful day it promised to be. But wait! As the sunlight shone on my clean windows, I was suddenly aware of streaks and spots that were entirely unnoticed the day before. The windows had looked clean until the sun shone through at just the right angle for a brief period that morning.

Just like those windows, we may "look" clean and think we are spotless, but when the light of the Holy Spirit shines in our hearts, we see blemishes that we were not aware of.

In light of the knowledge that Christ's return could be at any moment, what kind of people should we be? Peter tells us clearly that we are to live godly and holy lives (2 Peter 3:11); we are to be looking for and hastening His coming (3:12); we are to be spotless, blameless and at peace with Him (3:14); we are to be on our guard (3:17); and we are to grow in grace and knowledge of our Lord (3:18).

The daily cleansing by the blood of Jesus and the daily ministry of His Word can make us the kind of people we ought to be. LOIS NABORS

Sunrise Over Jerusalem

Weeping may remain for a night, but rejoicing comes in the morning (PSALM 30:5).

As a pilgrim to the Holy City, one of my most cherished memories is of a quiet and holy moment of sunrise high on Mount Olivet, looking down on an orange path of light bathing Jerusalem in brilliant splendor.

After our daughter's serious accident, there were many months of painful convalescence. Awakened often during the night or early morning by a telephone call, we would try to comfort her over the phone or by going to her bedside.

At dawn one morning a tearful voice pleaded, "Please come, Mom, I'm hurting so much." Though I was tired, I decided that I should go to her.

As I backed the car out of the garage, the tears flowed. Could I go through another day like the last few? I began to pray silently as I drove, *Lord, give me the assurance that today will be a little easier than yesterday, for Carol and for all of us.*

As I ended my prayer, I turned the corner of our street and just then an orange sunrise, so much like the one in Jerusalem, flung itself over the roofs and treetops and flooded my face and the car with its bright warm glow.

Immediately God's special presence strengthened me. I knew He was with me and my family and especially with our daughter. Then a line of a song came to me. "It's a brand new day." Moments later, refreshed and ready for whatever the day might hold, I stood at Carol's bedside comforting and strengthening her with those same words, "It's a brand new day!"   ARVELLA SCHULLER

Time for Loving

There is a time for everything, and a season for every activity under heaven: . . . a time to love (ECCLESIASTES 3:1, 8).

When our first grandson was just a toddler, I had the joy of being his babysitter on many occasions. Routinely, about mid-morning, I would announce, "Time for a tea party," and we would sit down to Ritz crackers with peanut butter and a small glass of milk. One day Jeffie came to the kitchen sink where I was working and announced to me, "Time for loving, Grandma." Joyfully I picked him up and we shared hugs and kisses, then away he went to his play. This became a happy ritual for the rest of my baby-sitting days.

I could not help but think how pleased our Heavenly Father must be when we come to Him and say, "Time for loving." This "time" is when we forget about our work and other interests and just take time to read His Word and communicate with Him by prayer, telling Him of our love for Him. We not only speak of our love, we also demonstrate it by our very act of using that time exclusively for fellowship with Him.

We have a good example in God's Word of one who took "time for loving." Luke 10:38–42 tells of Mary who "sat at the Lord's feet listening to what he said." We hear Jesus' approval of Mary's "time for loving" in these words, "Mary has chosen what is better, and it will not be taken away from her."

Let us take time to tell the Lord we love Him and make time to show it.   LUCILLE A. FRASER

Be Still

Be still, and know that I am God (PSALM 46:10).

In these pressure-filled days, this admonition is difficult to keep. There is such a feeling of restlessness and hurry all around us. "I must do this and that; I must go here and there. . . ."

We Christians find ourselves in a real battle. It is so easy to be distracted when so many activities are crying for our time and attention. God commands us to "Be still, and know that [He is] God."

In Luke's account of Mary and Martha, we see that Martha loved Jesus Christ, but she was greatly occupied with service. She became anxious and irritable and lost the joy that should be part of serving. While Martha was bustling about and complaining, Mary sat quietly, listening to Jesus' words, experiencing the joy of getting to know her Lord and the sweetness of fellowship with Him. Jesus commended Mary for her choice.

There has to be a *balance* of fellowship and service. We are not always to sit, but when we allow service to come before our fellowship, we lose the joy of serving.

In First Corinthians 1:9, Paul tells us that God has called us into the fellowship of Christ. Regardless of the demand of duty and the invitation of many activities, it is vital to our Christian growth and joy that we spend time with Jesus. We must *be still* and listen to Him speak through His Word. We must take time to express ourselves to Him in prayer.

The desire of Paul's heart was to know Christ. May this be the desire of our own hearts.   DANA JACOBSON

Transparency

And we, who with unveiled faces all reflect the Lord's glory, are being transformed into his likeness (2 CORINTHIANS 3:18).

A friend astonished me with a simple but revealing observation as we discussed a local women's group. "The trouble with those women is that they all act alike. No one is being real!"

Her statement revealed a problem that is prevalent today. Many women find it difficult to be genuine, to show others who they really are and how they really feel. In a world where imitations and look-alikes are common, many have learned to put on a facade that hides the real person.

When I was in high school, I considered myself a good actress. Without a doubt, however, my most convincing roles were performed offstage. I was very aware that my peers were engaged in the same subtle deceptions.

At age 17 I gave my life irrevocably to Jesus Christ. Almost immediately I made the frightening discovery that I did not really know myself. My fervent prayer became, "Lord, reveal to me what kind of person You created when You made me. Then help me to live out who I am, truthfully and consistently."

In order to be women of God, it is imperative that we stop putting on airs, being imitations and look-alikes, and become transparent. Jesus came to be the light of the world, and godly women must determine to reflect that light. This can only take place as we "remove the veil" and allow others to see us as we really are. At that point of total honesty and humility, the fresh, vital touch of our Lord will rest upon us. We will find His presence ministering to our deepest needs, and He will be free to reach out and minister through us to those around us.   NANCY MATHISON

Comfort in Christ

God is our refuge and strength, an ever present help in trouble (PSALM 46:1).

I memorized this psalm years ago and it has been a comfort on many occasions. I especially remember one day.

I received a letter from my youngest son who was attending college. In it he voiced his hurt, disappointment and loneliness at the loss of a dear friend.

I went out to the garden to gather strawberries, but my thoughts were of my son. So many times I had reached out to meet his need. It seemed only yesterday that I had held him in my arms after a fall or extended a hand to steady the little feet as they took those first tottering steps. We worked over math assignments together. Whether the basketball game was a victory or a loss, I was there to encourage him. But today he was far away and I felt helpless.

I decided to write to him, tell him I loved him and was praying for him and remind him that God was his comfort. Often he would close his letters to me with a Bible verse, so with my letter I added Psalm 46:1, "God is our refuge and strength," and 1 Peter 5:7, "Cast all your anxiety on him because he cares for you."

Friend, God is the God of all comfort. He wants to help you today. Call on Him; He is always near. MELBA STUMBO

Continual Care

The Lord will guide you always; he will satisfy your needs in a sun-scorched land . . . you will be a well-watered garden, like a spring whose waters never fail (ISAIAH 58:11).

The desire to do God's will does not originate in our own heart; it has been implanted within us by God. It is not that He is a tyrannical master who gloats over the blind submission of His subjects; He has given us this desire because He loves us and longs to continually care for us. In His all-knowing, deep-caring love, He understands precisely how to bring release from our nagging worries, paralyzing fears and troublesome confusion. He has promised continually to guide, satisfy and give us strength. The end result? We are to become like a "well-watered garden" and a "spring whose waters never fail."

To know that God will continually guide us is both reassuring and liberating. Since He has inspired us to do His will, surely He will show us what it is and free us from confusion. We say that we long to know His will, but we do not sufficiently study our Bibles where the principles of godly living are taught. We say that we want to hear His voice but do not quietly wait until other voices are silent. We rob ourselves of His loving care and grieve Him in the process.

The word "continually" implies that His care is given on a moment-by-moment basis. He will guide, satisfy and give strength as the need arises.

Scorched places and droughts will come, but God has promised to satisfy our desire in those times. He will make our lives like a fragrant watered garden and a refreshing spring of water.   ELIZABETH JACKSON

Spiritual Achievement Test

For God did not call us to be impure, but to live a holy life. Therefore, he who rejects this instruction does not reject man but God, who gives you his Holy Spirit (1 THESSALONIANS 4:7–8).

In April, 1983, the National Commission on Excellence in Education issued a report in which mediocrity in teaching methods and standards was cited as the cause for societal erosion in the United States. We learned that our nation was suffering from complacency. Its prior commitment to high standards of education had shifted. We determined to combat the enemy by stricter educational requisites.

Today we live in a society whose pace of life, level of stress and emphasis on self-satisfaction and achievement lull us into rationalizing away our lack of spiritual discipline. Is our knowledge and understanding of God's Word on a par with our spiritual age (years after second birth)? Or would we fail in a *Spiritual Achievement Test* whose aim was to determine our level of spiritual education and ethics in our everyday world?

We are aware that knowing what is right to do and then not doing it is sin (James 4:17), but we are so busy! And we argue that God understands and could not ask more of us. Yet the most thorough purity is the only acceptable kind in God's sight. He gives us the command as well as the means, but the choice is left to us. Is our Christian life being eroded by a mediocre understanding of and commitment to God?

L. BETH DUMMER

God Will Defend

Do not take revenge, my friends, but leave room for God's wrath, for it is written: "It is mine to avenge; I will repay," says the Lord (ROMANS 12:19).

How easy it is to strike back when offended and hurt — how hard to wait and let God work in the heart of the enemy and heal broken relationships.

As a young missionary, I taught in the Bible Institute of Armenia, Colombia. One of my students was always showing off and chose to humiliate me in front of the others. There were days when I went to my room and cried to the Lord for courage to go back into the classroom and teach.

Then the Lord spoke to me through Psalm 37:7–10 — "Be still before the Lord and wait patiently for him; do not fret when men succeed in their ways, . . . Refrain from anger . . . A little while, and the wicked will be no more; though you look for them, they will not be found." I claimed this promise and waited.

Meanwhile I treated my "enemy" with kindness. Suddenly his attitude changed. Instead of being brazen, he became so meek that he ran from me! Then came the day when I looked for him in class and he was not there. He disappeared from the institute and from the city.

There have been times since then when some have wished to destroy me with their tongues. When these enemies appear, I remember my experience in the institute and how the Lord taught me to trust in Him, to be silent and to treat my "enemy" well. Is there someone who is causing you grief? Be not overcome with evil, but overcome evil with good. You will rejoice to see that in His time, God will work through you to heal the relationship, or He will remove the hindrance.   BEVERLY BOON

Be Not Anxious

Is not life more important than food, and the body more important than clothes? (MATTHEW 6:25b).

How many hours do we spend worrying about finances in direct disobedience to Christ's command, "Be not anxious"? He cautions us against the drive to accumulate wealth or to indulge in luxury. We must not spend our strength in concern about secondary matters.

Anxiety is brought about by a lack of spiritual perception. The Lord points out that even the glory of Solomon could not be compared to that of the lilies of the field. Since man's effort in the case of personal adornment is so far short of nature's handiwork, we should cease to worry about so trivial a matter.

Having brought up the question of worry in relation to our health, the Lord tells us that no man can add to the length of his life. Often the person who works in quiet confidence, never doubting or fearing, retains his health, while the anxious person readily yields to illness.

Christians need not worry about the future. We have a hope that is steadfast and sure, for Christ has overcome sin, death and the grave by His death and resurrection.

We cannot by self-effort rid ourselves of anxiety, but we can build faith into our lives moment by moment and day by day through prayer, meditation, Bible study and worship until our longing for the Lord leaves no room for worry. We can live one day at a time with perfect trust in Him.　　　　　　　　　　　　　　IRENE STIRZAKER

The Parade of Life

For we are to God the aroma of Christ among those who are being saved and those who are perishing (2 CORINTHIANS 2:15).

I have always loved a parade. I remember well the "Parade of Nations" at the General Councils. As a child I marched in costume, representing the Arab Lands, where my parents served as missionaries. Later, with my husband, I represented Vietnam where we worked for 20 years.

I recall, too, the wedding processions in Syria and Jordan. I remember the excitement as, clapping and singing, we headed toward the bride's home for the wedding feast.

The Bible talks about a procession. "But thanks be to God, who always leads us in triumphal procession in Christ and through us spreads everywhere the fragrance of the knowledge of him . . . the fragrance of life" (2 Corinthians 2:14–16).

Picture that great triumphant parade — marching to Zion, captives whose purpose is to give forth a fragrance. This perfume is not the dime-store variety, or even an expensive essence, but a delicate, sweet aroma placed within His children by Christ Himself.

Just as spilled perfume cannot be undetected, neither can a life given to God hide the fragrance He instills. The beautiful blend of praise, joy, trust, peace, love and gentleness will speak of His indwelling.

A fragrant life is not aggressive, but submissive. It is not *take*, but *give*. It is not *mine*, but *yours*. It is not *possess*, but *share*. It is not *I*, but *Christ*. Our mission is to spread abroad His life-giving fragrance, thus attracting the lost to Christ.

EVELYN MANGHAM

JANUARY 16

The Lord My Portion

The Lord is good to those whose hope is in him, to the one who seeks him (LAMENTATIONS 13:25).

The Book of Lamentations is actually a postscript to Jeremiah — as though the author wished to add detail on the mourning of Jerusalem. But inside this little book lies a beautiful portion of pure hope and of God's great faithfulness to His people (3:22–25). His love, mercy and compassion are fresh and new and just as sure as the morning sunrise and the earth-refreshing dew.

Each of us can recall personal incidents when God's mercy was apparent — the time when a loved one was hovering between life and death — or when parents prayed earnestly and diligently for a child who had drifted far from the Father. God understands that love within our hearts and shows His compassion. How many times has He shown mercy to someone who deliberately and willfully offended Him?

In God's Word we see His faithfulness everywhere. From Genesis to Revelation He never alters what He says He will do. He is the same yesterday, today and forever.

Jeremiah gives a personal testimony in chapter 3 of Lamentations where, after reciting the afflictions he has suffered, he states, "The Lord is my portion; therefore I will wait for him" (verse 24).

If we have made the Lord our portion, we have assurance of His compassion, faithfulness and mercy. Such assurance is more than enough to see us through the problems of life.   SHELVA BLIGHT

Pray for Your Friends

After Job had prayed for his friends, the Lord made him prosperous again (JOB 42:10).

Think of the pain that Job suffered! First his family and his possessions were taken away, then his health failed. After that, his friends took him off of the list of the "spiritual." How he must have smarted under their constant accusations and intrusive, fault-finding interrogations. God Himself seemed to have cast him away.

Job longed to defend himself before God. Instead, God gave Job a vision of His majesty. Humbled, Job said: "My ears had heard of you, but now my eyes have seen you" (Job 42:5). His vision of God changed his perspective of his suffering and brought about his reconciliation to God.

There remained, however, the reconciliation with his friends. Vindicated by God, Job could have been tempted by thoughts of bitterness and vengeance. Instead, God told him to pray for his "comforters."

When as young missionaries, a series of setbacks put me and my husband in a difficult situation, a fellow missionary made an insensitive remark. It stung like acid and remained engraved in my memory. Then God began to work in my heart. My vision of Him pushed secondary considerations aside, but the relational problem with the other missionary was still there. I was tempted to avoid that person or even to drop an occasional "innocent" remark myself. Instead, I prayed for reconciliation and felt led to offer him encouragement.

God rewarded my efforts when the other missionary publicly acknowledged my encouragement. God also worked out the difficult situation, fully answering my prayers.   PAULINE REESE

Teamwork for Eternity

There is neither Jew nor Greek, slave nor free, male nor female, for you are all one in Christ Jesus (GALATIANS 3:28).

Successful teamwork is one of the highest hurdles faced either on the mission field or in the local church. We are a part of each other; we need each other, yet we often do not understand each other. In Galatians, the Lord points out the steps that we can take in order to work within our team in an attitude of peace and joy.

"Since we live by the Spirit, let us keep in step with the Spirit" (5:25). If the Holy Spirit has this job for me to do, then it does not matter how insignificant it is in the eyes of others. I do not have to look for the important job or the one with "honor." Because God has chosen my job, it becomes important.

"Each one should test his own actions. Then he can take pride in himself, without comparing himself to somebody else" (6:4). We should plan ahead, do the best job we know how to do and then relax. Maybe someone else could have done it better—who knows? What does it matter? We did the best we could, and God Himself does not expect more than that.

Realize, however, that there are some things others just naturally can do better. God has given others some abilities that He has not given to you, and they will have a ministry in some areas that you may never touch. It works the other way around, too.

Let us see ourselves as God sees us—our gifts and also our failings. Let us accept ourselves, always recognizing that God is continually at work within us, transforming us into the image of His Son.   PAULINE A. MORRIS

When Children Leave

But one thing I do: . . . straining toward what is ahead, I press on toward the goal to win the prize (PHILIPPIANS 3:13–14).

They left one by one over the years until only our twin sons remained at home. Each parting wrenched my heart, not because I wanted to keep the children with me but because they all took their gifts and interests with them and left in the nest an emptiness that was replaced only by happy memories.

Then the time came for the last two to say goodbye. As we began our trip back to the completely empty nest, my mood matched the weather — sad, dark clouds dripped their tears on us.

Though I was sad in the knowledge that this part of my life was over, I felt joy in knowing that each child had trusted Christ as his or her Savior and had yielded to His call to service.

As I mused, my thoughts focused on Mary, the mother of Jesus. Like her, I had chosen to do God's will. Her words, "I am the Lord's servant, . . . May it be to me as you have said" (Luke 1:38), often found an echo in my heart.

Now as I thought of Mary, I remembered that after Jesus' return to heaven, she went with the disciples to the Upper Room. Her home empty, she was now actively pursuing a deeper life than before. She was not bemoaning her lot but rather was moving toward new challenges.

My first new challenge came a few nights later when the doorbell rang. A brokenhearted woman had come to my empty nest to receive counsel, prayer and comfort. I thanked the Lord for showing me that He could bring hurting ones to my empty nest and make it a place to show forth His glory. MARY MCGARVEY

JANUARY 20

God Needs You!

Remember this: Whoever turns a sinner away from his error will save him from death and cover over a multitude of sins (JAMES 5:20).

All of us — even missionaries — face times of discouragement when we wonder of what value we really are in God's work.

As I read Romans 15:18–19 in the *Living Bible* I received a new understanding of these familiar verses. God showed me that through His power He *was* using me and would continue to use me here in Thailand.

Paul wrote to the church at Rome, "I dare not judge how effectively he has used others, but I know this: he has used me to win the Gentiles to the Lord." Notice the personal pronoun — God had used *him*. We need to be more aware that God can use *us* if we allow His power to work through us.

Paul continued, "I have won them by my message and by the good way I have lived before them, and by the miracles done through me as signs from God — all by the Holy Spirit's power." Paul was an example. He allowed God to use him — lips, hands, mind — and lives were changed, people were healed and prayer was answered.

Too many people are not accomplishing anything for God because they fail to realize that God wants their words, their hands, their feet, their lives.

Perhaps today He needs us to do a special work for Him. Is there a lonely one we could visit, an encouraging letter to write, a prayer burden we could assume?

Can we, like Paul, say, "I know this — *God has used me* to win people to Himself?"　　　　　　　　　　CORRINE SAHLBERG

Sentenced for Life

God, who has called you into fellowship with his Son Jesus Christ our Lord, is faithful (1 CORINTHIANS 1:9).

God has been faithful to me since the day of my conversion, and the fellowship of Christian friends has added much to my Christian growth through the years.

I remember a picture that hung on my bedroom wall during my teen years. It was called, "Sentenced for Life," and in it a lovely bride was coming down a staircase to start a new life with the man who had won her heart. That picture spoke to me like a voice from the Lord Himself, "You are mine always." God had a claim on my life.

In contrast to the life of peace and tranquility we Christians are privileged to live, we see about us iniquity and lawlessness. Even some who supposedly have received the Comforter display a meager amount of joy and victory. Our desire must always be to do whatever the will of God indicates for our personal lives.

Fellowship with the flawless Christ is absolutely essential. To some extent character is formed by earthly associations and Christians may make genuine contributions to our lives. Only fellowship with Christ, however, will bring to us all that is lasting.   IDA E. JOHNSON

Be Faithful

Be faithful, . . . and I will give you the crown of life (REVELATION 2:10).

Today I attended the funeral of a friend. The Lord's presence was keenly felt, and from many lips came the comment, "She was really a great person."

She could boast no outstanding abilities or achievements. High honors had passed her by. She did not possess an unusual personality, for she was clothed with a "gentle and quiet spirit" (1 Peter 3:4). She had no special charisma that made her a "star"; she always considered others better than herself.

It was not this world's good that made her great. There were resources sufficient to grant her every wish, but she chose simplicity in home and dress and used the surplus to help others.

There is but one answer to the reason for her greatness. She was faithful! Underscored passages and marginal notations filled her Bible, attesting to her faithfulness to her Lord and to His Word. She was faithful to her church. Her pastor could count on her and trust her in all matters. She was faithful to friends and filled her prayer list with requests of all kinds. She was faithful to her husband and to her family and to the larger family of believers. Her home was always open to God's servants. And she was certainly faithful to her trust. In the ways that were open to her, she responded to the cries of the lost and to the requests of missionaries.

Yes, she was a great person and we all knew it. But she herself did not know it—not until she heard the words of her Savior, "Well done, good and faithful servant! (Matthew 25:21).   ANNE EPPERSON

Marriage and Children

Sons are a heritage from the Lord, and children a reward from him (PSALM 127:3).

One of the greatest plans of God for His creation was marriage and, through that union, the birth of children. God instructs us in Deuteronomy 6:7, "Impress [my laws] on your children. Talk about them when you sit at home and when you walk along the road, when you lie down and when you get up."

Another blessed verse is Proverbs 22:6, "Train a child in the way he should go, and when he is old he will not turn from it." It suggests that there may be some wavering from the truth for a period of time, but God promises when the child is old he will not depart.

In Titus 2:4 we read, "Then they can train the younger women to love their husbands and children." I am so glad God knows the way that we take. There have been some dark days to walk through with my children. As yet I have not seen total victory, but God has given me two special verses to strengthen my faith: "All your sons will be taught by the Lord, and great will be your children's peace" (Isaiah 54:13); "I have heard your prayer and seen your tears; I will heal you" (2 Kings 20:5b).

What a privilege is ours as Christian mothers to *train* our children, *love* them, *pray* daily for them and, committing them to the Lord, *trust* His promises, for they are *sure* and *steadfast.*   LOUISE LETOURNEAU

JANUARY 24

Never-failing Promise

Be strong and courageous. Do not be terrified; do not be discouraged, for the Lord your God will be with you wherever you go (JOSHUA 1:9).

Only Christ in us can help us perform, with endurance, for His glory. In order to go and do God's work we need to have the promise that He will go with us. I found this promise and made Joshua 1:9 my life verse.

He may call you to leave home and loved ones, to sell a new car and purchase an old one, to go from one end of the United States to the other and over two oceans, trusting Him and believing His promises to see you through.

In every situation, even when the doctors say there will be no children, you trust. Psalm 128 was our special promise for this. We prayed, and before we could get His ear again there were six, all born during very important moves the Lord called us to make.

In our service for the Lord, we must depend on His promises and also try to bring our children to understand them too. "God will not tease us," said our little five-year-old one day. We had prayed in faith about an important matter and, as she met her daddy at the door, she was the first to know He had answered our prayer.

How good to know that He *is* the same yesterday, today and forever.   VIRGINIA MCGEE

Practical and Spiritual

Whatever you do, work at it with all your heart, as working for the Lord, not for men (COLOSSIANS 3:23).

I'll do anything but be a preacher's wife," said a girl who struggled to know God's will for her life. She had seen her mother cope with hours of entertaining and trying to counsel people in need. She just did not see how it could all go together. Either you entertain or you counsel—you cannot do both. But Mary and Martha, sisters in the Bible, are good examples of how it can be a happy combination if the Lord is glorified in it.

Four stages have been helpful to me as the wife of a preacher and district superintendent. They are things we must do.

Sitting. One of the most important acts of life is just to sit at the feet of Jesus and learn of Him. There must be that time of sitting alone with God before we can accomplish anything worthwhile.

Serving. To be able to keep so-called secular service in its right place, we must be conscious that both serving and learning are duties, and in both we should honor God.

Standing. He is able to undertake for us in all things, and we must trust Him with our cares, responsibilities and sorrows. When we think His help is delayed, it is important to remember that He is never before His time and never lags behind. We must trust Him enough to stand fast in Him.

Sharing. We must be able to serve and yet not be bogged down with home care, to sit and learn that we might share the learning, to stand upon a promise and share how God met a need in answer to our faith. Both practicality and spirituality are needed to complete the Christian character.

MARTHA MANGHAM

Ever-flowing Spring

Feed the hungry! Help those in trouble! Then your light will shine out from the darkness, and the darkness around you shall be as bright as day. And the Lord will guide you continually, and satisfy you with all good things, and keep you healthy too; and you will be like a well-watered garden, like an ever-flowing spring (ISAIAH 58:10–11, TLB).

For several years my husband and I have been involved in a ministry to refugees coming from Vietnam to Hong Kong. The Lord gave me these verses in Isaiah before we left the pastorate to return to missionary work.

During that first summer, we faced literally thousands of people living in cramped quarters and dark warehouses. I was reminded that we were to be as lights shining out in darkness because we were indwelt by the One who said, "I am the light of the world" (John 8:12).

At times the task seemed overwhelming — thousands of people with physical and spiritual needs. But we had the promise of the Lord's continual guidance. He led us daily to those in need and opened up unusual opportunities for service.

Just three months before packing for this assignment, I had undergone three surgeries, including a double mastectomy. We faced many "mountains," but as we walked with God, He satisfied us with all good things, and kept me in excellent health, despite the long days of ministry.

Each of us can claim this promise as we seek to bring His life and light to those who are in spiritual need. He has commanded us to reach out to those around us, and His commands are always accompanied by His promises.

ESTHER FITZSTEVENS

In His Image

To this you were called, because Christ suffered for you, leaving you an example, that you should follow in his steps (1 PETER 2:21).

While living in Nagoya, Japan, I met a lady who taught *shuji* (Japanese calligraphy). She wanted to improve her English and I wanted to learn how to write Japanese characters with a brush, so we made the happy exchange. Every week she came to my house and taught me *shuji*, and after the lesson she practiced conversational English with me.

The first step in each lesson was to watch her draw the Japanese character with a special brush. Since she was making the example for me to follow, she used bright vermilion ink. The next step was to mix the *sumi* with a small amount of water in the well to form jet black ink for my writing practice.

When her beautiful example was prepared, my teacher placed it in front of me. I tried to copy her work, but in spite of my efforts I could not match her artistic brush strokes. Her Japanese character was beautiful. Mine looked like the work of a six-year-old with a shaky hand!

One day the teacher took her red example and carefully laid it underneath my practice paper. With confidence, I traced the clearly visible strokes with my brush. After doing this on several practice sheets, the teacher removed her example and I was "on my own." The result was amazing. By tracing over her Japanese character, I had learned the correct pattern.

Through this experience, the meaning of Christ, our example, was indelibly inscribed on my heart. As I study God's Word, I see Jesus as my example. I trace my life over His life so that I can follow in His steps! ELEANOR J. PEASE

Hang Tough

But encourage one another daily, as long as it is called Today (HE-BREWS 3:13).

To the one who suffers from depression, nothing could be worse. People offer cliches like, "Just pull yourself together," "Snap out of it" or even, "Just read the Word and trust." It usually is not that easy.

I had seen tribespeople suffering from fear of evil spirits or from obvious depression, but they did not know God. If after they had been converted there was still depression, I would feel impatient. I wanted to tell them, "Christians don't get depressed."

Today I know better. It took nine long months before a doctor realized my deep depression was a side effect of a strong anti-malarial medication.

Satan's oppression took on several forms—because I had never before been bothered by this, I kept searching for the awful sin in my life. Then I became convinced that no one suffered as I was suffering. In addition, I felt sure my trial would never end.

Through my ordeal God taught me two great truths:
1) I could not flee from His presence (Psalm 139:7–18);
2) My position as child of God is in Christ, and that position is *secure*.

As these two truths began to dawn upon me, I would cry out, "O God, I cannot feel your presence, but I know You are here, and as Your child I am in Christ. Nothing can take those things away."

Child of God, whatever you are suffering now, grasp these two unshakable truths—His abiding presence and your guaranteed position—and look up!   FRAN BOZEMAN

JANUARY 29

Come

Come with me by yourselves to a quiet place and get some rest (MARK 6:31).

We say "come" to a baby or a small child, to a pet or to someone we love. We invite friends to "come" to our home for fellowship or fun.

The word *come* appears more than 700 times in the Bible. In Matthew 11:28 Jesus speaks of coming to Him for rest — real rest. He invites us to come. Only when we come to Him as our Savior do we have complete rest.

In Solomon's Song 4:8 we read, "Come with me." The implication is that we do not go by ourselves, but He invites us to *come* with Him. It reminds us of what was written about Enoch — that he "walked with God; then he was no more, because God took him away" (Genesis 5:24).

Jesus said, "Come, follow me, . . . and I will make you fishers of men" (Mark 1:17). He has already trodden the way, and He invites us to follow and to learn to win others.

Mark 6:31 quotes Jesus inviting us to *come* with Him and rest. He does not say *go* — rather, we are invited to *come with Him.* The resting is always with Him. It is His presence that makes the blessedness of the rest.

MARY ZONDERVAN

Charted Course

For our light and momentary troubles are achieving for us an eternal glory that far outweighs them all (2 CORINTHIANS 4:17).

Penny-Lou, whimpering and restless, obviously expected a trip to the veterinarian. I knew we were on our way to see my daughter, the dog's mistress, to whom she is deeply attached. But trying to comfort and reassure the dog was fruitless.

Then we arrived at our destination. Fear and frustration were replaced by happy barking and tail-wagging. Penny-Lou's fear was unfounded.

So often I find myself reacting as Penny-Lou did. As a Christian, I am on my way home. On my pilgrimage here I experience life's share of joy and fulfillment, perplexity and disappointment, pain and suffering. Sometimes I stumble onto untried paths. Occasionally I see no light ahead, no end to adverse situations and no solution to my problems.

I must remind myself that, unlike my four-legged friend, I am not without understanding. Mine, as that of all Christians, is a charted course, planned in His highest wisdom by One who loves me dearly and assures me of the outcome.

Surely our Lord rejoices when, instead of walking alone and fretting needlessly over the inexplicable trials, we walk with Him in faith, believing that all His ways are perfect.

Although we often do not understand, we can look forward to our arrival home, where we will not only understand but will be delighted with our Father's explanations about our journey.   MARGARET SANDELL

A Mother's Desire

Then I will give him to the Lord for all the days of his life (1 SAMUEL 1:11).

A s the mother of active, growing boys, I have thought much concerning my desires for them and their futures. My desire is that they will know the voice of the Lord for themselves and that they will respond in obedience.

Chapters 2 and 3 of First Samuel tell us about Hannah, who promised her son, Samuel, to the Lord for as long as he lived. She confirmed that promise by taking him to the house of the Lord to live under the spiritual guidance of the priest, Eli. There, in the spiritual atmosphere of the temple, Samuel ministered unto the Lord, but he "did not yet know the Lord: The word of the Lord had not yet been revealed to him" (verse 7). He did not actually know the Lord and had not heard God's voice to him personally.

When Samuel *did* hear God's voice for himself, when he became personally acquainted with the Lord, his service took on meaning and became effective and widespread.

Should we not then pray earnestly that each of our children will know the voice of God personally, first in salvation through Jesus Christ and then in a daily walk, listening to the voice of God's Spirit and actively obeying? John 10:27 tells us that God's sheep *hear* and *know* and *follow* His voice.

Claim that in prayer for your children today!

A. ELAINE GARDNER

Never Worthless

A bruised reed he will not break, and a smoldering wick he will not snuff out (ISAIAH 42:3).

Centuries ago, when there was a great deal of illiteracy, scribes were engaged to do the important writing for business documents or personal correspondence. The scribe used as his writing instruments various kinds of tall grasses having jointed, hollow stalks. Sharpened to a point, these reeds became his pens.

If, in the writing process, the reed was worn down and began to smear and blotch, the impatient scribe would throw it down, trample it under his feet and replace it with a fresh one.

How encouraging it is to know that God is not like that scribe. When we resist His hand and our efforts result in scratches and stains—making a mess instead of a message—He does not trample us, destroy us and replace us. Our failures are neither fatal nor final. Instead, in loving mercy He sharpens us again, forgives the blemishes, whitens the page and continues the writing. With God we can always begin again. And what He has forgiven and forgotten, we can forgive and forget.

"A smoldering wick" creates only enough fire to produce a dirty smoke—no flame. Snuff it out—forget it—replace it! But God says, "No, I will not quench it." The slightest bit of fire will be fanned into flame. The smallest bit of desire for God will be cherished and cultivated.

How often I have felt faint and smokey, useless to God and dry in my soul. And just when I am tempted to despair, the Lord lovingly encourages that desire for Him that He has put within me. He fills me with His oil and the flame burns again.   EVELYN PETERSEN

Women Who Followed Jesus

Many women were there, watching from a distance. They had followed Jesus from Galilee to care for his needs (MATTHEW 27:55).

Christ called disciples publicly. The men who left homes and work to go with Him learned much. They marvelled at His words, yet, for a time, misunderstood much of His purpose. And they made mistakes. Later, in Holy Spirit power, they would start the church and bear the salvation message of Jesus to the ends of their world.

Women followed Jesus too—many of them. He did not call them publicly: He simply crossed their paths at some point. With miraculous love He released them from the ravages of demons or illness, transforming dreary existence into meaningful, purposeful life. Drawn as by magnet, they remained with Jesus in His travels, and they served Him.

As Christ turned from the work in Galilee to face His ordeal in Jerusalem, the women followed and ministered. They grieved while darkness fell and death claimed their dear Lord at Golgotha. Had they also watched and prayed during His long Gethsemane agony? Such faithful vigil would have been consistent with their devotion.

A few women met an angel at the tomb resurrection morning and brought the apostles an astounding news flash: "He has risen!" After Jesus ascended to heaven, the women were among the community of saints who waited and prayed in Jerusalem for the promised Holy Spirit.

Like those women long ago, we may walk with our Savior, ministering to Him as we serve our families, our churches and the needy world around us.   SUE MULTANEN

Blessing

Blessed is the one who reads the words of this prophecy, and blessed are those who hear it and take to heart what is written in it (REVELATION 1:3).

That special music blessed my soul!" Have you ever thought that "blessing" in this context may be just a sanctified way of saying, "That music made me feel good"?

The underlying meaning of blessed — "to be happy" or "to be declared happy" — is a long way from "good feelings." Our casual misuse of the word, just because it is a convenient evangelical cliche, can make it more difficult for those going through experiences which may *result* in blessing but do not produce good feelings. A woman who has lost her husband to cancer, a family whose new baby is deformed or retarded, a man who has lost his job: we all know people in these situations. And none of them is "happy" either in the world's sense of that word or in the evangelical misuse of "blessing." Yet, each of us can know God's blessed gifts through such experiences.

We are told in Revelation 1:3 and in 22:7 that if we read, hear, take to heart and keep these writings, we shall be blessed. But as we read other portions of the book and ponder the pictures that grow increasingly horrifying, there is nothing that produces light feelings or "good vibrations."

"Blessed is the one who reads . . . and take[s] to heart what is written." It is of tremendous benefit to learn more of God's design for our own lives, suffering included, and of His control over the universe. As we truly begin to understand His sovereignty — so powerful, so terrible, yet so supremely comforting — we shall want to reserve the use of the word "blessing" to those times when we can convey that meaning.   BARBARA J. HAMPTON

Risking All

May the Lord repay you for what you have done. May you be richly rewarded by the Lord, the God of Israel, under whose wings you have come to take refuge (RUTH 2:12).

The streets of Bethlehem were dark. A heavily veiled woman hurried silently toward the home of the wealthy Boaz. Her heart beat faster as she made her way swiftly yet stealthily along. It was a daring thing she was about to do — she, the young Moabite widow, was risking all to present herself to Boaz at this hour of the night.

Perhaps he would make fun of her, mocking her before his young men. Perhaps he would take advantage of the secrecy of her visit for his own pleasure. But no — surely not. For Boaz was no ordinary man. Ruth had heard of him first from the harvesters. And then she had been made a special guest at his table and the object of his protection and generosity.

Yes — she had every reason to trust Boaz. And now, on her mother-in-law's advice, she was going to present her claim to Boaz for a levirate marriage, under the strange Israelite custom by which the first unmarried next-of-kin of a deceased husband was to marry the widow and raise a child to claim the inheritance of the dead man. Boaz was a near-kinsman, and he had no wife.

Ruth took the risk and was rewarded. There comes such a time for each of us. And when we take the risk of faith and say, "Lord Jesus, I give myself to You for all of this life and all of eternity," then and only then can the rewards of faith be ours — a life of fellowship, love and fruitfulness within the unbreakable enclosure of the love of God in Christ Jesus. MAXINE HANCOCK

Death

There is a time for everything, . . . a time to be born and a time to die (ECCLESIASTES 3:1–2a).

I have seen the face of Death;
It's not a stranger to me.
I have seen the pain and suffering,
Loneliness and misery.

The wooden cross in Tombstone,
The mausoleum where Napoleon lay;
A cemetery in Germany where fresh flowers
Were kept each day.

I saw the ovens at Dachau,
Where life was so very cheap;
The battlefields at Verdun,
Where skeletons were piled in a heap.

The rows of white crosses in Arlington,
Where our heroes are laid to rest,
As death rode on the battlefield,
Choosing our youth — our best.

Death came and took a baby,
The first daughter born to me,
Then my dad and mother,
And added to my grief.

I do not fear Death when it comes,
It is no stranger to me.
Oh, Death, where is thy sting?
Oh, grave, thy victory?

JEANNE BANKS

FEBRUARY 6

Ingratitude

Give thanks to the Lord, for he is good; his love endures forever (PSALM 107:1).

The winter had been especially cold. Snow covered the ground for weeks, hiding the grass and seeds that normally feed the birds. When there is snow, I try to keep birdseed in the feeder. I also melt grease, pour in seeds and freeze this into cakes. The birds love it and need it for warmth on the coldest days. When I throw out a new serving, it is not long before the takers swoop in. The crows and blackbirds come screeching and cawing, the busy starlings, grosbeaks and cardinals close behind.

Oblivious to me, they seem to say, "Look at what I found!" If I get too close to the sliding glass door, they fly to the nearest tree until I have backed off. They do not associate me with their meals at all.

Not long ago I visited a woman who had terminal cancer. A brilliant person, a former teacher and an avowed atheist, she was now fighting a courageous but losing battle with the disease. Yet she wanted nothing to do with God. She said she had no problem accepting the gifts—justice, kindness, love—but she would not credit God with being the provider of them. She said she herself had earned everything and had things well in control.

I could not help but think of the birds who thought the seeds and suet were their own clever provision. At least the birds reward me with their beauty and song. How sad when someone created in the image of God fails to acknowledge Him as the giver of every good gift.   ASTRID A. CATHEY

Self-Worth

Brothers loved by God, we know that he has chosen you (1 THESSA-LONIANS 1:4).

Six teenagers — Indian Christian girls — gathered around my dining room table at an after-school Bible study. They were in various stages of growth in self-esteem. I longed that they might grasp the truth that God loves and accepts each of them totally and without reservation.

When we fail in our behavior, we sometimes feel that God no longer accepts us. He does not always like our *actions*, but His acceptance of *us* is complete.

Satan is so quick to whisper, "You're no good! You can't do anything right! How can you call yourself a Christian?"

Someone has said that all spiritual battles are won or lost at the door of the mind. If we allow sinful thoughts to control us, we will fail. We need to be aware that Satan is out to destroy us, and he often attacks us through our thought life. Dwelling on thoughts of rejection, jealousy, bitter feelings, guilt or worry often leads to depression.

But we can shut the door of our mind and refuse to think about things that will lead us into sinful thoughts or actions. If we go by our feelings, by remarks people make or the way we were treated as we grew up, we may have problems accepting ourselves. Our feelings about ourselves need to be based on the facts in God's Word, not on the opinions of others.

When we are tempted to think about things that will lead to wrong actions or depression, we must, by an act of our will, refuse to allow Satan to control our thought life.

Remember: you belong to God, and He loves you.

LINDA WOOD

The Perfume Flask

Wherever the gospel is preached throughout the world, what she has done will also be told, in memory of her (MARK 14:9).

On the fireplace mantle in our home stands a glass case protecting a delicate, brilliant blue perfume flask, an antique that we purchased in Israel a few years ago.

This glass bottle was found in an excavation just outside the old wall of Jerusalem, near the Wailing Wall. Dated at the time of our Lord's ministry, the bottle is a rare treasure, believed to be one of a few glass articles brought to the Holy Land by wealthy Roman families during Roman rule.

According to some Bible scholars, the perfume flask that Mary broke over the feet of our Lord was not alabaster but a precious glass bottle, perhaps given to her by a wealthy Roman client in exchange for her services as a prostitute.

In a land where pottery vases and jugs were commonly used, you can imagine the shock when an unknown woman displayed and broke such a costly and rare object. This was too much for the bystanders who knew only a simple way of living.

But no treasure was too costly for Mary to demonstrate her love for her Lord. And if the gift she gave was associated with her past, then the giving became the gift of her life — her past, her present, her future!

Each of us must reach that juncture in life where, publicly and unashamedly, we give all of self to Jesus Christ.

ARVELLA SCHULLER

Found in the Field

It will be good for those servants whose master finds them watching (LUKE 12:37).

For the first time in months, Grandpa did not go with the trio that first weekend in December. It was to be an overnight trip, so he stayed behind on Saturday to finish the plowing before the freeze. It was less than two hours after the trio left that Grandpa was found in the field, fatally stricken with a heart attack.

The shock was doubly devastating because he had been in such good health. But far worse than the shock was the loss — and the emptiness that follows such loss — of a great man.

The next evening some friends dropped by and Bill was trying to tell them about this great life that had slipped from us. I was in the kitchen when I heard him, choked with emotion, say, "We loved him and needed him much more, perhaps, than he needed us. We have no regrets, but if only he had not been found in the field. . . ."

"Found in the field . . ." The words struck me! This man who died in the field had lived in the field. He loved people — all people — more than anyone I know. He never saw a crowd or a throng or a mob; he saw people — men and women and little children. And he loved them.

When I saw a group, he saw a lonely boy. When I saw a crowd, he saw the man who had worked for 37 years at the trailer factory and was worried about retiring. He saw them. And while I lived near the field, he was living in it.

Yes, he was found in the field. He would have been found in the field no matter where he died, for he knew Jesus and had heard Him say something about a field ripe for harvest.   GLORIA GAITHER

A Good Motto

The desert and the parched land will be glad; the wilderness will rejoice and blossom (ISAIAH 35:1).

The words on the motto read, "Bloom Where You're Planted." *That's for me*, I thought. My husband and I were facing an entirely new ministry of church planting as we returned to the Republic of Mali. I promptly purchased a copy of the motto and tucked it into our baggage. When I set up my office niche in our new home, my lovely motto rated a prominent place.

Here I was in a new city far away from co-workers, in a new ministry situation—and all ready to bloom. But the American community did not open their circle to me. Our embryonic church groups were not yet ready for women's classes; I could not even see the beginnings of a bud, let alone a bloom.

One day as I sat staring at my motto, I began to think about plants. I do not have the proverbial green thumb, but I do know there are some basic conditions necessary to produce a good plant. I watched my neighbor's gardener care for her roses. Beginning with cuttings, he watered, he fertilized, he carefully cut and snipped.

That began a personal "gardening" program in my own life. I found joy and new dimensions by spending additional time in prayer and Bible study. Though I found no joy in the necessary "pruning," it did bring spiritual growth.

Soon, without any effort on my part, there were opportunities for a Bible study and prayer with American friends and classes among African women.

My motto still hangs above my desk, more meaningful now than before, because I have now learned the joy of producing that bloom. DELORES BURNS

God's Sure Promises

He brought me out into a spacious place; he rescued me because he delighted in me (PSALM 18:19).

This promise has been very meaningful to me through the years. One morning at the breakfast table the children expressed their unhappiness due to conditions in the school, their lack of Christian friends and their dad's frequent absence from home because of his work. As I listened, my mother's heart went out to their cry. As soon as the four went to school and the baby was cared for, I sat down to have my devotions.

With tears I told the Lord all about the hardships the children were experiencing. I had never before noticed the promise that God would take me into a "large place." Where? How? But I believed God, and I still remember the joy and blessing of that day, for I felt God had something special for us.

When the children gathered around the supper table, I read the verse to them, and together we believed that God had answered prayer for us. I was anxious to see how.

I did not have to wait long. Only a short time later a large church extended a call to my husband. What a happy time and what a wonderful ministry God gave us in that place.

Twenty years later, after varied ministries, I look back on the "large place" the Lord has given me: two missionary trips, radio work, opportunity to speak for various programs, extensive travel as WMPF president and as wife of a district superintendent. The promise has been true for our six children also. God has blessed each one with a unique ministry.

Take God's Word for your guidance today! His promises are true.   MELBA STUMBO

FEBRUARY 12

Make Me Willing

As thou goest — step by step — I will open up the way before thee
(PROVERBS 4:12, Old Hebrew Translation).

After 28 years as a missionary in the Far East, (including more than three years internment as "guests" of the Japanese during World War 2), I was quite prepared to remain in the States. Then my husband presented me with the proposition of going to the Middle East where my parents had been missionaries for 43 years. Recovering from an illness and weary in body, I had absolutely no desire to pack up and go abroad again. It all seemed too much!

How I struggled! I really wanted to obey God if this move was His will — but it was just too hard for me. While in the throes of decision-making, we were invited to speak and show slides to a ladies' group. Taking her text from Deuteronomy 1, a woman, who could not possibly have known about us, challenged the group to move on in their Christian experience. She read, "You have stayed long enough at this mountain" (verse 6). (We were living at Nyack, the "mount of prayer and blessing.") She continued, "Break camp and advance into the hill country . . . and to Lebanon" (verse 7). (It was to Lebanon we had been asked to go.) "Bring me any case too hard for you" (verse 17). (Everything was too hard for me.) God let me know that my next step was to be willing to go and He would open up the way! I had to cry out to the Lord that the best I could do at that moment was to be willing to be *made willing*.

Needless to say, we went to Lebanon and saw God perform miracles in the lives of individuals. Now I can say that those 15 years in Lebanon, despite uncertainty, destruction and constant danger, were some of the happiest I have known.   MIRIAM TAYLOR

Never Too Little

Seventeen hundred able men — were responsible in Israel west of the Jordan for all the work of the Lord and for the king's service (1 CHRONICLES 26:30).

The vastness of outer space, a national debt in the trillions of dollars and the swelling global population — the comprehension of these immensities tends to diminish the importance of the individual person.

To dwell on our "littleness" in view of our situatiom can bring a feeling of hopelessness. As Christians we should be hopeful.

Consider David the shepherd boy who, with a little sling and God's help, went to face the giant, Goliath. Or the little maid, far away in captivity, whose simple testimony enabled leprous Naaman to discover that Israel's God could hear. A little lunch, a little boy, available and willing, and a great multitude were fed. We should be encouraged by the many incidents in the Bible where "little" spelled victory.

Henry Drummond, a beloved professor at Edinburgh University, relates this personal incident. The village hall was being decorated for an appearance of Queen Victoria. He was asked to go for more paper streamers. He flatly refused, until a young man came down the ladder, looked him steadily in the eyes and exclaimed, "Don't you know — it's O.H.M.S.!" That settled it — he was "On Her Majesty's Service," and he felt 10 feet tall.

Those same four letters should be written upon the life of each Christian: O.H.M.S. He who died to be our Savior rose again and now lives to be our King. Do you sometimes feel too little or insignificant to serve Him? Do not sell yourself short. Be available. Stand tall and never forget — you are On His Majesty's Service!   JANET BAKER

Come In

I tell you the truth, whatever you did for one of the least of these brothers of mine, you did for me (MATTHEW 25:40).

The owner of the store said, "If my brother bothers you, just tell him to get out." I could not do that, even if I were the manager. You see, this brother suffers from shell shock—the aftermath of his military service. He has had a life of suffering, of deprivation and of limitation. Because of men like him, I enjoy the freedoms of this great nation. He must always be welcomed, made to feel comfortable and included.

I know of Another who suffered that I might enjoy a freedom—the freedom from the penalty and power of sin. At the Last Supper Jesus said, "This is my blood of the covenant, which is poured out for many for the forgiveness of sins" (Matthew 26:28). My door is held wide to welcome this One who has done so much for me. My aim is to make Him welcome, comfortable and included.

The words of Jesus take on new significance: "If you do not forgive men their sins, your Father will not forgive your sins" (Matthew 6:15). And, further, the word spoken to the woman taken in adultry, "Then neither do I condemn you, . . . Go now and leave your life of sin" (John 8:11). Forgiveness—marvelous freedom. Is it any wonder, then, that I work at forgiveness?

I first confess, then systematically forsake every known sin in my life. Then, just as diligently, I must forgive each person who has wronged me. His part is to assure me that He takes away my sin and sets me free.

Knowing this truth makes me abhor the words, "Tell him to get out." Instead, I shout the loving welcome, "Come in."

DONA H. FERRELL

I Will Help You

For I am the Lord, your God, who takes hold of your right hand and says to you, Do not fear; I will help you (ISAIAH 41:13).

No time of day is more precious and helpful than that which I spend alone with my Lord. He is the One who gives me comfort, guidance, help, strength, hope and courage to live for Him.

How does one cope when her world falls apart? By trusting the Lord, praying and reading His Word. When the doctor revealed that my husband had cancer and that the prognosis was not good, the Lord supplied strength. He upheld me by His right hand (Isaiah 41:10) as day after day I drove to the hospital and cared for my husband. When there was little to delight in, we delighted in the Lord and knew we could trust Him to do what was best. Then God took my husband home to behold His glory (John 17:24).

When days were extremely difficult, the Lord reminded me that He loved me, my family and the congregation which my husband had pastored. His love is constant and unchanging.

The Lord did help me! Not only did he give of Himself to me in many ways, He also gave me part-time employment, a friend with whom to pray, guidance for the future, courage to do things I had never done before, fearlessness to live alone and much more.

There have been extremely hard places in the past few years, but I also have had many blessed experiences and joyous times. Praise His name for His presence in sunshine or rain and His continued message "Do not fear, I will help you."   WILDA W. NICHOLSON

Joy in His Presence

Because of the Lord's great love we are not consumed, for his compassions never fail. They are new every morning (LAMENTATIONS 3:22–23).

While visiting a glass factory in Monterrey, Mexico, I watched with great interest as the skillful artist worked. With long tongs he first held a piece of glass in a furnace until it began to melt. Removing it, he went quickly to work. With simple tools and with lightning speed, he created a beautiful blown-glass ornament. The finished product became a reality only after the glass was subjected to the intense heat of the furnace.

Even though we experience the heat of many trials, God is there to shape us in His beauty that we may be useful objects for His glory. That fiery furnace may be the loss of a loved one, a disaster resulting in loss of possessions, a financial crisis or the deep sadness of knowing a family member is unsaved. Our journey here may sometimes be lonely; there may be bitter tears of disappointment and pain, yet it is in the crucible of life's testings that we are reminded of the love of our Heavenly Father.

What a comfort it is to know that His mercies are new every morning and that there is real joy in His presence.

KATE ESPARZA

Why Fearful?

I sought the Lord, and he answered me; he delivered me from all my fears (PSALM 34:4).

When the disciples thought they were going to perish in the storm on the Sea of Galilee, they cried out, "Teacher, don't you care if we drown?" (Mark 4:38). After Jesus had quieted the storm he asked the question, "Why are you so afraid? Do you still have no faith?" (verse 40).

This question has often rebuked me in my walk with the Lord when, with pounding heart, I have watched at the sickbed of a loved one or spent sleepless nights worrying over problems with family or job. There have been some victories but many more failures as my faith has often been too small. The Lord reminds us, "Whoever listens to me will live in safety and be at ease, without fear of harm" (Proverbs 1:33).

It would appear to many Christians that we are nearing the last days where "men will faint from terror" (Luke 21:26). We are constantly being told of contamination—in the food we eat, the water we drink, the air we breathe. Crime and vice affect our communities and even our homes. The threat of nuclear war is worldwide.

Our concerns are many: the spiritual welfare of our children, the lack of harmony in many homes, the humanistic philosophies being presented in our public schools and the economic uncertainties in our complex industrial society.

But peace is what God has promised His children. Jesus said, "Peace I leave with you; my peace I give you" (John 14:27). This peace may be ours today if we completely trust Him. The psalmist said, "I sought the Lord and he answered me; he delivered me from all my fears" (Psalm 34:4).   LAVERN TAYLOR

Afraid — Who, Me?

The Lord Almighty . . . he is the one you are to fear (ISAIAH 8:13).

Our first home as missionaries in the Ivory Coast, West Africa, was quite small, except for the large, dismally dark bedroom. A scorpion had found a perfect hiding place there. It no doubt would have remained as an unwelcome guest had I not stepped on its back one evening and received a painful sting.

For days I was skittish and jumped at anything that moved near me. My language-learning informant, having taken as much of my jumpiness as he was able, quoted a Baoule parable: "If your grandmother was chased by a red bull, you will run when you see a red termite hill."

How perfectly that parable fit me! Red termite hills dotted the Baoule savannah. A person afraid of them would be living constantly in a state of fearful uncertainty.

God wants His children to live careful lives in the fear of the Lord. But my fear was misplaced, and misplaced fear is:

1. *Confusing* — It hinders a Christian from seeing situations as they really are.

2. *Contagious* — It spills over onto those near us. (Thankfully, my language helper was disgusted with my fear.)

3. *Confining* — It boxes the Christian in and keeps him or her from reaching out and attempting to do exploits for God.

Misplaced fear is a hindrance to us as Christian women, for it robs us of the joy of a life of perfect trust in God.

HELEN POLDING

We Need Deborahs

Go! This is the day the Lord has given Sisera into your hands. Has not the Lord gone ahead of you? (JUDGES 4:14).

Deborah, wife, mother, prophetess and judge, was able to sort out right from wrong not only for herself but for others. She held court under a palm tree, which reminds me of our front yard in Irian Jaya—a quiet corner where people could come to talk and ask questions. When the gospel first came to the Moni people, they had much "sorting out" to do. There were so many things in their lives they wondered about. What is right and what is wrong? What does God think about this or that?

Having been given the Lord's instruction to go up to battle, Barak replied to Deborah, "If you go with me, I will go; but if you don't go with me, I won't go" (verse 8). The presence of her godly life was what he needed in the thick of battle.

I think of the Moni Deborahs in Irian Jaya who have left parents and possessions and have gone with their husbands into isolated valleys, with tiny babies on their backs and toddlers by their side. They have ministered in malaria-infested lowlands where there is no medicine, sometimes coming back without those little ones or even losing their own lives so that frontiers might be pushed back for God.

Only eternity will tell of the battles that have been won, enemies conquered and exploits accomplished for God because of an optimistic woman of faith who said, "Go! Conquer! God is on your side!"

Deborah had that beautiful womanly ability to inspire those whose lives she touched. As women, we need not apologize for God's call or His anointing on our lives.

GRACIE CUTTS

Living Illustrations

In the same way, let your light shine before men, that they may see your good deeds (MATTHEW 5:16).

One Sunday afternoon, several years ago, my husband, Joel, was on his way to a preaching appointment when he was involved in a rear-end collision. Immediately upon impact both drivers emerged from their cars. The damage was slight and no one was injured. But the driver of the other car was a woman driving with a learner's permit. She was at the point of uncontrollable hysteria.

My husband talked kindly to her, assuring her that he did not consider her responsible for the accident. As they talked, he explained that he was a minister and that, having preached in a local church that morning, he was on his way to fulfill an evening preaching commitment. After a time, the lady regained her composure and left.

Occasionally my husband would mention the incident, wondering if the lady had since received her driver's license. Then several months later at a men's meeting, Joel was surprised to see the husband of the woman who had been involved in the accident. He told Joel that he and his wife had discussed the incident and decided that since my husband had shown such kindness and concern, they would go to the church where he had preached that morning. There they accepted Christ as their Savior and found the joy and peace for which they had been longing.

Sometimes the living illustrations of God's instruction to "love your neighbor as yourself" (Matthew 19:19) can be more powerful and earn more attention and response than a whole sermon of spoken words. IRENE MCGARVEY

Good — Better — Best

Do not conform any longer to the pattern of the world, but be transformed by the renewing of your mind. Then you will be able to test and approve what God's will is — his good, pleasing and perfect will (ROMANS 12:2)

A wise Christian teacher was instructing her students in the comparison of adjectives. When she came to the word *good*, she told them to remember this: "Good, better, best; never let it rest, 'till the good is better and the better best." Needless to say, this brief saying made an indelible impression.

Many times through the years I have thought of those words, especially in relation to God's will for my life and the lives of others. It is *good* to *know* the will of God, *better* to *do* the will of God, but *best* to *love* the will of God.

It is the will of God that we be saved. In Second Peter 3:9 we read, "not wanting anyone to perish, but everyone to come to repentance." It is the will of God that we be sanctified, for First Thessalonians 4:3 states, "It is God's will that you should be holy." It is the will of God that we behave ourselves, "For it is God's will that by doing good you should silence the ignorant talk of foolish men" (1 Peter 2:15).

In the midst of circumstances which could defeat us, we can go forward in victory in the will of God.

Know the will of God, do the will of God and love the will of God. Then it will make no difference where it leads us or what it costs us, for "faith is the victory" and the joy of the Lord is our strength.   RUTH KLINEPETER

God's Measurement

Cast your bread upon the waters, for after many days you will find it again (ECCLESIASTES 11:1).

I was a jogger. I ran each morning—exactly one mile. Well, actually, I often walked a bit of it. Every day? Well, not quite. I did not jog on Sundays—or Wednesdays—or when there were guests at my house—or when I did not feel well. I guess that is not a very good record.

A Christian? Well, of course! Perhaps God's record will show a better performance than the jogging chart.

What does God measure? "For I was hungry and you gave me something to eat, I was thirsty and you gave me something to drink, I was a stranger and you invited me in, I needed clothes and you clothed me, I was sick and you looked after me, I was in prison and you came to visit me" (Matthew 25:35–36).

"Lord, when?" "I tell you the truth, whatever you did for one of the least of these brothers of mine, you did for me" (Matthew 25:40).

"But Lord, I teach at the women's Bible study fellowship. Someone else with more time can entertain those new people."

"Teaching is good, but it doesn't take the place of person-to-person kindnesses which are the hallmark of My children."

"I can't quite bring myself to visit my friend who's just had surgery. I'm healthy; she might be dying. I don't know what to say."

"I'll give you words. She needs your honesty and love. If she's too sick to talk, just hold her hand."

Each of us has opportunities to show kindness to others. Let us not fail in this ministry to our Lord.

EVANGELINE DAVIDSON

Praise His Name!

The Lord is my rock, my fortress and my deliverer; my God is my rock, in whom I take refuge. He is my shield and the horn of my salvation, my stronghold (PSALM 18:2).

He is my rock. A rock is firm, secure and unchanging. It is the best foundation on which to build. These same characteristics belong to Jesus. He is the security in every situation because He alone never changes. Recently, during a period of great difficulty, God seemed beyond reach, and I felt that the battle was mine alone. Now that I have come out on the other side and can look back, I see that He was there all along.

He is my fortress. A fortress signifies safety and protection and conjures up a picture of strength and invincibility. And that is Jesus! It is to Him we can flee when we are threatened, when all around us is falling. It is He who will hide us from the worst of the storm and who will defend against Satan's attacks.

He is my deliverer. He is the one who comes to our aid, our Champion, the One who has Himself gained the victory and now causes us to triumph in Him.

He is my refuge. Jesus perfectly fulfills the psalmist's word picture. We can say, "In Him will I trust." But such commitment requires a deliberate act of our wills. To say, "In Him will I trust," means taking our hands off the situation and leaving our future, and that of our loved ones, to God. It is taking Him at His Word and holding Him to His promises.

MARGARET ZACHARIAS

Walking with God

Trust in the Lord with all your heart and lean not on your own understanding; in all your ways acknowledge him, and he will make your paths straight (PROVERBS 3:5–6).

Child of God, remember that living daily in communion with God will always be of unspeakable advantage to you. Jesus said, "Whoever has my commands and obeys them, he is the one who loves me. He who loves me will be loved by my Father, and I too will love him and show myself to him" (John 14:21). He shows Himself to us when we spend our lives constantly in communion with Him.

Living in the presence of God prepares us for the time when afflictions come; then we are able to bear them well, knowing that because we trust Him with all of our hearts, He who makes no mistakes will work them out for our good.

How human it is for us to lean on our own understanding instead of placing our whole dependence upon God, knowing that He does all things well. "He is the Lord; let him do what is good in his eyes" (1 Samuel 3:18).

In the night seasons we are to trust in the Lord, and faith in Him will bring us through to that desired haven of rest where there is unspeakable peace. We must not resist the working of God in our lives, for it is His plan and purpose to conform us to the image of His Son, Jesus Christ.

Walking with God is such a blessed way — the only safe way!

PHYLLIS MACINTYRE

FEBRUARY 25

Interceding

The Spirit helps us in our weakness. We do not know what we ought to pray, but the Spirit himself intercedes for us with groans that words cannot express (ROMANS 8:26).

Interceding is a word I have heard all my life, but not until May 1981 did it have a personal meaning for me. One day during my Bible reading this verse stood out, and I wrote it down and memorized it. Little did I realize that in a few weeks that small portion of God's Word would be a comforting, stabilizing force.

When our daughter had to be taken to the hospital, we had to help her cope with serious illness and surgery. During that time, the Lord answered many prayers for her, all the time helping us to accept the inevitable. There come times in our lives when we are so burdened we cannot form our needs into prayer, but I was constantly reminded that the Holy Spirit was interceding for us.

Just before surgery, our pastor and his associate joined our family at our daughter's bedside. Scripture was read, and we held hands as our pastor prayed. There was a sense of God's presence in the room and a peace and calm I had not thought possible.

Four hours later, the surgeon called us into a room and explained the surgery—not at all what we had expected. My first thought was that we had not known how to pray for that type of surgery because we did not even know it could be done. But the Holy Spirit knew, and He had been there interceding as He had promised.

I found then, as I had many times before, that He can work out our problems so much better than we can, if we will just leave it all to Him and let Him intercede for us.

FAYE SPEER

Glowing and Growing

But grow in the grace and knowledge of our Lord and Savior Jesus Christ (2 PETER 3:18).

Recently a family member expressed her sincere appreciation for a mutual friend with whom she had not been in contact for some time. She felt that he was *really* changed. He was more gentle, less critical and showed a genuine concern for others. In retrospect, I could also see the results of spiritual growth in my relative's life. Perhaps because she had grown in the Lord, she was now looking for biblical qualities in others.

The changes that take place in the lives and growth of God's children remind me of the ivy plant that hangs in the corner of our living room. Sometimes it grows very quickly, seemingly in every direction, and then all of a sudden it appears to stop growing and starts to wilt. Then I must pinch back the stems, cut away the old dead part and nourish it with water and plant food.

So it is with our spiritual lives. In order for there to be growth and beauty, there must be a pruning or cutting away of the non-essentials so that new growth can take place.

I wonder if family and friends see change and spiritual growth in our lives? Does the pruning and watering of the Holy Spirit and the nourishment of the Word produce lives that are healthy, growing and glowing? RAE A. TEWINKEL

I Do This!

I will go before you and will level the mountains; I will break down the gates of bronze and cut through bars of iron. I will give you treasures of darkness, riches stored in secret places, so that you may know that I am the Lord, the God of Israel, who calls you by name. I form the light and create darkness, I bring prosperity and create disaster; I, the Lord, do all these things (ISAIAH 45:2–3, 7).

Many times during my years as a missionary, I have cried to the Lord, and He has accomplished the seemingly impossible. Language learning — what mountains! Revision of the New Testament in Yipunu — gates of bronze! Preparation of manuscripts for the Bible Society — bars of iron! He did all that, always showing me clearly that it is "'Not by might nor by power, but by my Spirit'" (Zechariah 4:6).

He also promised to give us treasures of darkness and riches hidden in secret places. This He did and is doing for me. But often those treasures and riches have to be ferreted out of their hiding places, and this has meant entering into deep darkness. But He who created both light and darkness is there also; He brings prosperity and allows disaster.

And the years pass. His treasures of darkness — those precious gems hidden in secret places — are still to be found. Often deep gloom descends and all looks hopeless — the treasures that seemed secure slip away. And then His voice calls my name, and I remember He is the Sovereign Lord; the darkness and disaster are all part of His plan for my life.

"I, the Lord, do all these things."   GRACE NELSON

FEBRUARY 28

God Is for Me

For I know the plans I have for you, declares the Lord, plans to prosper you and not to harm you, plans to give you hope and a future (JEREMIAH 29:11).

One benefit of living in the Southern Philippines has been the marvels we discover in the Sulu Sea. While swimming in the salty water, we often enjoy the delights of looking into an awesome, beautifully ordered and designed aquarium.

Hundreds of exotic fish move about — some darting here and there, others gliding silently — each obeying God in its own unique way. There are myriads of creatures in this submarine world — all designed to match or starkly contrast with their environment. In it all we see the rightness of God's order.

How much more our Creator cares for us. How much more He wants good things for human creatures made in His image. Knowing ourselves to be God's special creation, do we nevertheless sometimes have questions and doubts?

We wonder why God does not intervene when we suffer. How can a loving God allow hurt and disappointment? Why do Christians sometimes sink to depths of despair? We have all probably had thoughts like these from time to time. I believe we can express our doubts to God. When we do, He will teach us a very positive truth — *God is for me and not against me!*

We all suffer in one way or another. In spite of how we feel, God is still at work in our world. And, through the operation of His Holy Spirit, He is at work in each of us. Setting out to discover what God is doing and cooperating with Him will bring to our lives the order and rightness we discovered in the Sulu Sea. SANDI WISLEY

FEBRUARY 29

Be Still and Know

Be still, and know that I am God; I will be exalted among the nations, I will be exalted in the earth (PSALM 46:10).

Because of my husband's career, it was necessary for me, as a young bride, to leave my hometown and move to Cincinnati, Ohio. Leaving my family and friends and moving from a rural area into a large city was an unpleasant and frightening experience. The adjustment was difficult.

In the five years we resided there, I still longed to be "home." When problems and difficulties arose, I found myself thinking, *If only I lived near my mom and dad; if only I were back home, then these problems wouldn't seem so bad or the hurts so deep.* It was during one of my times of self-pity, that I took my Bible and knelt beside my bed. I wept before God, confessing all the fears and hurt that filled my heart. After a time of weeping and questioning and informing God of the solutions to my troubles, *finally* I was silent before Him.

Led by God's Spirit, I turned to Psalm 46:10 and there, in just eight short words, I saw that my problem was deeper than just separation from loved ones. I read, "Be still, and know that I am God." How much I learned from that short line. In my rebellion I was *not* being still. I was *not* waiting upon the Lord. Worse yet, I was *not* allowing Him to be Lord of my life. As I thought about those words, my tears became an acknowledgment of sin and sorrow for my failure.

Often when I am perplexed, God speaks to me again through these same words. "Be still, and know . . ." and I rest anew in His sovereign Lordship.   VIVIAN M. SIMPSON

Fret Not

Do not fret — it leads only to evil. For evil men will be cut off, but those who hope in the Lord will inherit the land (PSALM 37:8b–9).

Whether in David's time or ours, there is much "fretting" going on. When we cannot find something in our own lives to fret about, we look elsewhere and still fret.

What is our attitude when we see people in our office, factory, school or even in our home, who make no profession of Christianity yet seem to have everything fitting together? They may even ridicule us or chide us for not "getting ahead" as they have.

Psalm 37 cautions us not to fret about the seeming prosperity and progress of the ungodly. When adversity or reversals come to these people, they often find it hard to cope. "Fret not," for you have so much more when you have Christ in your life — peace, joy and eternal life far outweigh and outmeasure anything belonging to the evildoer.

Four distinct phrases in the psalm outline the way a child of God ought to live: "Trust in the Lord," "Delight yourself in the Lord," "Commit your way to the Lord" and "Be still before the Lord." If we can put our life in the right perspective, we will "fret not."

If we put our trust and confidence in the Lord, we may enjoy His presence and find it a delight to walk each day with Him. EVELYN BOLLBACK

MARCH 2

One Goal

But one thing I do: Forgetting what is behind and straining toward what is ahead, I press on toward the goal to win the prize for which God has called me heavenward in Christ Jesus (PHILIPPIANS 3:13–14).

How many times have you faced a morning completely overwhelmed by the many tasks ahead? Too many jobs . . . too many goals . . . simply too much to do?

I remember the "golden olden" days, when women's lives revolved around the home. Life was simpler then—no agonizing decisions. Take Monday, for instance. It was washday, *period*. First, hot water and soap went into the old wringer washer. Then each load went through the wash, two rinses and out onto the line. By 3:00 P.M. all was folded and certain items dampened and rolled for Tuesday's ironing. Goal accomplished. Today's "labor-saving" automatic washers have merely guaranteed that every day is washday and the laundry is never done.

Of course, the "olden" days were not all golden. Women have always had so many demands on them that they often feel torn. This common frustration led me to choose for my life verse Psalm 27:4. "One thing I ask of the Lord, this what I seek: that I may dwell in the house of the Lord all the days of my life, to gaze upon the beauty of the Lord and to seek him in his temple."

Jesus had a goal. He set His face as a flint to go to Jerusalem, knowing He was to be our sin-bearer. "It was for *this very reason*," he said, "I came to this hour" (John 12:27).

No matter what our age or circumstance, what a comfort to have this single, worthy, lasting goal: to behold the beauty of our Savior all the days of our lives and to learn of Him.   MARY J. SELLER

True Contentment

I know what it is to be in need, and I know what it is to have plenty. I have learned the secret of being content in any and every situation (PHILIPPIANS 4:12).

This verse took on new meaning for me as my husband and I prepared to leave our homeland to minister in another country. We were not a young couple beginning a missionary career; God had opened this door as we reached our retirement years.

After the excitement of getting passports and visas, I began to comprehend more fully what lay ahead of us. As I looked around, I gazed at a house full of lovely things, the accumulation of 41 years of marriage and ministry. Many objects brought to mind family and friends who had enriched our lives. All these belongings now had to be sorted out. A few would be stored. Some we decided to take with us to New Zealand. Many things would have to be sold. How important were these things? In light of our circumstances we now had to renunciate them.

The key to contentment is learning to enjoy, with thanksgiving, those things the Lord permits us to possess, without allowing them to possess us. We must hold to things lightly, for possessing them does not bring contentment.

In the early years of our marriage, we had few of the earthly things, but we felt we had plenty and were content. Later we enjoyed the pleasure of abundance of things. Now we had to be content to part with some of them.

Jesus Christ is the source of true contentment. Paul held lightly to things that he might know Him. In this we may follow his example. Things can be lost, but Christ is our eternal possession.   DOROTHY MEASELL

Hooked by a Fish

Taste and see that the Lord is good; blessed is the man who takes refuge in him (PSALM 34:8).

One fringe benefit of being an MK teacher in Zamboanga was the city's seaside site. I went swimming often, yet it was 15 years before I discovered the beautiful underwater world.

One day I was urged to look through an underwater mask. Standing on a large piece of coral rock I peered into the vestibule of a whole new world. Subsequently, I went out and bought myself a snorkel and mask which have netted me countless hours of pleasure as I study God's amazing creation beneath the surface of the water.

In coral crannies I have often spied the gently waving, long, sharp spines of the sea urchin. From experience, I know that if the sharp points get stuck in my flesh they are quite painful. But I notice that the urchins do not pursue me; they only protect themselves. So one day, as I calmly floated above a cluster, I was able to observe the beautiful jewels amid the spines.

The sharp spines and tenacles of terrorism, kidnapping and political uncertainty in Zamboanga City also framed lovely, shining jewels: a small child holding my hand and declaring, "You are my best friend," because that day she found God's unspeakable gift of salvation. Another, about to leave permanently, declaring, "I'll see you again," for here she first heard and believed that heaven is real.

We are instructed to "taste and see that the Lord is good." So many times, however, we live on the surface, oblivious to the beauty that is ours for the seeking. Snorkeling has become my favorite sport, finding God's hidden gems, a lifelong pursuit.   ESTHER SNYDER

Why This Waste?

A woman came to him with an alabaster jar of very expensive perfume, which she poured on his head as he was reclining at the table (MATTHEW 26:7).

The shattered alabaster jar lay on the floor, every fragment lustrously beautiful. A subtle, beautiful fragrance filled the room. The woman who had glided in soundlessly, silently broken her treasured vase and without a word poured the expensive ointment on Jesus' head, stood back from the dinner party — half wishing she had never come, half ashamed at the impulsiveness of her gesture, half afraid that He would not understand.

Around the Master, the disciples showed their consternation. Nostrils flared, not in response to the heady perfume but in anger and indignation. Then came the question — short and rasping — "Why this waste?"

This — waste? Love expressed at great cost? Worship expressed with beauty? Personal devotion expressed at the risk of ridicule? This — waste?

"This perfume could have been sold . . . and the money given to the poor" (verse 9). Always, there are more practical matters than an expression of love and worship.

But Jesus' words cut through their criticism. "She has done a beautiful thing to me" (verse 10), He said quietly. He savored the sweetness of her gesture — one moment of beauty before the dark anguish of Gethsemane, before the stark horror of Calvary. "When she poured this perfume on my body, she did it to prepare me for burial" (verse 12).

Love, worship, devotion — expressed to God through Jesus — are the most precious things in this world. Of no value to the cash-register mind, they are priceless in the eyes of our Lord.   MAXINE HANCOCK

Who Are You?

We all stumble in many ways. If anyone is never at fault in what he says, he is a perfect man, able to keep his whole body in check (JAMES 3:2).

Do you really know yourself? Did you think it necessary to lose your personality when you became a Christian? The statement "Your attitude should be the same as that of Christ Jesus" (Philippians 2:5), does not mean we no longer think for ourselves. I have met many individualistic Christian men and women. Yet some would have us believe that we must be nebulous blobs floating through life, never hassling anyone.

Jesus said He came not to send peace but a sword; however, any conflict in our relationships with others must not be because of our abrasive personalities, but because we are standing up against the sin and wrong around us.

Jesus gathered around Him strong personalities — doctors, tax-collectors, rugged fishermen. They did not lose their personalities, but neither did they remain the same.

The apostles were not timid men who sat around after the Resurrection and hoped someone would notice their faithful church attendance and their quiet demeanor and come to God. Their commitment to Christ took on a whole new meaning. They taught in private homes, secret caves, public places — and they were martyred for their faith.

God may not ask us to quit our jobs or lay down our lives, but are we willing to let Him make a difference, willing to allow His Holy Spirit to enhance the good aspects of our personalities and to remove those that displease Him?

God will not force us to be like His Son; He wants us to love Him enough to desire this for ourselves. LEE A. SHORT

MARCH 7

Receiving Strangers

When an alien lives with you in your land, do not mistreat him. The alien living with you must be treated as one of your native-born (LEVITICUS 19:33–34a).

Strangers seem to have a special place in the heart of God. At least, significant attention is directed to them in His Word.

A harlot in ancient Jericho entertained two men — strangers, spies. And when their lives were threatened, she gave them refuge. In so doing, she laid her own life on the line. Had they been found, she surely would have been killed. Her courage and hospitality won her life and the lives of her family when the Israelites destroyed the city.

Then she became a refugee, a stranger in Israel. And God provided one to take her in as she had taken in the spies. It was Salmon, a descendent of Judah and of Abraham. Could he embrace one who was not only a gentile but a prostitute? But Rahab had already demonstrated her faith. She was a worthy bride, and Salmon took her as his wife. Soon a little boy was born, baby Boaz. As he grew, he must have wanted to hear over and over the exciting story his mother had to tell about how she hid the spies.

Many years later, when that little boy was grown and had become a wealthy landowner, he learned of a young woman, a widow, who had come from Moab to Bethlehem with her Israelite mother-in-law, Naomi.

Rich, influential Boaz took note. Kind, gracious Boaz acted. He married Ruth and eventually these two became the great-grandparents of King David and ancestors of our Lord.

What is your attitude toward strangers?

ASTRID A. CATHEY

Be Alert

Then he opened their minds so they could understand the Scriptures (LUKE 24:45).

The mind is the organ of intelligence, purpose, under-standing, opinion, choice and reason. It is able to re-ceive and understand news, facts and information.

In today's world there are books, newspapers, TV, radio and schools of learning—all vying for our attention. There are people and programs and publications ready to fill our minds with their ideas and thoughts. As Christians we have been given new minds to understand the Scriptures. We must, therefore, always guard against becoming dull, slug-gish or lulled into insensitivity about truths and issues that are vital to our new life in Christ. We must always be alert!

Life is short. It drifts by like a mist. We do not know what will take place tomorrow. We need to walk carefully, giving ourselves fully to the work of the Lord. Because our adversary, Satan, is always on the alert and ready to put us out of commission, we must always be clothed with the protective armor of God.

We do not know when Jesus will return. He has told us to be alert so that we are ready to meet Him. Constant com-munion with our Lord will keep us close to Him. Interces-sion makes us aware of others. Petition supplies our needs. Let us be alert and clear-minded so that we will know how to pray, and our prayers will be both powerful and effective.

Our new life in Christ came to us at great cost. Shall we not guard it with alert and watchful minds?   SVEA HENRY

The Marketplace

Live such good lives among the pagans that, . . . they may see your good deeds and glorify God on the day he visits us (1 PETER 2:12).

The market in Old Jerusalem is one of the most unusual and interesting places to see and smell. Yes, I said smell—because it is the odor that is the most impressive memory of the marketplace.

Today the long, narrow, crowded streets offer many tourist attractions and cheap souvenirs, but it takes only limited imagination to realize that it has changed very little since our Master walked those narrow lanes. The odor of meat hanging too long in the sun, of animals (sheep and donkeys) that brush past you and the mixture of mid-Eastern spices have robbed more than one tourist of his appetite. Add to this the aroma of many who do not have the luxury of a bath or even a change of clothing, and the experience of shopping in the marketplace is unforgettable.

Our Lord was not lord of the quiet retreat or mountaintop only, but He also went to the marketplace and ministered there where He was no doubt jostled, shoved and rudely treated.

Today, our marketplaces have become quite sophisticated; we have checkout counters, credit cards and shopping carts. But there are still crowded aisles, shoving, pushing and occasional rudeness on the part of someone "too busy" to be polite. Jesus wants to walk with us in our crowded marketplaces. If He is Lord of our lives, we must take Him with us there also.

It is easier to serve Him in our own quiet places, but others need to see that we belong to Him. Today He wants to help us show His love in busy streets or offices or stores.

ARVELLA SCHULLER

Sing Hallelujah

See! The winter is past; the rains are over and gone. Flowers appear on the earth; the season of singing has come (SONG OF SONGS 2:11–12a).

According to the weather forecast, "Winter is past and spring is around the corner, so take heart." I pray, "Lord it has been winter in my heart. These past months since my husband went into Your presence have left my heart cold and numb.

"I'm lying in my yard soaking up the warm sun and looking at what should be a large expanse of grass but what, in reality, is weeds. What an example of my life! The receding cold and barrenness of winter have revealed the weeds of self-pity and doubt. You know how I loved and needed him; his ministry with the church and the radio — they needed him. Why did You need him, Lord? How do I raise four very active children by myself?

"Suddenly I feel foolish and guilty. I know the answer, but it is not the answer I want. You, dear Lord, are sovereign. I prayed a year ago that I might learn how to praise You. I am learning, but it is a sacrifice of praise — a praise that costs and is painful.

"Last year when an acquaintance told me of *her* husband's sudden death, I saw the look of pain that crossed her face, but I could not identify with it. Lord, now I understand her pain!

"Examining the weeds more closely, I notice small flowers growing among them. Like miniature violets, they have a beauty all their own. Even out of ugliness comes beauty. As I look for Your continued leading in my life, Lord, I am learning, as C.H. Spurgeon suggested, to 'sing Hallelujah by anticipation.'" DIANA MORROW

He Is in Control

Like clay in the hand of the potter, so are you in my hand (JEREMIAH 18:6).

One of the hardest questions I have ever been asked was asked by a child. Because her mother, an alcoholic, was unable to care for her, she had been in our home for three years. Through tears of anguish she said, "I thought you said God answers prayers. I've been praying for a long time now, and my mom still hasn't stopped drinking."

The question was one with which I had also been struggling. When we took that little girl and her brother into our home, the chaplain in the hospital's alcoholic ward warned us that the mother might not recover. We dismissed his warning, feeling sure that God would answer our prayer. The mother had received Christ, and we were certain she would recover sufficiently to want her children.

Time passed and the woman was no better. Meanwhile, I met recovered alcoholics and began to question why, when God was doing the miraculous in many lives, there was no miracle for this mother. We had to face the hard fact of her disobedience and selfishness in refusing to deal with her problem.

Today that mother has lost custody of her children. In their formative years, when parents have so much influence, someone else will guide them.

God knows our lives from beginning to end. We have to rely on Him when nothing else makes sense, when our prayers do not receive the answers we long for. The knowledge that He is in control is the only thing that will being peace in certain situations.   ANONYMOUS

Born to Win

Put on the full armor of God so that you can take your stand against the devil's schemes (EPHESIANS 6:11).

I know that as God's soldier I am promised the whole armor of God and admonished to put it on. But sometimes I find myself shaking inside the armor. There are times when the battle is so fierce that I tremble.

At times I have thought of Jehoshaphat's cry to the Lord: "For we have no power to face this vast army . . . We do not know what to do, but our eyes are upon you" (2 Chronicles 20:12). God's answer of assurance came: "Do not be afraid or discouraged because of this vast army. For the battle is not yours, but God's" (2 Chronicles 20:15). In awe Jehoshaphat bowed down and worshiped the Lord. The next morning Jehoshaphat exhorted the people: "Have faith in the Lord your God" (verse 20). They were to trust Him completely as, singing and praising the Lord, they went forth into battle. There is no better way to put the enemy and his hosts to flight than by songs of praise. When they began to sing and to praise, the Lord set ambushes against their enemies and defeated them.

Encouraged by this example, I remember my position in Christ—"hidden with Christ in God," and seated in the heavenly places with Him (Colossians 3:1–3). With such assurance I need not fear any situation. I have the promise of His presence and of victory. Thus encouraged, I adore and worship, stand to praise Him, believe Him and then, singing and praising the Lord, turn to the battle knowing I am more than conqueror through Him who loves me (Romans 8:37). JANIS TIMYAN

Faith

And without faith it is impossible to please God, because anyone who comes to him must believe that he exists and that he rewards those who earnestly seek him (HEBREWS 11:6).

To some, faith may be as vague as the early morning mist that often rises only to vanish as the sun appears. To the Christian, however, it is as real as hope, fear, joy and sorrow.

To a world revolving in the realm of materialism, only those things which can be seen or felt can be accepted. Faith, because it does not fit into such a description, is therefore considered a figment of man's imagination. Yet, God calls faith *substance*. The Christian's honest acceptance of this substantive fact will lift him into a realm in which he can live and move and enjoy the provisions offered by God.

Faith is real. "For it is by grace you have been saved, through faith" (Ephesians 2:8). Not the prophetic utterances of some medium, not an inherent ability such as "an ear for music"—faith is a spiritual gift. We cannot acquire it by effort, but we can improve it by use.

Faith overcomes. Doubt may bring defeat and discouragement, but let the sun of faith begin to rise and it will push back the darkness. "This is the victory that has overcome the world, even our faith" (1 John 5:4). Faith refuses defeat.

Faith is spiritual vision. Faith is to the Christian's spiritual experience what eyesight is to his physical body. Faith sees with the eyes of the soul those things which cannot be seen by the eyes of the body. It is being "certain of what we do not see" (Hebrews 11:1).

Faith is yours for the asking, but it comes by believing, receiving, experiencing and living. Without faith, it is impossible to please God!   DOROTHY SHEPSON

MARCH 14

Do You Need Help?

I said to the Lord, "You are my Lord; apart from you I have no good thing" (PSALM 16:2).

The Psalms have brought blessing to people through the ages. In some, the writer in his anguish pours his heart out to God; in others he rejoices and sings God's praises. Sometimes he expresses how God has heard him and delivered him from fear, doubt and trouble.

In the psalms there is comfort for the believer, and they have ministered to me in recent days as my husband and I returned to India. After a one-year furlough, we were to begin our sixth term of service, and it was hard to leave our four grown children and one grandchild. I wept many tears and asked the Lord if we could not remain in the homeland, at least for a while longer. Although He indicated this was not His will, at the time of parting He gave us grace and strength, as He always does when He asks His children to do something difficult.

After we landed at the crowded, noisy airport, there were the usual procedures to go through, but finally it was over. As we rode toward Bombay City, rain fell in torrents, streets were dirty and people thronged everywhere.

That night, homesick and lonely, I began to reflect on why I had returned. The thought came that I had not come back because of my great love for these people. I had come because I loved the Lord, and I was obeying His command to come and minister to people whom He loved and for whom He gave His life. My prayer was that He might love them through me.

If today you need help, comfort, instruction or wisdom, a look into the Psalms may bring the message you need for this hour.   RUTH LEWELLEN

To the *Known* God

God did this so that men would seek him and perhaps reach out for him and find him, though he is not far from each one of us. For in him we live and move and have our being (ACTS 17:27–28a).

A beautiful friend heard the tragic news that her sickness was cancer. Before enduring the agony of extensive surgery, she declared publicly that "God is God." Her serene acknowledgement of God's total control brought a new submissiveness. Months of recuperation followed, but she was able finally to go overseas and vigorously work long hours among refugees. God has a plan. He is a true Father.

Paul's sermon on Mars Hill (Acts 17:22–25) graphically positions God — as God, as the decision maker, as the true Father. "Lord of heaven and earth . . . he is not served by human hands, as if he needed anything." God laid the plan of salvation. He determined the ministry of Jesus and the Holy Spirit to mankind. He had plans for Jonah even in the belly of the big fish, for the Israelites in captivity, for Joseph in prison in Egypt, and He has plans for us.

God is the true Father. We are the offspring of God not only by creation but by redemption. How wonderful to belong, to relax, to rest in Him. Mary Magdalene belonged to the true Father. She believed and received. The woman at the well believed and received living water. Lydia, Paul's first convert in Europe, heard the message and believed that Jesus was God. She and all her household received God's salvation.

Our God is the *known* God. His Holy Word verifies His reality. He is real. He is alive. We rejoice in His presence today.   DONA H. FERRELL

MARCH 16

Airborne

But those who hope in the Lord will renew their strength. They will soar on wings like eagles; they will run and not grow weary, they will walk and not be faint (ISAIAH 40:31).

There I was, seated on a powerful, majestic airplane — modern from tail to cockpit and moving at some 500 miles per hour. Only 10 minutes had elapsed since takeoff at Toronto's International Airport, where ground conditions were overcast, windy, wet and gloomy. In a matter of minutes, the powerful, birdlike machine had offered me a place of refuge and comfort and had lifted me heavenward to fluffy clouds and fathomless blue skies. The contrast was more than I can adequately describe. Only those who have experienced it know the feeling!

The Lord has allowed me to mother four precious lives, children who are now parents themselves. In the pain and agony of birth, the "skies looked overcast," but only for a brief time. That healthy cry, and the days that followed as I held my child and realized that here was God's precious, miraculous gift, made me appreciate how measureless and vast was God's loving care and concern for me — measureless as the endless blue I saw from the plane's small window.

As my life moves on to more mature years, to "grandma-hood" and freedom from many responsibilities, I marvel at the transitions of life. The nitty-gritty, earthly experiences are preparing me for the heavenlies. The hurting points occur to help me appreciate the "blue skies."

To reach my destination of ministry that weekend, it was in God's plan that I travel through some turbulence and discomfort. Through such practical experiences, He shapes our lives to bring us to a full appreciation of His heavenly riches.   MARION SYLVESTER

MARCH 17

The Source of Life

My people are destroyed from lack of knowledge (HOSEA 4:6b).

As medical science continues to unlock the secrets of the human body, we gain greater insight into the highly complex structure and functioning of that which reflects the image of God. If we would take time to look at the stars, draw a flower, compare the patterns on butterfly wings or describe the sensation produced by a summer's breeze or a winter's downpour, we would begin to hear the voice of nature speaking to us of the character of God.

If we would consider the patterns of family living, or note the depth of feeling in the faces around us on the street, or catch the fervent desire for change in those with physical or emotional difficulties, or see the often futile searching for something more, we would begin to glimpse the meaning of the God-shaped void within us.

As we turn to Scripture and take note of God's character and dealings with man, we begin to feel His image touching us through the pages of the Bible. We hear His voice as He addresses our needs and upholds our faith, challenges our weaknesses and demands our total commitment.

In the midst of all that bears witness to God and His work, how is it that people can still manage to spiritually starve to death? Is it empty indifference? Whatever it might be, let us not take the path of destruction but embrace the Source of Life!   L. BETH DUMMER

MARCH 18

And Be Ye Kind

And do not grieve the Holy Spirit of God, with whom you were sealed for the day of redemption. Be kind and compassionate to one another (EPHESIANS 4:30, 32).

As we start our day with God, let us pray that the fragrance of Christ will be noticed by the world about us. What does it matter if someone is sharp-tongued or irritable with us? Should we flare up and retaliate? Or should we answer rudeness with courtesy, surliness with cheerfulness and annoyance with patience?

How shall we win the lost if our actions are no different from theirs? How can we have an influence for good if we show meaness of spirit? How can we be an example of the best in this sinning world if we show the same spirit of vindictiveness to those who have wronged us? Only as we yield to God and ask Him to show us how to be kind, will the sweetness of our lives turn people to Christ.

Do you have trouble with members of your family, your husband, children, parents or relatives? Do you demonstrate your love for them despite their behavior? Or are you a negative, nagging, condemning, legalistic bundle of so-called virtue whose presence causes resentment?

Families can be upsetting, but if you bathe yourself and them in earnest daily prayer and if you obey the scriptural admonition, "Do not grieve the Holy Spirit. . . . Be kind," regardless of behavior, you will see a response from them that will be positive. Let love so fill your heart that your family is surrounded by its overflow. Behave in such a manner that even troublesome family members will think of you as one who really loves them. Love, prayer and kindness will triumph for God's glory, and you will be enriched in the process.   MARGARET TOMPKINS

Be Not Anxious

Do not be anxious about anything, but in everything, by prayer and petition, with thanksgiving, present your requests to God. And the peace of God, which transcends all understanding, will guard your hearts and your minds in Christ Jesus (PHILIPPIANS 4:6–7).

The threat of war, violence, crime and the open acceptance of sin in our world causes many to be anxious. We do not know what trials we may be called upon to endure in the future. The Lord says, "Do not be anxious!" Why? Because as we live in His presence each day, we know He is in control and is interested in every detail of our lives.

He has given us a formula for peace: "In everything, by prayer." The Lord wants us to bring everything, small or great, before Him in prayer. He wants us to come to Him in a spirit of humility and thankfulness and to be specific in stating our needs and desires.

Obedience to His instruction will result in supernatural peace, peace we will not be able to explain but which we will experience in our hearts and minds as we look to Him.

Remember when the disciples were in the boat with Jesus on the Sea of Galilee? Suddenly a storm came up, and the disciples were afraid. Then they cried to the Lord, and he rebuked the winds and the sea and "it was completely calm" (Matthew 8:26).

What is the tempest in your life today? Do you long for peace and calm? The Lord wants to speak peace to your heart. That peace will keep your heart and mind if you trust and obey.   HELEN MCGARVEY

In His Presence

You have made known to me the path of life; you will fill me with joy in your presence, with eternal pleasures at your right hand (PSALM 16:11).

You awaken so full of a sense of the presence of the Lord that you can scarcely contain your joy, and all that matters is to escape the mundane and to be with the One you love.

Then, suddenly, the hubbub of daily life wraps its tentacles about you as someone slams a door, clangs a kettle down on the stove or turns on the radio. Is your initial reaction, like mine, one of anger — anger at having what is private and precious and beautiful shattered by the cacophony of the ordinary? Is He still there, or have you lost that "other-worldly" feeling that is so special?

What does it mean to be in the Lord's presence? Is it really something so fragile and delicate that it can be broken by the everyday activities of life? Never! When Jesus said, "I will be with you *always*," that is exactly what He meant. Always — in the quiet moments with Him, in the comings and goings of visitors to the house, in the blaring of horns in a traffic jam, in the nasty intrusions of the evil one — always!

As Jesus was there with His disciples in the everyday activities of life — traveling, talking, paying the taxes, eating, visiting the sick — so He is with us. All that is lacking is our awareness of Him. And that is something that can be changed by a quick prayer ("Thank You that You're here, Lord."), or by a moment of thanksgiving ("What a beautiful flower, Lord. Thank You for creating it for me to enjoy."), or by a cry of distress ("Help, Lord! I can't cope with this!"). He is there *always*.   JUDI BRODEEN

On Revelation

Where there is no revelation, the people cast off restraint; but blessed is he who keeps the law (PROVERBS 29:18).

To be without revelation — what a pitiful state! Amos writes about the days of a famine of hearing the words of the Lord, a total lack of revelation from God. People were running here and there, searching for something meaningful in life. When people have cast off all restraints, they drift with every tide. They cannot see because they are spiritually blind.

Today we desperately need people with vision. Just as in the time of Eli, when Samuel was a boy ministering before the Lord, real vision is rare. We find few who are really open to God's revelation.

We are a privileged people. We have in our hands a complete written revelation of God, but do we — do I — allow God to reveal Himself through His Word? Am I well enough acquainted with His law to abide by it? Do I delight myself in God's laws?

Paul writes about our being "conformed to the likeness of His Son" (Romans 8:29). As followers of Jesus Christ, our whole lives should be a revelation of Him to those around us. Where this revelation is lacking, the people are unrestrained. Often we find people apologizing for their language or their conduct when in the presence of a true servant of the Lord.

In order for the Lord Jesus to shine through us, we need to be transparent like a glass lampshade that enhances the light and directs it where it is needed.

May Christ find us open and obedient so that He can reveal Himself to us and then through us to a needy world.

PENELOPE R. HALL

Spare Yourself

For whoever wants to save his life will lose it, but whoever loses his life for me will find it (MATTHEW 16:25).

When Jesus faced the cross, one of His disciples insisted that He spare Himself, but Jesus recognized this as a message from the devil and pointed out that it was not the way of God.

God ordained and intended from the beginning for a woman to find her highest joys and greatest fulfillment in giving of herself and sacrificing for those she loves and for those in need. A vain woman who lavishes all her energy and love upon herself may appear to be very beautiful and glamorous in the eyes of the world, but that mother scrubbing clothes, washing dishes or rocking a fretful baby in her arms is beautiful in the eyes of God.

Though we may have a true desire to fulfill God's purpose in our lives, we continue to struggle. Many times each day a choice must be made. The voice of the flesh and the devil whisper, "Spare yourself." The voice of the Spirit whispers, "Deny yourself. Give yourself." Which voice shall we obey?

The cross of Christ confronts each of us — the life of denial of self and of our own desires, wishes and ways. Christ's message is always give, spend and be spent. Will we spare ourselves or be spent for Jesus?

As we serve in the home, in the church, in the neighborhood and in the world, Jesus says, "Give, give, give!" Our enemy says, "Spare yourself. Hold back. Hang on to what you have. Live within yourself and for yourself." Jesus says, "Open your heart and life to selfless giving and living, and I will use you and bless you and fill your life with joy unspeakable."   MAURINE BERKNER

Try Praise

Give thanks in all circumstances, for this is God's will for you in Christ Jesus (1 THESSALONIANS 5:18).

I had been having difficulty with one of my assistants from an outstation clinic. We had requested that he and his wife, also an assistant, move back to our Pyramid Clinic after their temporary assignment.

Nap Yikwa refused to return. His wife came and helped us, but Nap said that he would rather do nothing at all than come to our area, that he did not like the people and did not want to help them. He was angry with me and told his wife if she continued to help me he would divorce her.

His rebellion and dreadful attitude weighed me down and affected the other clinic assistants, even though they did not agree with him. Our relationship became strained; every time I saw Nap I felt tense and frustrated.

But the Lord did not allow me to remain frustrated. Everything I read seemed to be on the theme of praise as the beginning of victory. I asked the Lord to help me to praise Him in this situation.

Every time I saw my assistant, I would thank the Lord for him. Throughout the day whenever I thought of Nap I would give thanks to the Lord and praise Him in obedience to His Word—even when I did not feel like it.

Now I no longer feel tense or frustrated when I see Nap. The heaviness I felt in his presence is gone. Though he still refuses to help us and is still in the same unhappy state of rebellion, I want to laugh sometimes because of my complete change of feelings.

Perhaps today there is a situation that is causing you tension and frustration. Try praise. It really works!

MAGARET RUPP

You, Lord

Lord, you have assigned me my portion and my cup; you have made my lot secure (PSALM 16:5).

You, Lord. Do we fully comprehend the beauty of this relationship? Almighty God, Creator, Alpha and Omega, is our Lord. "You have assigned me." This great God has taken our position in life as a serious matter of concern! He has gone so far as to assign our cup. God's beautiful plan for our lives is completely known to Him.

"But," we complain, "my cup is not as glamorous as another's. My portion is bitter." Remember, God has assigned that which comes to us. If He assigns, then He also equips! Life is a perfecting process through which we will someday be like Jesus Christ Himself.

For 12 years, I have been a missionary to Japan—a culture far different from that of the West. Although outwardly Western, Japan is inwardly very Eastern. Life here for me has been a perfecting process. I have cried more, hurt more and been more burdened during this missionary journey than in any other time of my transient life. My portion and my cup have been assigned. I know beyond any doubting that the perfecting process, though often slow, is taking place.

The psalmist goes on, "You have made my lot secure." Since our Lord has assigned us, we may rest perfectly secure. Whatever is poured into our cup comes from His boundless love's supply. What a source of comfort, healing and strength this knowledge gives.

Neither shrink in the face of trial or suffering nor be carefree in the face of blessing. Your cup and portion have been assigned. All has come to you from your Father's loving hand. Rest secure in that love. JANICE KROPP

Joy of Surrender

"Who for the joy set before him endured the cross" (HEBREWS 12:2).

As a Christian woman I am being called to a life of continual surrender in the everyday involvements of motherhood. At times it has brought about genuine crisis in my life and required me to lay aside my will, my rights, my time and even my priorities. It is in these very challenging times, however, that God has met me through His Word, encouraging me on in the joy of surrender.

One of the most recent examples God has used to reinforce this principle of surrender has been Abraham, who, with Sarah, faced many crises. The first of these crises was the call to leave their homeland, family and friends and go to a destination God would show them. What an encouragement to see the principle of surrender result in God's approval and blessing.

Then later, in the separation from Lot, Abraham had every "right" to choose first. He chose, however, to rest in the faithfulness of God and to surrender his right.

The highest call to surrender in Abraham's experience was God's command concerning Isaac. It was almost unthinkable. This was his only son. How could he surrender him back to God through sacrifice? Yet, expectantly, he proceeded toward that critical moment of surrender. Just as he was about to plunge the knife into Isaac, God provided a substitute. Victory through surrender!

Let us thank the Lord for His example, for His surrender, for new opportunities to trust Him, for pressing us into the joy of surrender.   JUDY CHAPMAN

How Well Do I See?

Do not judge, or you too will be judged (MATTHEW 7:1).

It was early morning. In the temple courts, Jesus was surrounded by an eager crowd of listeners. Suddenly the teachers of the law and the Pharisees forced their way to where Jesus stood. A disheveled woman, eyes red from crying, was half dragged, half pushed to the front. Her accusers hurled the facts of the case at Jesus and asked their question, hoping to trap Him.

Silently they awaited His response. Instead, Jesus stooped and wrote with His finger on the ground. As again the men told of the act of adultery and the demands of the law, they asked, "What do you say?"

Slowly Jesus straightened up and looked at them. "If any one of you is without sin, let him be the first to throw a stone at her" (John 8:7), he answered quietly, then stooped and wrote again.

Overwhelmed by the terrible awareness of their guilt, the accusers left one by one. What, then, was Jesus' word to the woman? "Then neither do I condemn you. . . . Go now and leave your life of sin" (verse 11).

Jesus' words ring in my ears—"Why do you look at the speck of sawdust in your brother's eye and pay no attention to the plank in your own eye?" (Luke 6:41). It is easy to delude ourselves that our vision is perfect. We feel competent to judge the attitudes and actions of others. Like the men in the story, we insist that Jesus pronounce judgment. Yet He shows us that our vision is distorted because we view everything through the grid of our own sin.

Let us ask the Lord to fill us with the same forgiveness and acceptance of others that He showed to that guilty woman.   GLENDA WELDON

The Lord Our Refuge

The eternal God is your refuge, and underneath are the everlasting arms (DEUTERONOMY 33:27a).

Sometimes in life's journey we pass through dark valleys of trouble. But in the midst of the darkness we have a refuge, a safe place, the eternal God our Savior. His loving arms uphold us and shield us all day long. This verse was a source of strength and comfort to me while I was going through one of the most difficult experiences of my life.

As my husband was driving our van homeward after an Easter service in a village church in India, a motor scooter with a side car came from the opposite direction. While passing us, he suddenly swerved and collided with our front wheel. The impact pulled our vehicle over to the wrong side. We immediately helped the injured passenger to the hospital and reported the accident to the police.

But when the relatives of the scooter's driver saw the position of our car, they decided to bring suit against us. I was falsely accused of causing the accident by reckless driving.

Following the initial hearing, I was shocked to discover that my lawyer did not believe I was not driving our vehicle. Soon after, however, he was convinced of the injustice of the case against me and defended me well.

God brought about my acquittal nearly a year later. But during those months, as I stood in the criminal stand and heard false testimony against me, I remembered what my Savior suffered for me. He understood what I was going through and gently drew me close to Him. His purpose was being accomplished as we witnessed of Him to lawyers and people in the court whom we would otherwise never have met. The eternal God was indeed our refuge. MURIEL ENTZ

God's Faithfulness

A righteous man may have many troubles, but the Lord delivers him from them all (PSALM 34:19).

What do you do when your daughter calls to tell you that because of a custody battle, your two grandsons, six and eight years old, were kidnapped by their father from a Christian grade school? What do you do when, after 26 months, you still do not know where they are or if they are alive?

What do you do when the doctor tells your husband he must have immediate surgery for throat cancer and that the larynx may be affected?

What do you do when your three-year-old grandaughter withdraws tearfully when playmates taunt her inability to hear or speak?

What do you do when, from miles away, your daughter informs you that an emergency trip to the hospital is required to save the lives of herself and her unborn child?

What do you do when the ambulance, sirens screaming, hurtles toward the hospital in a desperate effort to save your husband's life?

What do you do? You obey God's Word, "Call to me and I will answer you" (Jeremiah 33:3).

The Lord answered our call, and His miracles were the evidence. Our grandsons were returned to their mother. The cancerous throat tumor miraculously disappeared before surgery. Ears and tongue loosed, our grandaughter hears and speaks perfectly today. Daughter and baby were miraculously spared. Bypass surgery on my husband's clogged arteries provided a collateral blood system.

Truly we serve a faithful God of miracles to whom we should give all honor and praise!   GLORIA CARTER

Service

The Lord said to him, "Who gave man his mouth? Who makes him deaf or dumb? Who gives him sight or makes him blind? Is it not I, the Lord? Now go; I will help you speak and will teach you what to say (EXODUS 4:11–12).

God is not looking for our ability but only for our availability. In Exodus 4, God instructed Moses to go, but Moses drew back and began to make excuses. "Lord, I can't do that job; I don't have the gift of speaking. Lord, who am I? They won't even listen to me." The question really is not "Who am I?" but "Who is our God?" God answered "I am that I AM! I am Jehovah."

The question is not "What are my gifts?" or "What can I do?" but "What has God told me to do?" I am not responsible for what the people do or for whether or not they listen, but woe is me if I do not obey God.

There are two pastors in Soubre, but there are also some 60 villages. To enable the pastors to reach these villages, I sometimes have to fill their pulpits. I love to teach, but I have always felt that preaching should be done by preachers. Furthermore, in this area, people are not too ready to listen to a woman. Even though I am frequently troubled by the same questions that plagued Moses, I know I must obey.

We are to be the spoon or fork in the Master's hand, available to be used as He wishes and not as we wish. If a mother picks up a spoon to feed her child and the child spits out the food, that is not the spoon's fault. The spoon's only responsibility is to let the mother use it as she wishes. Let us be willing to be spoons in His hand, obedient and available for whatever He asks us to do, leaving the results with Him.   KATHLEEN SOLVIG

The White Orchid

Give, and it will be given to you. A good measure, pressed down, shaken together and running over, will be poured into your lap (LUKE 6:38).

As a token of their appreciation for speaking at a Ladies' Retreat in Irian Jaya, Indonesia, the women presented me with a lovely orchid plant. The single spray held six lovely white blooms, each the size of a medium rose. So I picked it and brought it into the house where I could enjoy it most. Very soon all the blooms were gone from the plant, and nothing remained but ugly roots and bare leaves.

The orchid bloomed again, however, and, not realizing its potential, I picked that also and brought it in to where its pure white beauty was the admiration of all who saw it.

Later another spray began to develop, and I eagerly watched its growth. To my amazement, a second spray appeared and the two began to bloom simultaneously. I showed it off to everyone who came.

One of our MKs was to participate in a final concert before going to the States for further studies. I thought it would be nice for Melanie to have an orchid corsage. I picked one spray, added delicate fern, wrapped the end in foil and attached a bow. It was gorgeous. When Melanie saw the lovely white orchids, she decided to wear them in place of the corsage she had already received.

I watched the remaining spray grow and bloom with more beautiful flowers than ever. Six months later, bloom number 12 was budding. And they continued to come.

May God help us that in every way we might give, not only to receive but to share that others may also have joy!

MARY CATTO

True Sacrifice

How can I repay the Lord for all his goodness to me? (PSALM 116:12).

The Africans have a proverb: "Mayimbi gave away the rat but held on to its tail!" These words have something to say to all of us, especially as they relate to our acts of sacrifice to God.

In the Old Testament, much emphasis is placed upon the burnt offering, an offering "made by fire, an aroma pleasing to the Lord" (Leviticus 2:2). Such sacrifice was meant to encourage the giver to gratefully acknowledge God's mercy and goodness. In essence, it indicated that the giver offered up his entire being in a voluntary surrender to God.

This idea is not exclusive to the Old Testament; we also read in Romans 12:1 the exhortation to "offer your bodies as living sacrifices, holy and pleasing to God." Hebrews also urges us, "Through Jesus, therefore, let us continually offer to God a sacrifice of praise . . . And do not forget to do good and to share with others, for with such sacrifices God is pleased" (13:15–16).

Today our affluent lifestyle often keeps us from fully understanding the true spirit of sacrifice. We tend to give out of our abundance rather than our poverty. We find it so much easier to give of that which costs us nothing. God, however, calls us to a life of giving, of giving until it hurts, out of a heart of love for Him. This sacrifice, then, becomes "a fragrant offering, an acceptable sacrifice, pleasing to God" (Philippians 4:18).

If God calls on us to sacrifice something today, may we be quick to respond and to offer it joyfully for His glory.

JANE RAFFLOER

A Promise from God

Train a child in the way he should go, and when he is old he will not turn from it (PROVERBS 22:6).

This beautiful promise contains a condition for us to fulfill. Training is a long and sometimes tedious job, but it is exciting to see God doing His part in the lives of our children as they grow.

A short time ago, I received a small piece of paper stuck inside a letter from our daughter, Renee, who was away at MK school. This is what it said: "Put a grain of sand into an oyster, and in time there grows around that grain a pearl of great beauty. The grain of sand is worth little, but what grows around it is valuable and lasting." *Lord, make me like that little grain of sand; make me something that will grow and become valuable and lasting, something that will be beneficial to all those whose lives I touch. Lord, make me like You, please.* At the end she wrote, "I copied the first part, and the rest is a prayer for me that I thought I'd share."

How exciting to see God working, molding and making little girls into women who love Him and spend time in His presence.

How often do you take time to pray for your children? Don't wait until they are grown; begin today — even before birth! Pray for them, teach them, show them your love for the Savior, and God will complete His part of the promise, "When he is old he will not turn from it."   RUTH BOWMAN

Reaffirm Your Love

Now instead, you ought to forgive him and comfort him, so that he will not be overwhelmed by excessive sorrow (2 CORINTHIANS 2:7).

We have all heard a lot about forgiveness. David, Hosea, Peter and many others wrote on the subject. Paul, however, leads us one step beyond forgiveness.

Many of us are quick to apologize and make restitution when we have offended someone. But what steps are we willing to take when we have been hurt? Paul says to comfort those who have offended us. Strangely enough, the act of reaching out in comfort has a healing effect in our own soul. This reaffirmation of our love may require some tangible expression — a warm hug or a plate of cookies.

My friend and neighbor in Ecuador became angry with my husband and me when her son expressed interest in going into the ministry. She told us to get out of her life and to leave her son alone. We tried to talk with her and apologized for having offended her, even though we were the ones offended. I waited a few days for her to calm down, then I sent her a jar of homemade jam with a note, "I hope our friendship will be sweet again." A few days later I sent her a package of seeds and a note, "May our friendship blossom like these flowers." When there was still no word from her, I sent her a set of pretty cloth napkins and a card, "Can't we clean up this misunderstanding?" The following Sunday I invited her to come for coffee. She came, and we laughed and chatted as though nothing had happened.

My friend never did ask my forgiveness for what she had said, but I was able to forgive her, comfort her and confirm my love to her.

Is there someone who needs to know you still love him or her? Begin today to reaffirm your love.   CONNIE D. SMITH

A True Picture

I will also give him a white stone with a new name written on it, known only to him who receives it (REVELATION 2:17).

If I were to place before you two white eggs, you would not be able to tell much about them. Are they hard boiled? soft boiled? rotten? fresh? You could, however, test them by floating them in water, spinning them on a flat surface or even dropping them.

We have people all around us every day, and there is simply no way we can tell who they really are except by testing them. Even then we cannot be certain.

While my husband's body was being invaded by deadly cancer, we received many tributes from a wide variety of people. Among them were students. These young people ran errands, did laundry, brought meals, notes, flowers.

One student often wrote beautiful cards and signed them with his first name only. At first I could not identify him. One day the following note arrived: "You may be wondering who I am. I am the tall, blonde fellow who used to help you in the library." Later I learned his identity and realized that his description of himself was not at all as I would have portrayed him.

Revelation 2:17 tells us about a white stone on which our new names will be written. In that day there will be no doubt as to who we really are. Our description will be contained in one name, a new name. In that day we will know ourselves as we really are known by our Creator, God. If, as someone has said, this is the true photograph of the soul, will it be a picture of the person God intended us to be?

BEATRICE CARTMEL

Erase Old Tapes

Bless those who curse you, pray for those who mistreat you (LUKE 6:28).

She was a really close friend, an older woman whom I greatly admired and respected, yet her words hurt me deeply. To make this trip to visit her and her family, I had ridden in the back seat of our car, cringing as every jolt sent pain to my injured neck.

As we traveled homeward, my pain was mental as well as physical. The "tapes" of my mind kept repeating her words, "My, you've gotten fat!" *Lord, how can I get victory?* I prayed. *I do love this woman, regardless.*

"Pray for her," the Lord seemed to say. And pray I did.

Waking in the night with neck pain and heartache I prayed, "Lord, restore our relationship. Let it please You again." Each time the "tape" replayed, I short-circuited it by praying for her. In time the heartache was gone, replaced by God's peace.

A few months later my older friend wrote to me about a severed relationship with one of her close friends. "How could she say those things about me? How can I get victory again?" she wrote. I shared what the Lord had taught me through my own problem, never revealing, however, that the problem had been with her.

Later she wrote, "I hope your friend and you have as good a relationship now as my friend and I do. Your suggestion works!"

Are you plagued by mental "tapes" that replay hurtful words? Pray for the one who hurt you. Ask the Lord to bless that one. He turns bitterness to peace and restores relationships. SHARON T. KENDALL

Take Time

The Lord your God is with you, he is mighty to save. He will take great delight in you, he will quiet you with his love, he will rejoice over you with singing (ZEPHANIAH 3:17).

I worked for a year in an orphanage in the Philippines. One of our charges was Mark, a husky two-year-old with a large head, square shoulders and sturdy, thick legs. He was so heavy that I could not pick him up and carry him any distance. He was also active, running here and there, grinning his big, foolish smile when he saw me and, in spite of his size, acting like a perfect coward, reduced to tears, when boys much smaller than he pulled his hair.

One day as Mark was running through the orphanage, intent on some errand of mischief, I called, "Mark, come here." He stopped, redirected his course and came toward me. I pulled up a chair, sat down and held out my arms to him. He grinned and climbed onto my lap, then flopped his heavy head against my chest and dangled his legs on either side of me. I put my arms around him and hugged him as hard as I dared.

I felt sorry that I had not interrupted his activity to do this more often. So many times I forgot that he was still a very little boy who, in spite of his eagerness to be on the go, needed to take time out to receive love. Mark would come and sit on my lap when he was hurt or sick. But when things were going well, he just wanted to run.

All of us get very busy in our lives and forget that we must take time to be with the Lord. Especially on days when everything is going right and we are busy, we need to climb into His lap and feel His arms around us. Then when it is time to return to our work, we are reassured of His love.   DEBBIE COWLES

An Apple a Day

In a desert land he found him, in a barren and howling waste. He shielded him and cared for him; he guarded him as the apple of his eye (DEUTERONOMY 32:10).

To be the apple of one's eye is to be cherished. Let us think of ourselves in that light.

An apple is round, representing the never-ending love of God. It is found in almost all temperate parts of the earth, reminding us that God's love is widespread. Whether we are a run-of-the-mill kind of person (like the more common varieties of pippin, or russet) or someone of distinction (like a cortland or rome), we are special to Him.

Apples possess seeds that make them capable of reproducing themselves. And the seed of truth that was planted in us at salvation makes it possible for us to reproduce and disciple other believers.

Apples have varying textures and flavors. Some are used for sauce, some for pies and some for juice and other purposes. God has a different purpose for each of us, depending upon talents and gifts.

Apples are attached to the life-giving branch by a stem. We receive our ability to please God and to produce fruit by abiding in Christ, the vine.

The old adage that a bad apple can soon ruin the whole barrel full is a warning to us that our lives have more of an impact than we think. Many people have been disillusioned because one of God's children has failed to live an exemplary life.

But even fallen apples are usable in making cider. When we err, disappoint our Father or fall into spiritual dryness, rescue is near at hand. Confession and contrition bring renewed fellowship. ETHEL K. HUTTAR

Everlasting Water

Come, all you who are thirsty, come to the waters (ISAIAH 55:1). *On the last and greatest day of the Feast, Jesus stood and said in a loud voice, "If a man is thirsty, let him come to me and drink"* (JOHN 7:37).

In the Holy Land we visited a village about 10 miles outside of Damascus. As we drove slowly down the road, we came upon a group of 5 or 6 young women walking together to the well to get water. Each woman deftly and confidently balanced a tall jar on her head, laughing and talking as she gestured freely with both hands. I watched with amazement at the feat these women performed with such ease. How many times a day did they come to get water? Once? Twice?

As I watched, I realized that these women were enjoying each other's friendship in the same way I did when I met my neighbor at the supermarket. Sometimes it is a real chore to do the weekly grocery shopping, but how much more difficult it must be to carry water each day to use for various purposes.

How unbelievable Christ must have seemed to the Samaritan woman at the well, when He spoke about the everlasting water and told her she need never thirst again.

Our Lord always comes to us in our extremity. It was a miracle that she stopped to listen to Him and another miracle that she believed. Surely she was lonely, for if she had had more than one "husband" she would certainly avoid the other women at the well. She was most likely the topic of their conversation.

Over and over in the ministry of our Lord we see that He came to help those who were in need. He came to seek and to save those who were lost.   ARVELLA SCHULLER

Patterns for Living

Do not conform any longer to the pattern of this world, but be transformed by the renewing of your mind (ROMANS 12:2a).

Our final, senior home economics assignment was knitting. I chose a fairly simple pattern for a long-sleeved, V-neck pullover sweater. Very quickly into the project, however, I discovered that knitting and I did not get along. In fact, we began to avoid each other, and soon time was running out. With graduation approaching, my sweater only vaguely resembled the pattern. I finished it just in time, but "it" was a mess!

Do you know what happened to that too short, too wide, sleeveless, "long-sleeved" sweater? No one ever wore it, or even admired it. My mother tucked it away in a drawer for purely sentimental reasons.

God's Word gives us patterns for living, patterns with clear directions for our speech, our thoughts, our actions and reactions. He has also given us the perfect pattern in His Son, Jesus. If we *know* Him well, if we *follow* Him closely and if we *love* Him above all else, His pattern will be duplicated in us. This requires allowing Him to make drastic changes in that sinful nature that pulls us toward the world.

We have all momentarily abandoned God's pattern and have had to deal with the consequences. Some have finally chosen to leave God's pattern and, sadly, their lives resemble my "sweater"—useless and laid aside, unable to bring glory to the Creator. If, however, we obey and daily follow His pattern, we will continually enjoy the work of His creative power in our lives—a peaceful, joyful life that will forever bring honor to His name.   CONNIE C. MCMASTER

APRIL 9

Doing vs. Being

Whoever can be trusted with very little can also be trusted with much (LUKE 16:10).

I spent several hours on my knees that day — not in Bible reading or intercessory prayer — but in scrubbing floors. There were times when my mind wandered to the correspondence on my desk, the number of people on my visitation list and the talk to be prepared for a certain church group. I knew that the task was not a glamorous one, yet it was necessary for the health of my family and as an example of order and discipline.

The mental battle continued as I completed the living room. I had often talked about this with the Lord — *doing* tasks versus *being* tasks, public ministry versus private training grounds. Halfway through the dining room, He reminded me of the 30 years in Nazareth which had as their primary purpose the molding of character and growth in wisdom and grace (Luke 2:40, 52).

As my arm grew tired and the blister on my knee enlarged, I became aware of a sense of stillness, a quiet communion with the Lord that is hard to achieve in the bustle of public ministry. He taught me about the stubbornness of stains and the beauty of cleanliness. The freshly scrubbed rooms spoke of the importance of renewal times when my Savior would root out cobwebs of doubt or ignorance and the hidden dirt of "sophisticated sins."

The arrival of my children, eager to share their day and ever forgetful of removing their shoes, served to remind me of the Lord's patience when my best intentions and eagerness to serve only muddy my pathway.

Even in the menial tasks we may learn spiritual lessons if our hearts and minds are open.   L. BETH DUMMER

Reaching Out

Therefore encourage one another and build each other up (1 THESSA-LONIANS 5:11).

Have you identified with Paul when he was under pressure far beyond his endurance so that he actually despaired of life? The loss of a child, a serious car accident, stinging misunderstandings and unwanted daily pressures have occasionally driven me to that point.

I remember times when I said, "Lord, I can't take any more." God met me through His Word, but He also used His children to minister to me. As I wrestled with the hurt of an unwanted move, the words of my son, "God will lead us, Mommy," brought courage to my heart. When the words of a very critical letter rung in my ears, that little note, "We believe in you" brought hope and joy.

Once, after some particularly hard news, I read Ecclesiastes 4:9–10, "Two are better than one, . . . if one falls down, his friend can help him up. But pity the man who falls and has no one to help him up!" I thanked the Lord for those who had helped me up so many times.

One day a young man got on the bus I was riding in Piura, Peru. He stood up front with a bag of candy, explaining that he was a university student in need of funds. One hundred soles (2 cents), the price of his candy, would not hurt anyone, he said, but it would help him. As he continued speaking, one phrase stayed with me: "Hoy para mi, manana para ti" (today for me, tomorrow for you). As he passed along the aisle, hands reached out everywhere, eager to buy. His expression, "Hoy para mi, manana para ti!" was in my mind as I reached for my candy.

Reach out and encourage someone today. Tomorrow you may be the one needing encouragement!   FAITH FIELD

Hope, Believe, Win!

Against all hope, Abraham in hope believed and so became the father of many nations, just as it had been said to him, "So shall your offspring be" (ROMANS 4:18).

Without weakening in his faith, Abraham faced the fact that his body, at about 100 years of age, was as good as dead and that Sarah was beyond childbearing age. Yet, Paul tells us that Abraham "did not waver through unbelief regarding the promise of God" (verse 20). He had complete confidence that God had the power to do what He promised.

Abraham can be held up as the ultimate example of hope to those of us who succumb to anxious moments while waiting for God to act. "Against all hope, Abraham in hope believed." When we are against all hope, it is so easy to waver in our unbelief. What we really need to do is to keep our subjective feelings in tow and to keep our eyes on the objective.

Like Abraham, we may frequently have to go back to God's promises to us. For example, if we were strictly honest, we would confess to moments of doubt when it seemed that our family's material needs would not be met. However, God in His Word promises us that He richly provides for our every need (1 Timothy 6:17). In faith, we can be sure of what we hope for and certain of that which we do not see (Hebrews 11:1). Then, like Abraham, we are strengthened in our faith. God does richly provide.

What has God promised to you that is against all human possibility? Has He given you the chance to strengthen your faith by placing you against all hope? If so, rejoice and be an Abraham! Stand faithfully on the promises of God, and in hope believe.   DONA SCHEPENS

APRIL 12

The Weaver

Be still, and know that I am God; . . . I will be exalted in the earth (PSALM 46:10).

One of the ways of God that continually amazes me is how He weaves the pieces of my life into one fabric. This fabric has become a protective covering, and the feel of it can only be described as knowing Him.

For years I was beautifully sheltered by my pastor husband. We were a team in marriage and ministry. I was just getting the hang of this wife bit when he died of inoperable cancer at the age of 60. It was not hard to give him back to the One to whom he had always belonged. We recognized that God had given us to each other for a time, and our confidence in Him held steady.

I was sure that my ability to adjust to my aloneness came from Christ's own life in me. But my acceptance was shattered when I became ill. During one long night of dialogue, my Father asked questions of me, gently but firmly, and then comforted me as I faced the answers.

"What are you saying on the inside?"

For the first time I realized that down under the outward calm I was yelling incessantly, "I won't have this . . . this inability to make decisions . . . this physical weakness that sends me to bed . . . this need to depend on others."

"Didn't you tell Me that you wanted above all else to know Me in this new role? If I choose that you be laid aside in order to know Me, why do you resist My way for you?"

Then I saw the reason for my anger — my personal independence was in jeopardy. That tendency to run with the bit in my teeth had resurfaced.

God dealt with me until I could say to Him, "I want to be still and know that You are God!"   MARY A. DUNLAP

APRIL 13

Trials Make Us Strong

Consider it pure joy, my [sisters], whenever you face trials of many kinds (JAMES 1:2).

No one looks forward to trials. We hope life will go along relatively smoothly. Yet in reality this is not good; as someone wisely said, "If all our life were sunshine, it would become a desert."

Why are trials necessary? "Because you know that the testing of your faith develops perseverence" (James 1:3).

When the Israelites fled from Egypt, why did God lead them through the desert rather than by a shorter route? The young nation, just freed from slavery, was unfit for battle. God knew they could not withstand their enemies. They needed first to learn about Jehovah, so He made His presence visible among them in the pillar of cloud and fire. Later in their journey they faced fierce enemies. Under Joshua's skilled leadership they fought decisive battles.

In our continuing walk with the Lord, we will surely face trials that we could not have endured as young believers. The Bible is replete with examples of those who faced trials like ours. James reminds us of the prophets and mentions Job and Elijah (James 5:10–17). Add to this list of those who endured trials, Ruth, Esther, Deborah and Mary Magdalene. God's strength in their weakness is available to us today (2 Corinthians 12:9).

As we "fix our eyes on Jesus," we can experience pure joy in trials. "Blessed is the [woman] who perseveres under trial, because when [she] has stood the test, [she] will receive the crown of life that God has promised to those who love him" (James 1:12).   ELIZABETH I. ARNOLD

APRIL **14**

What Do We Do?

You will not have to fight this battle. Take up your positions; stand firm and see the deliverance the Lord will give you. . . . Do not be afraid; do not be discouraged. Go out and face them tomorrow, and the Lord will be with you (2 CHRONICLES 20:17).

As a first-term missionary, Second Chronicles 20:1–38 became very precious to me.

I soon realized that I had no natural language ability and that I must depend upon the Lord. I would pray each principle of this prayer back to my Heavenly Father.

1. We must *look at who He is* (verse 6) — the God of the universe, powerful and mighty. No one can stand against Him.

2. *Remember* past victories (verse 7) — God's faithfulness to Israel, to the church and to us.

3. *Appeal* to the honor of His name (verses 8–9). His name is at stake, not ours. It is His responsibility to maintain its righteousness and holiness.

4. *Present* the problem (verses 10–11). Notice that the problem is not even mentioned until verse 10.

5. *Admit* weakness (verse 12). We need to tell Him that we cannot do it. We must humble ourselves.

Language study was very humbling. Imagine babbling like an infant and being laughed at for the way you talk. God had spiritual lessons for me to learn in language study.

6. *Focus* your eyes on Him (verse 22).

7. *Trust* in Him (verse 20).

8. *Sing and praise Him* (verse 22). Notice that the victory was not attained until singing and praising were done.

I am so thankful for these lessons in prayer that God gave me through language study. DONNA G. DIRKS

The Gift of Friendship

May the Lord deal with me, be it ever so severely, if anything but death separates you and me (RUTH 1:17b).

The philosopher, Ralph Waldo Emerson, said that the only kind of people who are fit to be true friends are those who are magnanimous. Webster defines magnanimous as "noble in mind; high-souled; generous in overlooking injury or insult; rising above pettiness or meanness." Putting it more simply, magnanimous people are those who truly know how to love.

As we look at the book of Ruth, we find an example of this in the person of Naomi. She had an extraordinary ability to draw out devotion and respect from others, and in this case it was from her daughter-in-law, Ruth. In Ruth 1:16–17, we have an expression of affection of such magnitude that this passage has often been used as part of the wedding ceremony. What characteristics must one possess in order to call forth such total dedication from others as these words describe?

The Earl of Clarendon said that such a person should have "the skill and observation of the best physician, the diligence and vigilance of the best nurse, the tenderness and patience of the best mother." Bishop Jeremy Taylor further added that friendship is "the greatest love, the greatest usefulness, the most open communication, the noblest sufferings, the severest truth, the heartiest counsel and the greatest union of minds of which brave men and women are capable."

There are sacrifices to be made in attempting to raise our friendships to their highest potential, but the effort is made easier when we remember that to love and be loved is worth all our best efforts. MARTHA BUSS

Sacrifice of Praise

Through Jesus, therefore, let us continually offer to God a sacrifice of praise — the fruit of lips that confess his name (HEBREWS 13:15).

My cheeks were flushed and my pillow wet with tears as I cried out in anguish to God. My younger sister who was seven months pregnant had just confirmed to me that the lump found in her breast several days earlier was malignant. Why God? How could it be, God? My thoughts ran in circles. Just two months earlier, two of my older sisters had died within two weeks, and I was still grieving. Now the thought of losing another was almost more than I could bear.

I had always believed that God has a purpose for everything He allows to come into our lives, but as I prayed, my heart questioned whether God could not use some other way to teach us the lessons He wanted us to learn. These seemed so very difficult.

As my sobbing subsided and my anguish calmed, it was as though the Lord Himself stood by me saying, "My child, I just desire that you praise Me. Praise Me for I am still in control, and I do all things well, for My way is perfect."

I began to praise Him for who He is, for His love and faithfulness, even though I could not understand all the circumstances. As I praised Him, the burden lifted and peace and joy once again began to fill my soul. That night I began to realize what it meant to "offer to God a sacrifice of praise" — not only to offer praise when everything is going well, but praise in the midst of sorrow, conflict and hurt. That is the *sacrifice* of praise.   MARY G. BLOCK

Home's Loving Aroma

Above all, love each other deeply, because love covers over a multitude of sins. Offer hospitality to one another without grumbling (1 PETER 4:8–9).

Looking down my private memory lane I not only see a large white frame structure called "home," I also remember the many wonderful aromas of popcorn, fudge and homemade bread. I am grateful that my childhood occurred before the instant, fast-food age and that it included those cherished times spent in the kitchen, learning, experimenting, tasting and sharing a time-worn recipe with family and friends.

As a result, I had a desire to open my home and communicate love and hospitality to many world travelers, musicians, young people and close personal friends. More importantly, it encouraged me to place my own immediate family high on the priority list of favorites for special dinner invitations and celebrations.

I believe it is the right of everyone in my family, when coming into the house, to smell freshly baked buns or cookies. Such treasured moments can be interpreted as "Someone here loves me — I am important to her." My finest lace cloth, crystal and a candle add a fragrance to the atmosphere of an otherwise long and often trying day.

As the nest empties and a family of four begin to establish their own homes and build their own family memories, I trust they will often refer to lessons well learned around table and fireplace, to the aromas and special settings that were a way of saying, "I love you." May they often apply the principles of First Peter 4:8–9 to one another and then to lonely, hurting people as well as loving brothers and sisters in Christ. MARION SYLVESTER

APRIL 18

A Purified Heart

The Lord does not look at the things man looks at. Man looks at the outward appearance, but the Lord looks at the heart (1 SAMUEL 16:7b).

Our first term as missionaries was spent at the Ambachico Bible Institute in Colombia. Omar Valencia had earned the title of foreman of the little farm that was part of the property.

When Omar was a little boy, he was asked to bring the cows carefully down the mountains from their grazing meadows to the milking shed. Day after day he performed his task without error. One day, however, a cow slipped and fell and broke her neck on the way down.

It was the best cow in the herd, so the owner became infuriated and, for punishment, pushed Omar into a dark room and locked him in. The owner then went and cut the heart out of the cow and made Omar eat the raw meat so that he would learn how to have a more concerned heart of his own for things of value.

Omar did eat that heart and, in his childlike way, he believed that it filled him with compassion.

As Christians we are to have a heart like Christ's. Compassion like His comes not through a physical ordeal, such as Omar endured, but through abiding in Christ and feeding on His Word. Can God look inside our hearts and find the desire to love, obey and serve Him in His harvest field?   WANETTA GROENEWEG

Our Protector

Without warning, a furious storm came upon the lake, so that the waves swept over the boat. But Jesus was sleeping. The disciples went and woke him, saying, "Lord, save us! We're going to drown" (MATTHEW 8:24–25).

Fears come in many forms: fear of not having a job, of not having good health, of not being successful, of not being accepted. People also fear that they may become victims of fire, flood, earthquake, famine or accident.

This thing of fear and uncertainty is not simple. Our Shepherd, and Guide . . . can be *in* the boat with us and we can still cry out in fear. We may even make decisions based on that fear, turning away from Him without analyzing it, instead of looking only to Him and trusting Him to give us a solution in the face of sudden danger, sudden fear.

What was wrong with what the disciples said? On the face of it, they were calling to the right Person, the Lord, for help. We know, however, that their attitude did not please the Lord, nor did their lack of faith.

We cannot fool God with our words. He knows our attitudes, our thoughts, emotions, feelings. He knows our fears and doubts. We may pray with very right-sounding words for God's direction and help while we are mentally working out our own solutions.

What we do about our fears and uncertainties needs to be constantly examined and reexamined. The message to Isaiah was: "The Lord Almighty is the one you are to regard as holy, he is the one you are to fear, he is the one you are to dread, and he will be a sanctuary" (Isaiah 8:13–14a).   EDITH SCHAEFFER

(Excerpted from the *L'Abri Newsletter*, 7/4/85, and used by permission.)

Walk in the Light

But if we walk in the light, as he is in the light, we have fellowship with one another, and the blood of Jesus, his Son, purifies us from all sin (1 JOHN 1:7).

L et us consider what it means to walk in the light: "God is light; in him there is no darkness at all" (1 John 1:5) and "Just as you received Christ Jesus as Lord, continue to live in him" (Colossians 2:6). Light is the opposite of darkness. There is much darkness and sin in the world. Paul exhorts us to "put on the armor of light" (Romans 13:12). He continues, "Clothe yourselves with the Lord Jesus Christ" (verse 14). "For you were once darkness, but now you are light in the Lord. Live as children of light" (Ephesians 5:8).

To illustrate, think of walking on a dark road with a friend who is using a flashlight to shed light on the path. You must keep close to that friend and follow carefully. Jesus has told us that He is the light of the world and that if we follow Him, we will not walk in darkness (John 8:12). In order to walk in the light, we must keep close to the Lord and follow where He leads.

"It is a life of dependence and communion, step by step, receiving Him afresh as our all-sufficiency, our wisdom, strength and holiness" (A.B. Simpson).

We must take every opportunity, in word and deed, to be a witness for Christ to the unsaved. We should walk in love and in the Spirit, that the fruit of the Spirit may be evidenced in our lives. Then, with clean hearts, we shall have fellowship with one another. "Come . . . let us walk in the light of the Lord" (Isaiah 2:5).   HELEN MCGARVEY

He Knows Best

This is what the Lord says — your Redeemer, the Holy One of Israel: "I am the Lord your God, who teaches you what is best for you" (ISAIAH 48:17).

Have you ever doubted that God really knows what is best for you? Dealing with some of the uncertainties of missionary life in a third-world country has brought me nose to nose with this temptation.

Some of my most persistent doubts have come, not as a result of great spiritual upheavals, but because of the common, ordinary household "snafus." After all, I reason, how could God's best be forthcoming in a recalcitrant washing machine that seems to look forward to breaking down in mid-washday? And what were His purposes the day the piano tuner removed the piano's action to replace a broken string and knocked the whole apparatus off the table, breaking hammers and scattering pins and calling for a major repair job?

As I analyze my feelings, I realize that I am not unlike the rich young ruler who was unwilling to part with his prized possessions in order to follow Jesus. I ask the Lord to teach me how each grievance makes me more dependent on Him.

Now I can sympathize with the majority of Peruvian housewives who have no washing machine and have to use a scrub board or a stone to clean their clothes. I can better understand my piano students whose lessons are less than perfect because they have no piano at home on which to practice.

As the Lord teaches me what is best for me, I am able to see even the mishaps as part of His plan!   MARY HIXSON

He Gives Victory

For the Lord your God is the one who goes with you to fight for you against your enemies to give you victory (DEUTERONOMY 20:4).

As we seek to obey our Lord's commands and to live according to His will, we experience all kinds of resistance and hindrance. Satan, our arch-enemy, uses many means and agents to fight against us and defeat us. As he did Eve in the garden, he tempts us to disobey God and to doubt His love. He seeks to keep us from laying up treasures in heaven by luring us after the world's pleasures and by keeping us preoccupied with the cares of this life.

Whenever we enter Satan's territory to proclaim God's liberating gospel and to make disciples, he opposes, delays and hinders. We have found this true throughout our years of missionary work in India.

Seeing the ripening harvest and great need of workers here in Gujarat State, we became aware of the need for a suitable discipleship training course. God led us to use the Navigators' material, "The 2:7 Series." With their permission, we began the translation. The only experienced Christian man available to help us put this difficult manuscript into the Gujarat language accepted the challenge willingly. A few weeks later, however, he returned the manuscript saying he could not do the work due to health problems. There was no one else who could do it. We turned to our Lord, reminded Him of His promise to fight for us against our enemies and claimed His victory.

About a month later, the worker who was so needed returned to tell us the glad news that God had healed him and that he would do the work. "But thanks be to God! He gives us the victory through our Lord Jesus Christ" (1 Corinthians 15:57). MURIEL ENTZ

APRIL 23

Love and Hospitality

The end of all things is near. Therefore be clear minded and self-controlled so that you can pray. Above all, love each other deeply, because love covers over a multitude of sins. Offer hospitality to one another without grumbling (1 PETER 4:7–9).

I t is nice to have visitors whom you have invited — or even three or four strangers with whom you can fellowship. It is another thing when you have your house arranged and clean for the chairman and his wife and two guests from America and then must also receive 100 men who will walk through your living room with dirt on their shoes and spill water from the water cooler.

On Friday, as I approached such a circumstance, I knew I faced a challenge. My American visitors were to arrive on Sunday, but all day Saturday, a hundred men from the villages would be meeting in our carport.

In my devotions that day, I came across the above verses and put them on a card on my refrigerator to memorize. I prayed, "Oh, Lord, help me to use hospitality without grudging." As I thought about the verses, I noticed that we are not only to have love one for another but that we are to have *fervent* love. This love is not in me but must come from God. It is only such love that covers a multitude of sins.

May the Lord give us such love, not only for the brethren but for the strangers who may come at inconvenient times.

KATHLEEN SOLVIG

APRIL **24**

Self-sacrifice

His divine power has given us everything we need for life and godliness through our knowledge of him who called us by his own glory and goodness (2 PETER 1:3).

There were once two porcupines who lived in Alaska. Desiring to get warm, they drew close to each other. As they did, they needled one another. It hurt so much that they pulled apart. But when they did, they got cold again, so they drew close once more, and hurt each other as before. Their predicament—they were either cold or hurting.

All too often this is the situation even in Christian homes. Personality differences are like the quills of the porcupines. They can get tangled and cause hurt. We must work at our relationships so that we will demonstrate the Christlike qualities of love, compassion, self-sacrifice and a forgiving spirit. The motto for our homes should be: "Be completely humble and gentle; be patient, bearing with one another in love" (Ephesians 4:2).

Love demonstrates itself in action. Have we done something today to demonstrate our love for our families? Love takes pleasure in its object. Jesus' example of love and compassion teaches us that it is possible for these qualities to be part of our Christian homes.

Self-sacrifice is against our human nature, yet it should be part of our "new nature." If each of us had an attitude of self-sacrifice, what a change would come about in the atmosphere of our homes. Self-sacrifice is total unselfishness.

Loving unselfishly does not mean making the least of ourselves but making the most of someone else. We view the other person through the eyes of Jesus.

This thought can transform relationships in our homes, especially with our unsaved loved ones! JO ANN LEMON

APRIL 25

The Prophet Elijah

Yet I reserve seven thousand in Israel — all whose knees have not bowed down to Baal and all whose mouths have not kissed him (1 KINGS 19:18).

Once each year Arab Christians make a pilgrimage to Haifa to visit Elijah's cave on Mt. Carmel range. There they remember his work as a prophet of God. Elijah is still thought of by both Jews and Arabs as one of the most important prophets of God. Each Passover Seder, the Jews prepare a place and anticipate the coming again of Elijah.

This great prophet spoke up to King Ahab about the false prophets of Baal and in a contest slew all of them. When Ahab's evil wife, Jezebel, sought to take his life, Elijah fled into the wilderness so discouraged that he wished to die. Here God miraculously provided for him, and he was strengthened in body and spirit.

Elijah complained to God that the children of Israel had forsaken His Covenant and he, only he, was left. He must have felt that not another loyal heart was left in the land. Then God answered His servant, Elijah, and assured him that he was not the only faithful one. Indeed, there were 7,000 who were serving the one true God.

Even today there is in Israel a remnant of Jews who have put their trust in Jesus, the Son of God, and are faithfully speaking up like Elijah. We can pray that these believers will not be discouraged but will realize they are not alone in their faith and witness.

Also, let us take warning from Elijah's failure and remember we are not alone in our witness. May we be faithful and willing to speak out wherever God wants us to, so that all people will hear the gospel and many will be saved.

CLAIRE LIVINGSTON

Hannah's Dedication

So now I give him to the Lord. For his whole life he will be given over to the Lord (1 SAMUEL 1:28a).

Corruption was rampant in Israel at the time of Elkanah and Hannah. The people were "religious" and went faithfully every year to Shiloh to worship God and to present their sacrifices. But even Elkanah had problems. He had two wives, and there was dissension in the home.

Hannah's life was difficult. Even as she worshiped, she could not forget how Peninnah constantly taunted her about being childless. Satan knew where Hannah was weak and vulnerable.

What did Hannah do? She went to the Lord in her anguish and cried out to Him. She then prayed specifically for a son and promised the Lord that he would be given back to the Lord for all of his life.

Again Satan attacked her. The priest accused her of being drunk. When she poured out her heartbreak, Eli saw her earnestness and gave her good counsel.

Hannah's circumstances did not change. Hannah herself was changed. If God would give her a son she was now ready. She had passed God's test.

In due time Samuel was born. Then came the time for the costly sacrifice. Though she could have found many reasons not to give him up, Hannah did not go back on her promise to the Lord. God saw Hannah's heart of obedience and blessed her with three more sons and two daughters.

What are you holding close to yourself, afraid to dedicate to the Lord? Your family? Your time? Your home? Pleasure? Temper? Bitterness? Trust God with *all*. He will not be one of many treasures, or even chief of all treasures. He will be all in all or not Lord at all.   BARBARA SCHAEFER

Human Love

I have set you an example that you should do as I have done for you (JOHN 13:15).

"Mother, could you?" "Mrs. G., do you think you would have time to . . . ?" "Sweetheart, I forgot to tell you that I invited _____ for supper tonight." Does that sound familiar?

Sometimes my reservoir of "human love" runs dry with the continual drain of daily relationships, cares and responsibilities. I am aware of the shallowness of my little pool of love, but God is ever willing to fulfill my request for love from His vast reservoir. He fills me to overflowing when in a moment of truth I realize my complete inadequacy.

For example, the doorbell rings just as the family is sitting down to dinner. Two (or three or four) young military men have just arrived home from sea duty and are dropping in to say hello.

My emotions say, "Oh, no, Lord. Not tonight. I don't think I can cope." My heart says, "Lord, I committed the day to you early this morning; be my strength." As I open the door, my mouth says in sincerity, "Welcome home, fellows, we've been praying for you. Come on in. We're just sitting down to eat, and there's plenty for all." In a split second the Lord pours in His strength and love and I find them sufficient.

That takes care of the constant emergencies, but what about long-term endurance required when the aged or ailing come to live with us? Or what about the child that is so difficult and triggers an ongoing battle of wills? Christ *was* and *is* sufficient. Whatever the demand—immediate or ongoing—His strength is made perfect in our weakness (2 Corinthians 12:9).   HELENA GARRICK

APRIL **28**

Don't Miss God's Best

I have come that they may have life, and have it to the full (JOHN 10:10b).

To encourage daily Bible reading among our Zairian high school students, we all use a calendar prepared for us by Scripture Union. What terrific lessons it contains for teacher and students alike.

This morning we looked again at the life of Joseph. I thank the Lord again for revealing Himself to me the night I first met Him, even as Joseph revealed himself to his guilty brothers. God changed my tears of fear to those of joyous recognition and brought me to the place where I could forgive myself (Genesis 45:5a).

And what a marvelous provision God has made for us because His Son went before to prepare the way for us. Why do we even give one thought to the old life in the desert where we were starving or try to hold on to some earthly treasure and miss the very best God has prepared for us? What we hold on to looks so worthless when we see the accomplishment of His purpose (verse 20).

The forgiven brothers went back home to their father with this amazing story, "Joseph is still alive! In fact, he is ruler of all Egypt." And what was poor Jacob's reaction? He was stunned; he did not believe them (verse 26).

Our faith is as weak as Jacob's when we just "hear" the good news, but when we begin to see and experience the firstfruits in our own lives, then we know that our Redeemer is alive!

Let us not be like Jacob. Let us not sit here "starving to death," trying to hold on to something of this life and missing the very best God has prepared for us, as we stay close to Him.   NORMA HART

On Romans

And we know that in all things God works for the good of those who love him, who have been called according to his purpose (ROMANS 8:28).

O ur first years as missionaries in Irian Jaya were spent at an isolated station on the edge of Lake Tigi. Every day I talked to the women, I witnessed their joyless, burdensome life. I saw their sorrow over the death of loved ones—especially their own babies. I longed to convey sympathy but was hampered by my lack of language skill.

Then I became pregnant. As the months passed, my friends in the village rejoiced with me. As I reached eight months, I left for the coast to have our baby in a Dutch hospital. All the village women waved goodbye as we boarded the plane. Of course they anticipated, as we did, the day when we would return with our child. But when that day came, our arms were empty. After living only two days, our infant was taken, leaving me with a keen realization of the sorrow and grief so often experienced by my Ekari neighbors.

The look on their faces revealed their unspoken question, *Where could it be?* I explained, "Jesus took my baby. He is in heaven, and someday we shall see him again." As they wept with me they said, "We thought we were the only ones who suffered like this. Does God really love us too?"

"Yes, He loves you too. He loves everybody," we eagerly told them. "And He comforts us in our sorrow."

Was this ability to share mutual sorrow the reason God took our son? Only He knows. But one thing I do know—it worked for good to those Ekari women who realized for the first time that God loves everyone and that He is the healer of broken hearts! MARY CATTO

Find Rest in Him

In repentance and rest is your salvation, in quietness and trust is your strength (ISAIAH 30:15b).

Some of the most profitable times for me have been the mornings I spent reading, writing and studying while on family vacations.

On two occasions we went to Hawaii, where I was to cut an album — once with the Alliance Trio and once a solo album of songs I had written. Finding a quiet place out by the pool or on the patio, I would spend two or three hours every morning alone with the Lord.

Years ago, family vacations did not afford me this luxury. We spent the mornings trying to get everybody's clothes organized for the day. Each child (four in all, but at times it seemed more like eight) had his own camera — loaded by Daddy every morning. Planning where to go and what to do each day usually ended in my wanting to take the next plane home.

My husband, Roy, would lead the way with them, and I would bring up the rear, grumbling and mumbling (talk about Miriam, I expected to wake up any morning and find myself snowy white with leprosy). Then there was no time for rest and relaxation, but now I can thoroughly enjoy vacations. Even though our children still go with us most of the time, we tell them we will meet them for dinner. Roy sleeps late, and I enjoy my meditating.

In returning and rest, in quietness and confidence, we can find what we need — Himself!   DELORES TAYLOR

Let Me Carry That!

A man of sorrows, and familiar with suffering. . . . Surely he took up our infirmities and carried our sorrows (ISAIAH 53:3–4).

We were home on furlough and nicely settled in a big roomy house in downtown Toronto. My husband was on missionary tour in British Columbia.

The children and I loved being with my dad, and it gave them a sense of belonging after the long separation from family.

Then suddenly he was gone! Stricken with a heart attack, he died late one night, all alone. No more loving, laughing Grandpa. No more dear, understanding Dad.

Letters, phone calls and visits helped me greatly. Yet the real comfort lay in reading in God's Word such passages as, "A man of sorrows, and familiar with suffering."

To be familiar with a subject is to know it thoroughly. Jesus saw, He knew and He identified Himself with a suffering world. He watched the widow of Nain as she followed the casket of her only son. He heard the sobbing of Mary and Martha at the tomb of Lazarus. He watched it all. He became acquainted with grief—*their* grief, *our* grief.

But it does not stop there. "Surely he took up our infirmities and carried our sorrows." How precious to tear-stained eyes are those words! If we are carrying a heavy bag up the stairs and someone says, "Here, let me carry that," and he takes it from us, who is carrying it? Is it not the one who took it from us?

The passage does not say that He took it away, thrust it from us or stamped it out. He does that with our sins. Sorrow is very different. He *lifts* our sorrows to His shoulders and walks right along beside us. He just comes to us and says, "Let *Me* carry that!"   MURIEL KELLY

Jesus, Multi-faceted Treasure

In order that they may know the mystery of God, namely, Christ, in whom are hidden all the treasures of wisdom and knowledge (COLOSSIANS 2:2–3).

A rare jewel is often so because of its many facets, each one catching light or adding dimension to give it depth and clarity. So too, is Jesus, the rarest of jewels, multi-faceted.

During recent travels, I became aware of these many facets. When gazing on the awesome beauty of rising mountains in West Virginia and lush evergreens and snow-capped peaks in Washington, I saw the majesty of God, revealed in His glorious creation. Such majesty cannot compare to the majesty in which Jesus will return.

In a boat that seemed minute by comparison, I viewed Niagara Falls from its base. In the awesomeness of that occasion, my soul responded in song. I knew that surely all nature would praise God for His power in creation if I did not praise Him first.

Canadian gardens were filled with flowers — each colorful blossom perfectly made. Yet Jesus, Rose of Sharon, is lovelier than those blossoms.

The peaceful, clear blue waters of Bermuda pale in comparison to Jesus' clear, unclouded vision. Seeing the ruins of ancient Greece only reminded me that Jesus is timeless.

Though majestic, powerful, clear-visioned and timeless, Christ is even more — my Savior, my Friend. Think of it — that we may own so rare a jewel, Jesus in our hearts, a multi-faceted treasure!   SANDRA MINTNER

What Is in Your Bag?

Do not have two differing weights in your bag—one heavy, one light (DEUTERONOMY 25:13).

Just like in Old Testament times, we find people today who are sometimes unfair in weighing out measures. But what about us, as Christians? Do we, in the same way, deal from the bag of our lives different measures for different people? Does our treatment of others vary? Does their position in life have anything to do with the way they influence our attitudes?

God told the Israelites not to be unjust in weighing out the grain and supplies they sold to others. They were to use perfect and just weights. He promised long life to those who conducted business in absolute honesty.

Let us ask the Lord to give us the ability to treat all men alike—not with certain actions toward those whom we consider prominent and other actions toward those who are not. "Here there is no Greek or Jew, circumcised or uncircumcised, barbarian, Scythian, slave or free, but Christ is all, and is in all" (Colossians 3:11).   DELORES TAYLOR

By God's Appointment

But he knows the way that I take; when he has tested me, I will come forth as gold (JOB 23:10).

Are you often puzzled about what to do in difficult situations? Do you wonder what God expects of you? Do you struggle to find an answer or a way out?

It seems that Jonah faced this same problem. He wanted to evade responsibility. Jonah's soul even fainted within him, and it was then that he remembered the Lord (Jonah 2:7). Your prayers are the God-ordained means for turning trouble into blessing. Instead of fleeing here and there and turning to people who cannot help, turn to God.

While undergoing a difficult experience in his own life, Andrew Murray learned the following lesson:

> In time of trouble, realize that God put you here. It is by His will that you are in this place. You may rest in that fact. Next, He will keep you here in His love and give you grace to behave as His child. Then, He will make the trial a blessing and teach you the lessons He wants you to learn. And finally, He can bring you out again—how and when He knows. We need only remember that we are here—(1) by God's appointment, (2) in God's keeping, (3) under God's training and (4) for His time.

These thoughts have been a blessing to me through the years.   CLAIRE LIVINGSTON

Crossings

Be assured today that the Lord your God is the one who goes across ahead of you like a devouring fire (DEUTERONOMY 9:3a).

I stood on the river bank watching the muddy water toss great logs like so much sawdust, remembering how just a few weeks ago, I had stood on the opposite shore dreading the crossing. It was not the physical crossing of the Mekong River from Thailand to Laos that I feared — especially since the trip was made by plane. It was what the crossing signified.

Initially, there was the ideological crossing from capitalist to communist society, part of which meant going from a society where consumer goods were abundant to one where even the most essential items were scarce or unavailable. Would I remember to take the right things with me? What if my daughters got sick? Would I think to include all the medicines we might need?

I would also be making a spiritual crossing from the warm Christian fellowship of church and friends. In Laos I could have little open fellowship with national believers and would find few English-speaking Christians.

Finally, there was the emotional crossing of leaving the familiar — friends, activities, home — to face the unknown. Would the girls find friends? How would they occupy their time? Could we be content in two gloomy hotel rooms?

But as I read the passage from Deuteronomy about God going across ahead of us, He gently reassured me that He would cross all my rivers ahead of me and be with me on the opposite shore.

Life is full of crossings. As you face your next one, remember that "the Lord your God is the one who goes across ahead of you."   JEAN ANDRIANOFF

Why Worry?

Who of you by worrying can add a single hour to his life? (MAT-THEW 6:27).

Philippians 4:6 cautions us not to be "anxious about anything . . . ," in other words not to worry. But how many times in our daily lives do we find ourselves worrying about a host of things including finances, our children or the future? There is an old Chinese proverb: "Why worry about how to cross the river if you have not even arrived at the shore yet?"

Anxiety is said to be undefined fear. When we find ourselves worrying or being anxious, it is very important to clarify what we are afraid of. Commit it to the Lord, and then act upon truth. Do not live according to the feelings that accompany worry or anxiety.

How good it is to know that we can pray and not worry, realizing that we are praying to a God — *our* God — who is all sufficient!

"Do not be anxious about anything, but in everything, by prayer and petition, with thanksgiving, present your requests to God. And the peace of God, which transcends all understanding, will guard your hearts and your minds in Christ Jesus" (Philippians 4:6–7). NANCY MARTINEZ

'Tis My Duty!

See to it that you complete the work you have received in the Lord (COLOSSIANS 4:17).

We met in far-off Rangoon, Burma. Petite, black-eyed Nellie, wife of the local pastor, was a busy mother — marketing, cooking, caring for her family. Known for her good works, she visited the sick, cared for the bereaved and ministered to the many needs of their precious flock.

When we first visited Rangoon, Nellie had everything organized for our comfort and pleasure — a smiling welcoming committee at the airport, a man who took time to show us the sights, trips to the markets and temples and a delicious meal served in her home. When I would remonstrate with her for going to so much trouble, she would always respond, "'Tis my duty, Madam."

Nellie had a strong sense of duty to the Lord she loved and served. She remembered His words: "Whatever you did for one of the least of these . . . you did for me" (Matthew 25:40).

So many times I remember Nellie's words, "'Tis my duty, Madam," said with an air of dignity and a sense of highest privilege, never of odious responsibility. When I feel like "the drudge in the kitchen" or am called upon to do something I would really prefer not to do, I hear her clipped Burmese English: "'Tis my duty, Madam."

Today as you face the many demands upon you, perhaps from your children, your employer or from your congregation (if you are a pastor's wife), I hope you will remember these words, "'Tis my duty," from Nellie, who was proud to be a soldier of the King of kings, proud to have the privilege of putting others first, proud to serve! BETTY HUNT

The Promise of Comfort

What is the matter, Hagar? Do not be afraid; God has heard the boy crying as he lies there (GENESIS 21:17).

Word had come to us via a telephone call from Kinshasa, Zaire, that our 20-month-old grandson had died. How would our Heavenly Father comfort our son and his wife and their other small son? With my eyes full of tears, I threw myself into the arms of Jesus and asked Him to show me afresh that God is alive and caring — a personal God who cares for His children.

As I leafed through my Bible, the Father of all comfort fixed my eyes on Genesis 21:17 first, and then I understood anew how God is dealing with human beings — even little boys — in this present time. It was as if God was saying to me, "I also heard your little grandson cry."

Further on, two more verses caught my attention, Genesis 45:7 and Genesis 50:20. Our Father makes no mistakes. He is the same faithful, loving and caring Father, teaching and disciplining us as we go. In those moments of precious fellowship with Him, He comforted me with the thought that this little boy is safe with Jesus; never again will he be sick or sorrowful. Not a soul can harm or hurt him, for he is safe in the arms of Jesus.

How wonderful that we can come into the presence of Jesus, who comforts us, teaches us and helps us to glorify Him, even in times of sorrow and trial. Trials test our faith in God, but we have His promise that all things will work together for our good (Romans 8:28).   BETSY STRINGER

Where Are the Servants?

Humble yourselves, therefore, under God's mighty hand, that he may lift you up in due time (1PETER 5:6).

In 1 Peter 5:5–10, God teaches the ultimate lesson in humility and submission. We are to *humble ourselves* even as Christ chose to humble Himself.

There is a time to pray, and there is a time to act. We need to put our prayers for humility into practice. Begin to serve. What needs to be done is usually pretty obvious. What is lacking is someone who is willing to put on the servant's uniform and pitch in.

God knows us very well. He knows how we hate being treated as servants, how we resent being lorded over. Therefore, immediately after giving us the clear command to serve humbly, God begins to reassure us.

He will give us special blessings for obeying; He will lift us up; He constantly has His eye on the situation. No one puts us down without His knowledge. No one stomps on our "rights" without Him taking notice. He is intensely interested in the minute details of what happens as we carry out His order.

To put all our concerns to rest, He tells us the end of the story. If we are determined to remain humble, if we are determined to serve others, keeping a watchful eye out for the devil and his traps, then God, at just the right moment, will lift us up and set us firmly in place. How is that for a promised promotion!   PAULINE A. MORRIS

God of All Comfort

Who comforts us in all our troubles, so that we can comfort those in any trouble with the comfort we ourselves have received from God (2 CORINTHIANS 1:4).

That Almighty God, the Creator of the universe, will comfort us in times of deep distress and sorrow is an awesome thought. I experienced His comfort and grace when my husband went to be with the Lord, and now I am able to comfort others who suffer loss.

I often wondered if the Holy Spirit would comfort and give grace to those of another culture as He had done for me. My husband and I worked for many years among the Quichua Indians in the northern jungles of Ecuador. Three years after his death, a tragedy struck our small town of Pano.

Pastor Santiago, along with a group from the church, boarded a small motorized canoe to go harvest corn at a nearby outstation along the Napo River. As they neared their destination, the waters became very turbulent and the canoe capsized. Among the seven who drowned was Santiago's wife, Beatriz. Would the Holy Spirit work in His same comforting way no matter what the nationality or the culture?

Santiago, in the wake of that river tragedy, suffered severe satanic attacks on his mind, but I saw the Lord wonderfully deliver him and give him the very mind of Christ. He continues to live victorously, as the Holy Spirit comforts and guides.

He is the God of all comfort who guides and gives grace just when we need it most.   MARY KADLE

Stir Up the Flame

For this reason I remind you to fan into flame the gift of God, which is in you through the laying on of my hands (2 TIMOTHY 1:6).

Having been reared in the country, I know a little about making a fire! My mother's kitchen stove was not the "drop in" builder's unit that can be found in many kitchens today. Rather, her range was an enormous black and white enamel wood stove with four places for pots and a reservoir which provided hot water. The large oven took up a major part of this kitchen appliance, and it devoured wood ravenously.

In the combination living room, study, den, playroom and library, we had a potbellied coal-burning stove with a glass door on the front. The only thing central about this heating system was its location in what we called our "great room."

When my mother got up in the morning, she always built the fire in the kitchen stove and then stirred up the coals in the potbellied stove. These coals had been smoldering all night, so she only needed to stir them a bit, add a piece or two of kindling wood and shortly the fire was burning brightly. At various times during the day, she would call me to "stir the coals." When she did, I knew to obey or else the corner where I was sitting reading my book would soon become quite chilly.

I thought about this one morning when I was reading where Paul told Timothy to "stir into flame" that which was in him.

Before someone can stir into flame, there must have been an original fire built. Jesus brought that fire to our hearts when He saved us. When we obey and stir the flame, others will benefit from its warmth.   DELORES TAYLOR

A New Garment

But seek first his kingdom and his righteousness, and all these things will be given to you as well (MATTHEW 6:33).

As a young, clothes-conscious missionary, I arrived in France acutely aware that at one time it had had a reputation for being the fashion capital of the world. Not having a lot of money for clothing, but determined to impress, I began to spend time window-shopping and pattern-book browsing. I was hoping to find an efficient, economical way to look nice.

Insult was added to injury when I compared myself to a fellow missionary who was endowed with more natural beauty and better economic resources. Oh, the distress I felt when I tried to compare myself to her. What frustration I felt as my schemes to impress by creativity became tangled in the sewing threads. I spent — wasted — many precious hours in agonizing, resewing and rescheming.

Conviction came and a crisis was reached. God spoke to me concerning the time that I had been devoting to what had actually become an obsession. He encouraged me to praise Him for creating me exactly as I was. I now felt that God would have me give more of myself in responding to the needs of others. And more time must be spent on grooming my inner, spiritual self.

Chastened, I began to obey that inner voice, and an amazing thing happened as I spent time actively seeking the kingdom of God and His righteousness. Neighbors gave me nice clothes which they no longer needed. Parents lovingly gave clothing gifts. God helped me to become a wiser shopper. The most beautiful result, though, was that I began to long to be dressed in the most appealing style of all — to be clothed in God's righteousness!   PAULINE REESE

Be a Prayer Warrior

Pray in the Spirit on all occasions with all kinds of prayers and requests. With this in mind, be alert and always keep on praying for all the saints (EPHESIANS 6:18).

Years ago, while serving as a missionary in Colombia, South America, I was taken to the hospital suffering a severe blood loss from a miscarriage. The emergency was so serious that the doctor told my husband I would not have lived until dawn if it had continued.

We learned later that a member of one of our churches felt the burden to pray for me at the precise time of the emergency. She was alert to the voice of the Lord. She did not say, "It is too late to pray for Jane. I will pray in the morning." She prayed then, and I am alive today!

Do we really believe that God will answer when we pray? A recent experience confirmed this for me.

During a Billy Graham Crusade I served as a counselor. One night my assignment placed me beside a lovely lady. I discovered before the service that she had attended church most of her life but had not received Christ. She told me she was thinking about going forward that night but that she was very shy. I assured her that I would go with her.

When the invitation was given, we walked the long aisle, and she put her trust in Christ. At the 24-hour follow-up call, she said: "I have such wonderful peace! Is this what it means to be born again?"

There is one additional thrilling piece to the story. Soon after the crusade, she went home to visit her father who was ill with cancer. When she told him about her decision to follow Christ, tears came to his eyes. He said: "I have been praying for you for five years!" Does God answer prayer? Indeed He does!   JANE COGGINS

Unfinished Vessel

But we have this treasure in jars of clay to show that this all-surpassing power is from God (2 CORINTHIANS 4:7).

Lord, many years ago
You placed your encircling arms around me.
During the ensuing years
You have guided me through tunnels, green pastures,
dark valleys.
But you always brought me back
to the mountains.
Today you have brought me
literally to the mountains of Irian Jaya.

Like the clay to which the potter
continues to apply pressure to form the vessel,
so I feel each day
pressures that are forming me
to Your image.
But that same potter who uses one hand
to apply pressure from without
uses the other hand within the vessel
to keep it from collapsing.

I am ten thousand miles away
from my homeland
but I am still turning
on that potter's wheel
like my fellow Christians.
Lord, mold us, form us, shape us,
that some day we all may be placed
on our Father's pedestal
as finished vessels.

CAROL MCDONALD

Only the Beginning

Therefore, I urge you, brothers, in view of God's mercy, to offer your bodies as living sacrifices, holy and pleasing to God—this is your spiritual act of worship (ROMANS 12:1).

The church which my husband was pastoring in Ohio chose for its annual missionary conference the familiar words of Isaiah 6:8, "Here am I, Lord. Send me." We cut out the letters for each word in the text and hung them over the sanctuary door so they could be seen by people as they left the services.

On the last night of the conference just before the congregation arrived, we noticed that the letter "S" on the word "Send" had fallen to the floor. My husband promptly got out the stepladder to replace the letter, when we suddenly realized that the sentence now read, "Here am I, Lord. End me."

What a powerful one-line sermon! So challenging was the new message that we decided to leave it for all to see and hoped that it would be implemented in their individual walks with the Lord.

How vital it is that we end ourselves before we can be sent. It has been said that a cross is simply an "I" which has been crossed out. Paul said, "I have been crucified with Christ and I no longer live, but Christ lives in me" (Galatians 2:20). So often in our service for the Lord, we feel that to be effective we must be clever, talented or bold, when actually these factors are of little importance. What really matters is that the vessel be empty for God to fill with His Spirit then use for His glory.

May our prayer today be, "Here am I, Lord. End me." Only when we come to the end are we really beginning.

JUDY WOLFE

Are You Awake?

Carry each other's burdens, and in this way you will fulfill the law of Christ (GALATIANS 6:2).

In the 20th chapter of Acts, Paul was in Troas where he and the believers met to break bread together and conduct a church service. After eating, he began to preach to his Sunday "dinner on the grounds" crowd. Because he was leaving the following day, his message lasted until midnight, and a young man named Eutychus fell asleep in the window. He was sleeping so soundly that he fell three stories to the ground. The crowd thought he was dead, but Paul embraced him and pronounced him alive.

Verse 8 says that there were many lights on in the meeting place. What a beautiful picture! Oh, Lord, grant that many lights are burning in our churches—not only those powered by the utility company but those who are lights to a darkened world and who keep in touch with the Source of power.

Even though, in our churches, lights are on, the Word is being preached and there is much activity, there are still those who are asleep. Eventually they fall away from the assembly. But like Paul, someone should go to their aid, caring enough to constrain them, embrace them and nurture them back to a relationship with God.

Not one word of condemnation was spoken to Eutychus about being alseep. The believers just loved him and broke bread with him.

Verse 12 says they were "greatly comforted." In other words, the church was ecstatic about this miracle. May God help us to be caring and compassionate toward those in our churches who are in the *windows asleep.* May we not condemn, but care. DELORES TAYLOR

Anticipation

Set your hope fully on the grace to be given you when Jesus Christ is revealed (1 PETER 1:13).

Observers say that there are fewer deaths in retirement and nursing homes just before the holidays or when relatives or friends are expected to visit.

We have all experienced what planning a trip does to us. Sometimes the excitement keeps us awake the night before we start. It is also true that when we are getting ready for a visit from a son or daughter or some close friend, we seem to have extra energy.

If we are going to live healthy lives, we need to plan ahead for joy and satisfaction. That means to make sure we see the bright side of life.

When we look back at our lives, it should merely be to see what lessons we have learned. It is, after all, the future that should concern us. Joseph Addison said in his poem:

> When all Thy mercies, O my God,
> My rising soul surveys,
> Transported with the view, I'm lost
> In wonder, love and praise.

To be in good spirit, we need to have a goal ahead of us. When my husband was asked what were the 10 best years of his life, he would reply, "The next 10." At age 78, he was still planning ahead rather than living in the past.

Asking God to help us keep a bright outlook on life and counting His blessings every day will bring excitement and more robust health to our lives. God's promise is, "Never will I leave you; never will I forsake you" (Hebrews 13:5). What better word could we find for confidence, health and happiness?   EVELYN LETOURNEAU

God's Wisdom

If any of you lacks wisdom, he should ask God, who gives generously to all without finding fault, and it will be given to him. But when he asks, he must believe and not doubt (JAMES 1:5–6a).

The young Christian mother wept as she spoke of her divorce. With a hopeless gesture, she cried, "Why do I always have 20-20 vision—hindsight! Now I know that everything was wrong—my attitude, what I said, what I did. Why didn't God give me wisdom when I prayed?"

How many of us remember with tears the things we should have done and how we should have done them? Do we wonder why we did not see things then as we do now? Naturally, as we follow Christ, His Spirit does impart grace and wisdom for the battles of life. Yet too many of God's children confess a lack of wisdom. Too many tears are shed in retrospection.

In James 3, the author describes two kinds of wisdom. He tells us that wisdom from above is, first of all, pure. God's wisdom cannot come to a sinful heart. Sin causes us to make decisions that bring hurt and failure.

Wisdom from above is also peaceable. "For where you have envy and selfish ambition, there you find disorder and every evil practice" (verse 16). How can wise decisions be made when there is contention and strife in the heart? God comes to hearts that wait until they are quiet enough to hear His still, small voice.

James further describes this wisdom as "submissive"—"It allows discussion and is willing to yield" (verse 17, TLB). A know-it-all attitude obstructs God's wisdom.

If we, as women in His presence, are to face the challenges of life in a troubled world, we need the *genuine* wisdom from above.   HELEN CONSTANCE

Promise of Comfort

Do not be afraid; do not be discouraged. Go out and face them tomorrow, and the Lord will be with you (2 CHRONICLES 20:17b).

All of us have experienced fear at one time or another. These fears have their basis in many different things. Sometimes we fear people, circumstances, the outcome of circumstances or the unknown. Fear of the unknown can be the greatest single fear.

The vast armies of the Moabites and Ammonites were coming to make war against the people of Judah. Jehoshaphat, king of Judah, was *afraid*. How did he handle his fear? He proclaimed a fast for his people, and together they sought help from the Lord. God gave them this promise: "Do not be afraid or discouraged because of this vast army. For the battle is not yours, but God's" (20:15b).

After more than six years as missionaries in Ecuador, we were preparing to take an eight-month study furlough, and I was filled with fear. My husband and I were going to be studying at a state university far from friends and relatives. Would we be able to find a place to live? Would we have enough money to meet all of our needs? Could we find proper schooling for our four children ages 8 to 15?

One night, unable to sleep, I called upon the Lord for help. He gave me the same promise that He had given the people of Judah. "Do not be afraid; do not be discouraged. Go out and face them tomorrow, and [I] will be with you." What a promise! I claimed it every time I felt afraid.

Just as the Lord took care of Judah in a most unusual way, He provided for us. It was exciting for our family to see God bless us with even more than we had asked.

Why should we be afraid when we have God's promise that He will fight our battles! JOYCE RENICKS

Sounds of Distinction

Even in the case of lifeless things that make sounds, such as the flute or harp, how will anyone know what tune is being played unless there is a distinction in the notes? Again, if the trumpet does not sound a clear call, who will get ready for battle? (1 CORINTHIANS 14:7–8).

Paul says that it is better to speak five words that people can understand than to speak volumes that they cannot comprehend. What good is a flute, harp or a trumpet unless they play the notes written on the score? But when each player plays the notes written for his instrument, the result is beautiful harmony.

Paul adds that if the trumpet does not give a clear sound, men will not know to prepare for battle. How interesting that Paul mentions both types of instruments. The flute and harp are soft, melodic instruments. Some people are like that — so gentle, kind, comforting and calming. But there is also a need in God's musical ensemble for a trumpet. The church needs the effect of the harp and flute, but she also needs the trumpet to alert her to battle. Satan is like a roaring lion. I doubt whether the soft melodic instruments could be heard above his roar, so we need the trumpeter to warn us of his approach.

When the "notes" are sounding clear, the unbeliever who comes into our Christian gatherings will be convicted of his sin, and his heart will be laid open to the Word of God. Another lost one will have joined God's family.

May He help us to live according to the notes in the "Book."   DELORES TAYLOR

Praise the Lord

*Let them give thanks to the Lord for his unfailing love and his
wonderful deeds for men* (PSALM 107:8).

In 1964 we were assigned to Minnesota to plant another
church. At that time, the congregation was meeting in
the chapel of a funeral home. We were able to give it the
appearance of a sanctuary by furnishing pews, a pulpit, an
organ and a piano.

One Friday evening the news came that the furniture
store in front of the chapel was on fire. We soon discovered
that the fire had done extensive damage to the chapel,
furniture and instruments.

At that time our new church was still under construction.
Our congregation's first reaction to the bad news was,
"Why did this happen? Where will we meet until the church
building is finished?"

All the sub-contractors and laborers gave our construction project first priority. This meant that within two weeks
we were ready to have our first worship service in the new
sanctuary — at least two months ahead of schedule!

Praise the Lord! We believed Romans 8:28, and we saw
God at work. "And we know that in all things God works for
the good of those who love him, who have been called
according to his purpose."

Today He invites us to trust Him and prove the truth of
that promise.   JOYCE STRECKER

MAY 22

Going Home

In my Father's house are many rooms; if it were not so, I would have told you. I am going there to prepare a place for you. And if I go and prepare a place for you, I will come back and take you to be with me that you also may be where I am (JOHN 14:2–3).

O h, the joy that is mine when I know the kids are coming home. The house gets a fresh cleaning, surprises are planned and the baking and cooking begins. Much thought is put into those favorite family-pleasing recipes and special dishes that were made over the years. The kitchen is filled with the aroma of apple pie and homemade cinnamon rolls (with lots of raisins). What a sense of satisfaction to know, finally, that I am ready now, and my family is on their way home.

In our Scripture, Jesus has returned to heaven and is making His plans and preparations for His family. In Luke 12:32 we are told, "Do not be afraid, little flock, for your Father has been pleased to give you the kingdom." When I read in God's Word of the streets of gold, the precious jewels and all that He is preparing, none of these will compare to the bliss of seeing my Savior face to face.

Just as I cannot wait to see my children — to hug and kiss them and be around them once more, sharing stories about all the good times that have made our store of memories — Christ stands ready to welcome us home. And I am looking forward to everlasting life with Him.   JUDY FREELAND

Praise

I will extol the Lord at all times; his praise will always be on my lips (Psalm 34:1).

PRAISE: *P*roperly *R*ecognizing *A*lmighty God *I*n *S*acred *E*xpression

To praise is to worship or glorify someone because of who he is, not because of what he can do for us. It is *proper* that we praise the Lord because of His attributes and characteristics. There is none other like unto our God.

It is important that we *recognize* God as He is. As we recognize Him as the Creator and Controller of our lives, we will say "You are worthy, our Lord and God, to receive glory and honor and power" (Revelation 4:11a).

Our offering of praise is directed toward *Almighty God.* Our Lord is great and worthy of praise. He is to be feared above all gods (1 Chronicles 16:25). There are innumerable "gods" in the world — gods of wood, stone, brass or even people, jobs, possessions. But our Lord, the Almighty God, is the One whom all nations will come and worship.

In is a very small word but one which indicates a function. It tells us how we will properly recognize Almighty God: by means of or through the use of sacred expression.

One definition of *sacred* is holy. We often hear people flippantly say, "Praise the Lord." It is right that we praise Him, but we should do so reverently.

There are various ways in which we can *express* our praise — song, prayer, testimony. Whatever means of expression we choose, our praise must be directed toward our Lord — for His honor and glory, not for any self-recognition.

Have you taken time to praise Him today?

PHYLLIS WESTOVER

MAY 24

Run the Race

Therefore, since we are surrounded by such a great cloud of witnesses, let us throw off everything that hinders and the sin that so easily entangles, and let us run with perseverance the race marked out for us (HEBREWS 12:1).

Lord, You know I love You. You know that I have committed my life to You. Yet, I am struggling and do not know why. I look at Your Word. I believe it. I claim Your promises; the truth is there, yet I struggle.

"Lord, I want to lay aside those weights that hinder me. I want to run a steady course — not fast, not slow, but steady. But I am entangled in my own pride. I depend too much on my own abilities. The responsibilities of family, the work of the church, my duty to my husband; it is all too much. It seems too heavy to bear. My emotions are so undependable.

"I know that these sins, these burdens, keep me from running the race You have called me to run. You alone, Lord, can give to me the faith that I need to keep my eyes on You. You made me and know exactly what it takes, or will take, to make my faith strong enough to run this race and win.

"You are the prize, Lord — victory in day-to-day living and then life with You eternally. These truths help me, but I need to live out my faith daily. Help me to lay aside everything that hinders me in my daily race. Keep working on me, Lord, so that in Your time I will be able to complete this race You have called me to run." MELINDA COLLMUS

Path to Greatness

Grant that one of these two sons of mine may sit at your right and the other at your left in your kingdom (MATTHEW 20:21).

The mother of James and John would have blended in very well with our 20th-century women. She wanted important positions and other fine benefits for her children.

One day she came to Jesus with a request. She wanted Him to promise that one son could sit on His left and the other on His right in His kingdom. She was even willing to wait until His kingdom came. She felt that her sons certainly were deserving. After all, had not each of them given up an incredible business to be one of Jesus' followers?

Jesus understood this mother's desires and goals for her children. He also knew that these same two sons would one day enter into His sufferings. They would discover that discipleship is costly. But He also wanted James, John, their mother and the other 10 indignant disciples who were listening to realize that position does not make greatness. Servanthood is what makes us great! "The Son of Man did not come to be served, but to serve, and to give his life as a ransom for many" (Matthew 20:28). Serving was the lifestyle of Jesus, and we are never more Christlike than when we are genuinely serving other people. This was the pattern He wanted for their lives—to be like Him.

In the 20th century, Christ's call and example are still the same. He is asking each of us to stop worrying about our positions. He wants us to serve Him by serving others. Service, not position, is our path to greatness, because it is in serving that we are most like Him.   DELORIS BUBNA

Learn the Secret

The Lord God took the man and put him in the garden of Eden to work it and take care of it (GENESIS 2:15).

As the saying goes, I feel closer to God in my garden than anywhere else. The Lord uses my gardening to teach me some practical truths.

One of these truths became clear to me as I watched the growth of my carrots. Every year I would sow the seeds, and every year I would have a nice, thick, healthy stand of carrots. Unfortunately, carrots do not develop well if they are growing too thickly. I knew that, but I did not have the heart to pull out many of the perfect plants. Weeds were easy to pull, but those carrots . . .

As a result, very few of the carrots ever developed to normal size; many were misshapen due to lack of growing room. When I learned to thin my carrots ruthlessly, those that remained were able to grow and looked like the picture in the seed catalog.

The laws of nature which God developed also apply to His human creation. I had allowed my life to become over-crowded with activities. Caring for four small children did not allow me to add very many more commitments without being overwhelmed. Had they been "weeds," these activities would have been easy to root out, but actually, they were good church-related activities. I had to make some hard, thoughtful decisions and learn to say no. As a result, I felt less uptight, less guilty and more in control. I had learned the secret of thinning, both in my garden and in my life.

As we encounter the many opportunities to serve our Lord, may He show us how much we are able to do without being overburdened and then give us the energy to do the things we have prayerfully chosen.   PHYLLIS EAGEN

Is That You, God?

The voice of the Lord is powerful; the voice of the Lord is majestic (PSALM 29:4).

Have you ever thought about the powerful voice of God? In creation, God spoke, "Let there be light," and there was light! He had only to speak, and all creation was formed.

In Psalm 29 God's voice is described as sounding like thunder. When Moses brought the Israelites to the foot of Mt. Sinai to meet God and receive the Ten Commandments, the whole mountain quaked violently. Moses spoke, and God answered with thunder. The people trembled. God was impressing on them that when He speaks, His people *must* listen!

Many, many voices clamor for our attention today, including the news media, politicians, rock stars, educators. These tend to block out the voice of God. It is difficult to take time to read God's Word in order to hear His voice today, but it is essential!

It is one thing to "hear" God's voice, but another to respond in obedience. Adam and Eve heard God's voice in the garden, but they hid because they knew they had responded to the wrong voice. Their disobedience resulted in the Fall of man and his separation from God. Failing to listen to God's voice will always bring consequences. Hearing and obeying bring gracious rewards.

Through the Bible, God speaks to us today. If we want to hear His voice, we must take time to read it and then act upon His words. Which voice is having the most influence in our lives: God's or another's?   DONNA BECHTEL

MAY 28

That I May Know Him

I want to know Christ and the power of his resurrection and the fellowship of sharing in his sufferings, becoming like him in his death (PHILIPPIANS 3:10).

Shared suffering brings an amazingly sweet closeness. During pregnancy and childbirth, mothers and daughters often grow closer. Cancer survivors can encourage others who have the same illness. Support groups of all kinds are successful because one who has been through an experience can share with another.

Consider some of Jesus' suffering—

Leaders of His own religion misjudged Him

His family did not understand Him

A friend betrayed Him; others deserted Him

He was humiliated and rejected

He experienced physical abuse and agonizing pain.

What you are suffering, Jesus understands. Some pain is so intense that it nearly conquers our will to live. If it brings about death to self, it will bring fellowship with Christ. When nothing else matters but knowing Jesus, we can look into His face, sense His loving arms around us and hear Him say, "I feel your pain; I will bear it for you." Self gasps its last as it surrenders to His loving power and strength.

When we face the worst that life offers and conquer through the power of His Holy Spirit, we taste the resurrection. Restored by the Lord Jesus Christ, we can walk triumphantly toward that day in heaven when we shall know Him fully.   L. JEAN ROWETT

Treasures of Darkness

I will give you the treasures of darkness, riches stored in secret places, so that you may know that I am the Lord, the God of Israel, who calls you by name (ISAIAH 45:3).

These ancient words leap from the text. What *hope* and *help* they give in life's complexities and sorrows!

How can there be treasures in darkness, when it is so overwhelming? The astronomers know this pervasiveness as they focus on "dark holes" in space; the anthropologists are aware as they study with a new perspective a dark continent; the theologian perceives humanity — by choice roaming in darkness.

Even more benumbing is the darkness that envelopes a Christian in time of tragedy! Is there a treasure to be found when a man's eyes are blasted out, when a child is claimed by death, when a young wife and mother is accidentally killed or when a partner is abandoned?

There is but one direction in which to look and that is toward the God-Man whose greatest triumphs came out of darkness! From the agony in the garden came the magnificent sacrificial cup! From Calvary's place, where nature drew its shroud over the earth, came a cry heard across the centuries — *It is finished*! From the blackness of the tomb sprang resurrection victory. Our blessed Lord found His treasures in darkness!

This same Lord said, "Follow me." He is with us in the crucible of smothering grief or in the narrow aisles of pain, when we stand on cliffs of unbelief or walk in the valley of the shadow of death. He is there in the darkness.

Where is this treasure? With joy we exclaim, "The treasure is in the Holy Presence of the Lord!" CURTISS BEDFORD

Dig Deeper

Then you will understand the fear of the Lord and find the knowledge of God. For the Lord gives wisdom, and from his mouth come knowledge and understanding (PROVERBS 2:5–6).

All that Scripture has to say about God's command-ments, truth and statutes stresses the importance of using His Word as a guideline for living. It emphasizes how vital it is for each of us to search for truths that directly benefit us in our daily needs.

Much of our "spiritual food" is prepared by others through television, radio and books—a veritable banquet from which to choose. It is good to get others' ideas on a situation, but how refreshing it is to let the Lord speak to us and to reveal our need as He sees it. Let us be challenged to dig out for ourselves the special truths God has for us.

What then is the formula for understanding "the fear of the Lord"? How can we be of more use to Him in our everyday contacts with people?

Proverbs 2:1–5 contains several verbs which present the outline for understanding "the fear of the Lord." They are the fundamental elements of Christianity, the basic re-quirements for living the Christian life.

1. Accept my words—read and study
2. Store up my commands—memorize
3. Turn your ear—meditate and pray
4. Apply your heart—apply truths to your life
5. Cry aloud for understanding—have a desire to know more of Him.

Let us follow our Lord more closely by "digging deeper" and discovering what He wants us to learn each day.

BARBARA A. BARKER

My Garden

Awake, north wind, and come, south wind! Blow on my garden, that its fragrance may spread abroad (Song of Songs 4:16a).

Mom, look!" My child came bursting through the door on one of those luxurious spring days, holding in her hand a fluffy, yellow dandelion surrounded by perky, lavender violets and a few tiny, white daisies.

"Aren't they pretty, Mom? Smell. Aren't they sweet? Here. These are for you!" I fetched my tiny vase bought especially for such offerings and tenderly placed the flowers by my kitchen window. Each time I looked at them, sweet memories of my daughter's love wrapped me in delight.

It is this kind of love that warms the heart of Jesus as we minister to Him. Often we are so caught up in the tediousness of the world, its weighty problems encompassing us, that we forget our primary reason for being—to glorify Him. This glorifying can take the form of doing noble deeds in Jesus' name. It can also mean simply *being*—sitting at the feet of Jesus, adoring, and even ministering to our Lord.

A friend of my mothers, who was once a gardener in England, said that the flower beds and herb gardens there are specifically laid out to catch the north wind. This wind, the mention of which can conjure up images of bitter cold, directs the aromas from the garden toward the master's house, providing fragrant pleasure for the family. I want my life to bring such pleasure to my Lord.

Ephesians 5:2 tells us to "live a life of love, just as Christ loved us and gave himself up for us as a fragrant offering and sacrifice to God." How is God asking us to present ourselves as a "fragrant offering" to Him?   SUSAN BLISS

JUNE 1

Our Unfailing Strength

Let us throw off everything that hinders and the sin that so easily entangles, and let us run with perseverance the race marked out for us. Let us fix our eyes on Jesus (HEBREWS 12:1–2).

An evangelistic meeting was planned in Kenya, and on the appointed date, a large crowd gathered at the site. Pastor John, a greatly loved elder, was to preach. When his turn came, Pastor John read Hebrews 12, verses 1 and 2 and spoke concerning the need to be born again and cleansed from "the sin that so easily entangles." He then turned to the running of the race with perseverance and climaxed his message with this illustration.

"All of us Africans like honey," he said. With typical gestures he continued. "Let us say that I carve a honey box out of a log. I find a thorn tree which has deliciously sweet flowers. I hang my honey box in the tree and wait and wait. Finally, I am sure the honey is ready, and as I approach the tree, the saliva begins to flow because of my great anticipation. Sure enough, I can smell the honey! I begin to climb. Soon thorns prick my hands and feet, but I continue climbing. The bees object to my intrusion and begin to sting. It becomes quite painful. The bees would be happy if I became discouraged. But do I stop climbing? Do I quit? No! Why not? Because my eye is on the *honey!*"

This story carries a message for us. We need the Lord to help us this day to keep our eyes fixed on Him and to persevere without wavering, knowing that in everything, He is our unfailing source of strength.　　LILLIE M. AMMERMAN

JUNE 2

Do Good!

Trust in the Lord and do good (PSALM 37:3a).

A body of water becomes stagnant if it does not have an outlet. So it is with our lives. Once we are saved, we must begin to do good works, or we will become increasingly frustrated.

A young mother came to me weeping because she had neither the time nor the energy to work in the church. There is comforting news for women like her! Our Heavenly Father knows our emotional and physical limitations. As we talked, she began to realize that her first responsibilities were to be a good wife and mother and to help her elderly father-in-law who lives with them. Part of that responsibility was to make sure that her family regularly attended church services. While there, she could take her turn tending the nursery and let her cheerful smile and sweet spirit reach out to others. As her children matured, she could be involved in more things.

We have many opportunities for service. We can spread cheer by our inward joy even if outside circumstances are not favorable. Perhaps we may brighten the day of the cashier at the store with friendly good humor, hug the lonely widow or put a comforting arm around the abused wife. The Lord may ask us to show interest in the teenagers' achievements and young loves or to kneel down to the level of a little child and explore his world.   VERNICE HAZLETT

Through the Storms

So do not fear, for I am with you; do not be dismayed, for I am your God. I will strengthen you and help you (ISAIAH 41:10).

What a beautiful sunny morning! It was one of those rare days in early June. But by early afternoon the clouds began to come up very fast. The sky grew darker and darker, so black that only the streaks of sharp lightning gave any light. It was the most furious storm I had ever witnessed. The wind and rain beat against the house, and thunder rumbled until the earth shuddered.

A small, tearful voice called, "Mommy, are you afraid?" I held my child tightly in my arms, not wanting to admit that I *was* afraid. "Can we pray?" asked the small, trembling voice. She prayed a few simple words, telling Jesus that we were afraid and asking Him to take care of us. Then, in a trusting voice, she said, "Now I can take my nap. Jesus will take care of us."

When the storms of life overwhelm us, when death robs us of the one we hold dear, when loneliness sweeps in, when we feel friendless, when pain envelops us, when our faith is faltering and we are fearful, how do we react? Do we cry out, "Why has God permitted this affliction and pain? Why has He taken my loved one? I do not understand why my plans have been overturned."

Has the sweetness vanished from life? Are you troubled and afraid? God longs to heal our hurts and give victory over our fears, but He waits for us to cry out to Him. He responds to our most desperate needs as we trust Him during the storms of life.   MILDRED SCHLEH

JUNE 4

There All the Time

I can do everything through him who gives me strength (PHILIPPI-ANS 4:13).

Have you been sitting around waiting for the Lord to change you by doing some miraculous thing in your life? Then, you would be the Christian you should be. Then you could stay on that diet, be a better wife and mother, lead that women's group or sing in church without shaking.

The Lord spoke to me about this "Let go, let God" concept I had. I was sitting around doing nothing, waiting for God to give me the power to do things for Him. The Lord showed me that the power I sought, prayed for and waited for was already there, waiting to be used.

I read somewhere that it is like driving a car with power steering. I have to take the wheel and turn it. Then the power steering takes over and does the work. This is true when the Lord wants us to do something; we have to put forth the effort, set our wills to do it and then let the Holy Spirit take over and give us the power we need to do it.

I felt the Lord leading me to sing in church, but I was terrified of getting up in front of people. So when I got up to sing, I kept saying to myself, "God said He was with me and He would help me, and I stand on that fact." Slowly, but surely, I felt the Holy Spirit giving me more and more power and boldness.

So instead of waiting around for that zap from heaven to change us, let us get started on that upward path. The power is there; the Lord is there. It is up to us to believe and to do something about it.   KITTY HAVENER

Follow Jesus

But small is the gate and narrow the road that leads to life, and only a few find it (MATTHEW 7:13). *Come out from them and be separate* (2 CORINTHIANS 6:17).

Fifty-one years ago, I went to the altar and asked Jesus into my heart. As I read the new Bible that was given to me, I found out that we must walk the straight and narrow way and that we are to "come out from them and be separate."

A few years later at Old Orchard Beach Camp in Maine, I went to the altar and told the Lord I would go anywhere and do anything that He wanted me to do. From then on, I asked *Where do you want me to go and what do you want me to do?* I found out that we must be *willing* to follow as the Lord guides us.

My pastor husband and I, with our nine children, have lived in eight southern states. The children were born in five of those states. I have been amazed at the many different ways that the Lord has provided for our needs. He surely does provide the exceeding abundantly above all we can ask or think.

I can look back and see how the Lord has led each step of the way. Each day we must pray, read and study His Word and be willing to do what our Lord and Savior wants us to do (Luke 9:23–24).

I would not change any of it. I rejoice that I came to know my Savior, Jesus, God's Son.　　ELEANOR DAMRON

Work or Worship

As Jesus and his disciples were on their way, he came to a village where a woman named Martha opened her home to him (LUKE 10:38).

Martha loved her friend Jesus. I believe He was more than a friend to her; I believe He was her Lord. Sometimes we tend to be too critical of Martha, perhaps even believing she was not as good a Christian as Mary. I do not believe this for one minute. They were His special friends. Jesus had visited their home many times. He was so special to Martha that she wanted things to be extra nice for Him.

Verse 40 tells us that "Martha was distracted." She had a great reputation as a fine cook. She was busily at work preparing the food, but at the same time, agitation was growing inside her because Mary was not helping. At this point, it was not just Martha possessing a good reputation, but her reputation possessing her. Even though she felt she was doing what was necessary, the Lord chides her.

In verse 42 we read, "Martha, one thing is needed." This was a mild rebuke to Martha. Jesus wanted her to see that what she was doing was only temporal, while Mary's actions were lasting. Do we spend as much time on our spiritual well-being as we do on the material?

"Seek first his kingdom and his righteousness, and all these things will be given to you as well" (Matthew 6:33).   ELSIE J. MCILRATH

JUNE 7

A Life of Giving

Charm is deceptive, and beauty is fleeting; but a woman who fears the Lord is to be praised (PROVERBS 31:30).

Dorcas gave so generously of herself to others that today, almost 2,000 years later, her name is linked with acts of charity.

As a disciple of Christ, Dorcas displayed faith, humility, diligence and perseverance in ministering to others. Widows, being the poorest and most helpless, were the chief objects of her charity. When she became sick and died, the people were expecting Peter to come and console them. Instead, they witnessed the miracle that restored her to life.

Like Dorcas, you too can give of yourself to help those in trouble or in need. As you do, there will spring up a rare, unconscious beauty and inner peace within your life.

There are many who are ready enough to give money but not willing to give of themselves in any way. There are some who would give willingly but have nothing to offer in the way of assistance. Actually, there are innumerable ways of giving. Are we willing to say, "Silver and gold I do not have, but what I have I give you"—our prayers, our tears, our ears, our hands, our feet and even our hearts?

"Now about brotherly love we do not need to write you, for you yourselves have been taught by God to love each other. . . . Yet we urge you, brothers, to do so more and more" (1 Thessalonians 4:9–10). ARBUTUS BARR

By All Means

I have become all things to all men so that by all possible means I might save some (1 CORINTHIANS 9:22).

Build a bridge," the speaker at the women's spring retreat admonished us, "if you are being confronted with difficulties in reaching your family or friends for the Lord."

My prayer, as we went home, was that the Lord would help me do this very thing to reach my neighbor. We had lived in the parsonage next door to her for several years, but she would never acknowledge my greetings when I saw her. If our boys played ball in our yard or in the street, her windows and doors would slam shut. And woe betide them if the ball went into her yard.

That spring, our eldest son, Sam, bought me rose bushes for Mother's Day. We decided to make a rose bed in the side of the yard next to hers, so we could enjoy them as we looked out the dining room window. One day as we worked in the rose bed, her window flew open, and she began to tell us how to dust and care for the roses for better results. What a wonderful day that was—our neighbor had spoken to us!

From that time on her attitude changed, even toward the boys. When her husband died quite suddenly, we were able to comfort her. We became friends and have kept in touch with her since we moved away.

In the most unexpected way, God built my bridge! Ask Him to build a bridge for you as you seek to show His love to others.   SALLY M. DITTMAR

JUNE 9

Envy: Root of Defeat

No eye has seen, no ear has heard, no mind has conceived what God has prepared for those who love him (1 CORINTHIANS 2:9).

A new Bible study was being organized in our neighborhood. As I entered the hostess's house, I sat down near a friend and chatted until the study began. It was about halfway through the lesson that I noticed it, the most beautiful rocking chair I was sure I had ever seen. It had deep wood grain and hand-painted designs. A high back and wide arms were an invitation to comfort, and its occupant was taking full advantage.

During the remainder of the study, I was absorbed in my thoughts. *Why had I not chosen that chair when I came in? Why did I elect to sit in this old seat?* As envy set in, my chair grew harder and harder. I decided that the next week I would come early and take that lovely chair.

The study over, I prepared to leave. As I did, I glanced at the chair in which I had been sitting. To my surprise, it was of the same rich stain as the rocker I had jealously admired, and the designs were remarkably similar. A closer look revealed that the two chairs were identical. I had wasted all that time coveting something I already had.

How often envy blinds us to the blessings we possess. We waste time and energy wishing for other things and missing out on the joy of all that God has given us. It is possible to spend one's whole life looking across the room, when we already have all we need for contentment and joy.

Are we envying what others have, or are we thanking God for all He has given to us? Close examination may prove that we have just as much if not more to rejoice in than do those whom we envy.   DENISE S. HAMMER

JUNE 10

The Source of Peace

You will keep in perfect peace him whose mind is steadfast, because he trusts in you (ISAIAH 26:3).

What a magnetic aura of peace Jesus must have possessed as He moved among people. His mind was centered on God, and He trusted His Heavenly Father perfectly. Jesus spoke many times of this peace which He possessed and which we so desperately need. His perfect peace can actually become an integral part of us when Christ is alive in us.

There are elements that can destroy our peace: worry takes over our mind; turmoil engulfs our emotions; doubt clouds our soul. Peace can replace each of these destroyers when our minds are totally focused upon the great power of God. Peace is not found in what is going on around us but in what is going on inside us.

In calming the seas, Jesus revealed His power over nature. He displayed His power over circumstances as He divided and multiplied the bread, over people as He healed the issue of blood, over life as He released the demon possessed, over death as He raised the widow's son.

When, as Jesus instructed, we fully trust this great God and are fully confident that He is capable to care for our individual lives in each circumstance and to bring the ultimate good into our lives, we shall have peace.   RUTH DAVIS

A Mighty Fortress

Jesus replied, "You do not realize now what I am doing, but later you will understand" (JOHN 13:7).

When our lovely 17-year-old daughter, Cathy, became ill with Crohns' disease, we were certain that with the help of the Lord and that of medical science she would have a fast recovery. But days turned into weeks and then into months as she failed to respond to every treatment given her.

We prayed continually, and our friends held us up in prayer as well. At our annual church council, 8,000 people lifted her up to the throne of grace. Our confidence was in Him.

Many nights we were at the hospital until midnight. We would come home exhausted, too weary to pray or read our Bibles. But God never failed to bring to our remembrance Scripture verses we had memorized through the years. Romans 8:26–27 became precious to us when neither prayer nor praise could be uttered.

After almost a whole year of treatment and two surgeries, it was evident that Cathy would not recover. Her suffering was so intense that I cried to the Lord to take her to be with Him, where all pain and suffering would be ended, and she would be with her dear Heavenly Father throughout all eternity.

Through her death, seven people found Christ as their personal Savior. We rejoice in this miracle of love. "Oh, the depth of the riches of the wisdom and knowledge of God! How unsearchable his judgments, and his paths beyond tracing out!" (Romans 11:33).   HARRIET SPEECE

JUNE 12

A Mother's Prayer

Watch yourselves closely so that you do not forget the things your eyes have seen or let them slip from your heart as long as you live. Teach them to your children and to their children after them (DEUTERONOMY 4:9).

When Benjamin was born, my prayers as a new mother were usually cries to the Lord for the ability to care for a newborn. My days started with an "Oh, Lord, help me not to drop his slippery body after I bathe him," and usually ended with a quick plea for *one* night of uninterrupted sleep.

After a few months of adapting to my new role, I found that caring for an infant really was not so difficult, and the tone of my prayers shifted toward a deepening concern that Benjamin have a happy life. I prayed that he would have a happy, well-adjusted childhood, do well in school, have a successful career and, of course, marry the girl God had chosen for him. I prayed, too, that he would be spared pain and heartache.

Today, I still pray those things for him . . . sometimes. But now my little boy is almost two, and his character is forming. Suddenly I am aware of so many more important things I need to pray for him. So I pray Micah 6:8 for him which says, "He has showed you, O man, what is good. And what does the Lord require of you? To act justly and to love mercy and to walk humbly with your God." My prayers also include First Kings 3:6–14, Solomon's magnificent prayer for wisdom, and I echo with all my heart John's words in Third John 4: "I have no greater joy than to hear that my children are walking in the truth." But most of all I pray that Benjamin will live Deuteronomy 6:5 and love God with all his heart, mind and soul.   CAROL ROBERTS

Unspoken Prayer Requests

In the same way, the Spirit helps us in our weakness. We do not know what we ought to pray, but the Spirit himself intercedes for us with groans that words cannot express (ROMANS 8:26).

When I see a dear brother or sister lift their hand in a prayer meeting to indicate an "unspoken prayer request," I am always deeply touched. No doubt these requests are, at times, for grave and weighty concerns. Perhaps they hesitate to voice them because they are too proud, too shy or intimidated by the presence of others in the room whom they assume are more spiritual. How precious it is to know that our Lord did not leave us comfortless and that we have His promsies. "Before they call I will answer; and while they are still speaking I will hear" (Isaiah 65:24).

King Hezekiah, regarded as an ideal monarch, made a covenant in his heart with God — very quietly and privately (2 Chronicles 29:10). Some of us feel uneasy in a prayer meeting, thinking that we are not the stuff out of which spiritual folk are made. When coming to Him by way of the cross, however, we all have equal access to the throne of grace, to the heavenly promises.

In matters of prayer, I cling to a beautiful promise found in Isaiah 59:1, "Surely the arm of the Lord is not too short to save, nor his ear too dull to hear."

At times we cannot pray at all, but He is there; the Holy Spirit is speaking for us and through us whether or not those around us can hear.   ALIA M. KAISER

JUNE **14**

Freed through Grace

But thanks be to God, who always leads us in triumphal procession in Christ (2 CORINTHIANS 2:14).

While in seminary preparing to become a missionary, I was required to write several sermons to fulfill the requirements for preaching class. Perplexed by this passage (2:14–17), I decided to study it further.

The imagery here is that of a military procession. According to protocol, the slaves came first, strewing flowers, spices and other fragrant material along the road. The victor followed, and after him came two different classes of captives: some who, when they reached the end of the parade, would be going to their death and others who would be given their freedom. All trample on the aromatic material, releasing its fragrance and announcing to the crowd the presence of the victorious conqueror.

The Apostle Paul includes himself and other Christians in this procession. We are the captives who have been set free by our victorious Jesus. Our bodily presence is a sweet fragrance to those who are hearing about Him and deciding whether to follow Him. We are, however, an unpleasant odor to those who are rejecting the Savior, to those who are fabricating a god according to their own ideas.

Many Christians weep bitter tears over their inability to witness for Christ. But this passage clearly teaches that our very presence is that testimony, that fragrance.

See how easy and natural the Lord has made it for us? He is indeed the Victor who leads us all the way. All we need to do is be aware that we are His captives. Then, when the opportunity presents itself, we respond to the questions others ask us about the Lord with simplicity and gentle honesty. It is as easy as that! ALINE LAFLAMME

JUNE 15

Love One Another

All men will know that you are my disciples if you love one another (JOHN 13:35).

On the night before Jesus died, He gave His disciples a new commandment: they were to "love one another." So also, Jesus comes into our busy lives today and gives us the same commandment.

How did Jesus show His love? As the disciples' teacher, friend, counselor and servant, Jesus acted in love. He made and served the disciples breakfast; He spent time talking with them; He prayed with them; He ate with them in their homes; He cried with them in their sorrow. Jesus displayed His love in all His contacts with people. He hugged the children; He fed the multitudes; He healed the sick and hurting; He suffered and died because of His love for them and for us. And now, He lives in us, so that in simple everyday living we have the privilege of expressing the very same servant love to those with whom we have contact.

Recently a friend whom I had not seen for three years had a birthday. I sensed a need to talk to her. When she picked up the phone, I sang "Happy Birthday." She thanked me and said, "How good of you to think of me; I was sitting here crying." As we talked, we encouraged each other by sharing the things God was doing in the lives of our families. I hung up, thanking God that I had listened to His quiet nudge to call my friend and let her know I loved her.

Why show love? So all men will know we are followers of Jesus Christ. What word of kindness, gift of love (or even a hug), can you share with someone whose name comes to your mind today? PRISCILLA SCHWALM

JUNE 16

Not How but Who

When the enemy shall come in like a flood, the Spirit of the Lord shall lift up a standard against him (ISAIAH 59:19, KJV).

During my first term on the mission field, I went through a bleak period of darkness and heaviness of spirit. Something had happened that sent me into despair. How could God cause this to work together for good? How could God bring any glory to His name by this happening? How could God bring deliverance? The doubts and questions plagued me.

One day I sat at the door of an African hut and watched while my husband tried to get our pickup out of the mud. Though he rocked the truck back and forth, its wheels only spun around and around until they were deeply mired. As I sat there still dwelling on thoughts of despair, God spoke to me. "Kathy," He said, "you are just like that truck. Your wheels are going around and around, but you are not going anywhere. You are stuck in the mud of doubt. Just as that truck must be helped to get out, so you are not going to go forward until you let Me push you out."

Later, I returned to my station and read an article in *Alliance Life,* "Not How but Who," by Dr. R. Edman. Suddenly I realized that I had been asking the wrong questions. When I stopped asking *how* and turned to *who,* I saw the Lord. He was able to give me beauty out of the ashes and joy and praise for the spirit of heaviness.

From that unfortunate situation, God taught me that no matter how dark the night, He is there, and it is He who will turn our night into day.   KATHLEEN SOLVIG

Trust Only in the Lord

By day the Lord directs his love, at night his song is with me — a prayer to the God of my life (PSALM 42:8).

The psalmist had just experienced a difficult time. He had known tears, thirst for God and agonizing prayer. Wave after wave of sorrow rolled over him. But through all of this, he was encouraged to take heart and remember the days when he led the congregation in praise and worship. He asked himself, "Why am I staying in this condition?"

We only need to look back a little to see how God has provided for us. "He knows the way that I take" (Job 23:10). He laid it out for me. This places a big responsibility upon us, but if we are resting in Him, He will flow through us. Even in the dark times of life, His song will be with us.

Two years ago I had bypass surgery. I had just had my pre-op medication and was in the "twilight zone." As I was being rolled down the hall on the way to surgery, my husband and children followed me as far as they could. I did not know what I was doing, but they told me later I was singing "Trust and Obey" as loud as I could. I even invited them to join in! (Needless to say, they let me carry it alone.) His music surfaced at this dark time. His Spirit brought peace and comfort.

Most of my songs were written after the "night" had passed. This line from one of them expresses the idea very well: "But when the clouds begin to roll, bringing darkness to my soul, will my song remain the same? Yes, my song is still the same; my song will ever praise His Name." His song surfaces whatever our circumstance.   DELORES TAYLOR

Freedom in Love

If you, then, though you are evil, know how to give good gifts to your children, how much more will your Father in heaven give good gifts to those who ask him! (MATTHEW 7:11).

Is there anything more beautiful than a mother's love? While that love can be a steady and secure anchor for a growing youngster, it can also become suffocating and possessive, robbing that young person of his freedom of expression and experience. The very love that once nurtured and supported can cripple and damage his ability to face the "real world." There must be freedom in love.

The Lord taught me this very lesson. When our first child was still in diapers, I would fret over the day when he would have to start school. Having come from a rural area to a large city, I worried about the busy streets he would have to cross, the size of his classes and whether or not his teacher would be harsh. But before Scott's school days commenced, we moved to a small community. You would have thought that my fears would have subsided, but not so.

The night before his first school day, I cried and cried. Though we had dedicated Scott to the Lord as a baby, and though I knew in my mind I should release him to the Lord, I could not. Then I sensed the Lord speaking to me, "Aren't you glad Scott can go to school, that he has no mental or physical handicaps preventing him from going?" As I thought over several promises from Scripture, my heart was at peace. With new understanding, I once again dedicated my son to the Lord.

Scott is now grown, and over the years I have at times started to "take him back," but the Holy Spirit reminds me to leave him in God's hands. There is no safer or more secure refuge for our children.   VIVIAN M. SIMPSON

The Perfect Gift

When he ascended on high, he led captives in his train and gave gifts to men (EPHESIANS 4:8).

The words, "Here is a gift for you," bring a surge of happy anticipation. Perhaps this is the reason everyone enjoys Christmas and birthdays. To receive a gift means that we are remembered in a very special way by someone dear to us. Sometimes the gift is less than perfect. Perhaps it is too large or small, or the color does not suit us. But let me suggest the perfect gift.

Just as the kings brought gifts to Jesus at His coming, Jesus came bringing gifts to us from the Father. Jesus' first gifts to us are redemption and forgiveness through His blood (Ephesians 1:7).

Another gift is our new membership in God's royal family (1 John 3:2). Being a child of the King gives us great security and self-worth. It is a relationship encompassing an eternal family of choice brothers and sisters.

Jesus brought the gift of light (John 8:12). God did not leave us alone in darkness, trying to make our own way in this new life. The Bible is our operational manual and guide to successful daily living.

By nature, we are social beings, and we like to have friends. The Holy Spirit is our constant companion to comfort, teach and encourage us (John 14:26).

Finally, Jesus came to bring not only the present abundant life but everlasting life (John 3:16). Jesus came that we might have a new life, a new family, a new guide, a new companion and a new (forever) future. Jesus, God's perfect gift, is all we need.   AUDREY P. BROWN

Pray Bible Prayers

Devote yourselves to prayer, being watchful and thankful (COLOSSIANS 4:2).

Creativity is not one of my big talents. I like to find someone else's idea, say "Why didn't I think of that?" and really go with it.

For some time, the Lord has been teaching me to *pray Bible prayers* and make them my own. This is not an original thought. Along the way, some saint of the Lord put out a challenge to pray God's Word back to Him in prayer.

My prayer list has grown to include not only family, friends and neighbors but also God's people who work near and far. It is such a joy to remember before the Lord His people whom we have met on many continents and islands.

For myself and others, I use one phrase from a Bible prayer each day for one week. Beginning on Monday, I might use Colossians 1:9, asking God to make His will known in all wisdom and spiritual understanding. I pray the same for people, ministries and needs every day that week.

On the next Monday, I use Colossians 1:10. Here, perhaps, just the first phrase is sufficient for that week, asking the Lord to grant that I and others may walk worthy of Him, pleasing Him in every way.

God hears and answers prayer. He has given us His Word. Does it not seem that if we pray His Word back to our Heavenly Father, it certainly would be praying according to His will and for His glory?

Do you feel satisfied with your prayer life? I did not and still do not, but the Lord has given me a "track to run on."   SUE JACOX

JUNE 21

For All the Saints

And pray in the Spirit on all occasions with all kinds of prayers and requests. With this in mind, be alert and always keep on praying for all the saints (EPHESIANS 6:18).

Scripture very clearly tells us of the responsibility which we have to continually pray for one another. We are commanded to carry each other's burdens (Galatians 6:2).

Allowing no occasion to pass, whether it be a time of prosperity or adversity, we should covenant to pray for each other privately and collectively. Through the Holy Spirit's insight, the necessities of our fellow believers should be allowed to touch us deeply. Reflect on how others may be worn out by heavy affliction or weighted down by intense anxiety or guilt. Watch for those who are lonely and distressed.

Someone has said that only persevering unceasingly with a heartfelt prayer of intercession can bring quiet fortitude to the soul in need. Prayer, as designed by God, is our communication system. It should be used as the chief exercise for building faith. Indeed, it is the way we obtain from God every blessing.

Fervently pray, asking that all the saints may live with the *purpose* of glorifying the Lord and with *purity* of heart and mind. Pray also that they may have *provision* and *protection* and *power* to work the will of God.

Intercession for one another is not only a responsibility but is among our most precious privileges. We will observe the victories resulting from earnest prayer, and because of our obedience to the command to pray, we will have deepened our own faith and commitment to the Lord Jesus Christ.   ARLISS M. ALLEN

JUNE 22

Light through Trials

And we know that in all things God works for the good of those who love him (ROMANS 8:28).

There is an African proverb that says, "That which blinds the blind man also feeds him." Its literal meaning is that those who are blind are expected to beg to gain their daily food. For me, that proverb has a very precious spiritual application. Difficult things may come to us during our lifetime, and the world may see those things as being very destructive and cruel. If, however, those things are accepted as part of His sovereign will, then, because of the growth and depth we gain in the Lord Jesus, they will have an opposite effect.

The husband of a young Christian woman was shot as he fled from their mud house during border disputes in our area of West Africa. He had just completed one month's study in literacy training so that he would be able to read the New Testament in Red Bobo. Just two days earlier, he had been baptized and had given public testimony that he was a new creature in Christ and was obeying His command to be baptized. What a difficult thing for his family and those village church people to accept the death of this zealous new believer in Christ.

Three months after his death, his wife attended one of our women's conferences. She told of God's sufficiency in her life and of the assurance she had that God loved her, would provide for her and never leave her comfortless.

What a testimony to all of us! Those "blinding" blows that may touch us will, in the hands of our loving Father, nurture and "feed" us and bring new life to those around us. May God help us to always be fed and not just blinded by our trials and difficulties.   BARBARA SORENSON

JUNE 23

Changes and Choices

But you remain the same, and your years never end (HEBREWS 1:12b).

Recently my life has been filled with changes and choices. I guess that can be said of all of our lives. Would it not be good if we could choose a period of our lives that was enjoyable and let time stand still? But we cannot. Ecclesiastes 3:11 and 14 tell us, "He has made everything beautiful in its time," and "Everything God does will endure forever."

If our childhood was a happy time, we did not want it to end. Everything was new, fresh and meaningful. We wanted our teen years to be over soon so we could be adults. In young adulthood, there were many changes and choices: college, marriage, the birth of children or the choice of a job. In middle age and even in our "golden years," there are still changes and choices.

My parents are in their golden years. Both of them have had severe physical problems. Because of this, I have had to make many choices and to endure a lot of changes. But Christ was and is precious, and His Word has been very real. When it became necessary to consider retirement housing for my mother and father, it was a difficult adjustment for all of us. But each day, as I went to God's Word, He had something just for me. For example, "Now go, lead the people to the place I spoke of, and my angel will go before you" (Exodus 32:34).

Yes, life is filled with changes and choices, but the right *choice* is Jesus Christ. He will take you through all the *changes*.   JANET C. JONES

JUNE 24

Better by Far

I am torn between the two: I desire to depart and be with Christ, which is better by far (PHILIPPIANS 1:23).

Our six-month-old son, Rob, lay fast asleep in his crib. His three-year-old sister, Scottie, slumbered in her bed. Their daddy was out of town.

Suddenly the phone rang, bringing word that my dad had gone to be with the Lord. Needing to talk with someone, I entered Scottie's room. I called and gently nudged her. Finally she awoke. "Honey, Grandpa Sundell has gone to heaven." Sitting up, she said, "Oh, Mother, isn't that wonderful! Just think, when we get to heaven, Grandpa will say, 'Good morning, May! Good morning, Scottie!' and he won't be sick anymore." And with that she lay back down and fell asleep. This small child had the firm assurance that to be with Christ is "better by far."

We lost one of our children at birth. Though surrounded by the love of husband, children, our families and by flower arrangements and sympathetic letters, I could not stop crying. Then from Isaiah 53, God spoke lovingly to me, "Surely he took up our infirmities and carried our sorrows" (verse 4). Slowly I learned that to be with Christ is far better.

Within one year from the time my mother comforted me in the loss of our baby, she went to Glory. I loved her and missed not being able to telephone over the miles and say, "Mother, I need your prayers today." For my mother, suffering the agonies of cancer, "to depart and be with Christ [was] better by far."

He will wipe every tear from their eyes. There will be no more death or mourning or crying or pain (Revelation 21:4).

MAY S. BROWN

United in Him

I pray also for those who will believe in me through their message, that all of them may be one (JOHN 17:20–21).

Can you sense the heart cry of Jesus as He prays for unity and oneness in His body? What are we doing as agents to bring about that oneness and, thus, the answer to Jesus' prayer?

But, you say, we have to be so careful. Today there are so many denominations, so many different ways people express their faith. There are cults teaching other gods, promoting other gospels, listening to other spirits. With whom are we to be one?

Jesus says that he is praying for those "who will believe in me through their message." Those are the ones Jesus desires to be brought into oneness — all who believe that He is Jesus Christ, Lord and Savior. Do you have such people in your life, in your home, at your church, where you work, socialize and shop? Are you at one with them in your central belief in Jesus as Savior, or is there separation because of prejudice and unforgiveness? Ask the Father to show you His family and how He loves and forgives each member. Now ask Him to show you those in your life from whom you have been separated by a gulf of unforgiveness. Think of your parents, brothers and sisters, other relatives, husband, children, neighbors or your pastor. Have you acknowledged the deed and forgiven the doer?

I do not believe Jesus would pray a prayer that could not be answered. Each of us needs to seek to be co-workers with God in seeing Jesus' prayer realized in our circle of associates. Let us help, not hinder, the process of reconciliation.

JEANNE MCKINNEY

JUNE 26

I Like Getting Up Early

Very early in the morning, while it was still dark, Jesus got up, left the house and went off to a solitary place, where he prayed (MARK 1:35). *And all the people came early in the morning to hear him at the temple* (LUKE 21:38).

Jesus was an early riser. I like it that He loved the morning. Maybe it is because I grew up on a farm, and I know how lovely the morning is. Everything is hushed. The earth seems refreshed. The light appears gradually, and there is a special excitement about the beginning of a new day. The Bible extols the morning and tells us to make a commitment to it.

I will awaken the dawn (Psalm 108:2).

Morning by morning, O Lord, you hear my voice; morning by morning I lay my requests before you and wait in expectation (Psalm 5:3).

From the rising of the sun to the place where it sets the name of the Lord is to be praised (Psalm 113:3).

This is the day the Lord has made; let us rejoice and be glad in it (Psalm 118:24).

If this were your last day on earth, would you not get up early? CHARLOTTE LEONARD

JUNE 27

Rejoicing Brings Joy

This is the day the Lord has made; let us rejoice and be glad in it (PSALM 118:24).

A surgeon was standing over his patient on whom he was about to perform surgery for cancer of the tongue. He said to him, "My friend, if you have anything to say, you now have the opportunity. I must warn you that these words will be the last you will ever utter; therefore, consider well what you wish to say."

Everybody listened very carefully as the man became pensive, choosing his last words. Finally he responded, "Thank You, Lord, for enabling me to use my tongue to praise You until now, and I shall continue to thank You with my heart."

Day after day we hear the expression, "Have a good day." We usually are told this by a salesperson, and the reaction to it could be anything from a mumbled answer to no answer at all. When I was in the work force, a favorite expression was "Another day, another dollar." I frequently see a car bearing a sticker which reads, "I owe, I owe, so off to work I go." We are constantly bombarded with complaints, problems and all sorts of negative statements from Christians and non-Christians alike. Many are the result of wrong actions and attitudes. Some Christians even look to the wrong source for help with their problems.

In an editorial entitled "The Greater Freedom," written for *Alliance Life*, Maurice R. Irvin states, "The person who is in Christ Jesus is guaranteed an absolutely endless eternity of bliss and blessing. Thus each day on this earth for him is just one of an inexhaustible supply of days."

If this is the day that the Lord has made, how can we not rejoice in it?   HAZEL HIERS

JUNE 28

A Change of Attitude

Find rest, O my soul, in God alone; my hope comes from him. He alone is my rock and my salvation; he is my fortress, I will not be shaken (PSALM 62:5–6).

Stella and I met while I was traveling around the United States on a missionary speaking tour. She and another elderly friend picked me up at one church and drove me to another for meetings.

As we rode along, I marveled at the laughter and cheerfulness of those two women. Everything delighted them. I later learned that they were loved by people in the church, and people tried to be in their company as often as possible.

Finally I had to ask, "How do you manage to stay so positive and cheerful about things?" Stella's answer was immediate, "I don't tell anyone about the aches and pains."

I had occasion to think of Stella earlier this year when I was at a difficult place in my missionary life. It really did seem as if everything was going wrong, through no fault of my own. At that point I wrote out a list of things that were bothering me. The list filled almost two pages!

Pessimism is prolific. Once I started worrying about something, many other things also seemed to go wrong. I decided to be optimistic and positive and firmly told myself that I would not complain. I began to look at those same circumstances in a different light.

Several months later I came across that list. Those complaints now seemed small and amusing. They had not changed, but I had.

"I don't tell anyone about the aches and pains," said Stella. As I grow older, I hope I can continue to grow as strong and beautiful as that woman.   DEBBIE COWLES

Why Things Go Wrong

Trust in the Lord with all your heart and lean not on your own understanding; in all your ways acknowledge him, and he will make your paths straight. Do not be wise in your own eyes; fear the Lord and shun evil. This will bring health to your body and nourishment to your bones (PROVERBS 3:5–8).

God wants us to trust Him completely. Problems cannot overwhelm us when we trust God. Things go wrong when we try to take over and do it our way. Sometimes we do not realize that we have taken over the controls until problems develop. Then a close look may reveal who is really in the driver's seat.

If we spend time getting to know God through His Word and through prayer, He will show us when to move and where to go.

We must not take pride in our own wisdom; rather, we must fear the Lord and turn away from what is harmful. Some of us go out to meet the evil instead of turning out of its path. Here is where the trouble often begins, especially when we have a little knowledge and do not wait for God to show us how to use it.

A healthy body and strong bones are spoken of as the rewards of trust and obedience. Many people long and pray for good health, but how many of us meet the requirements? Although it is not easy to trust and obey, it is absolutely necessary if we are to experience the fullness of life in Christ. LAURA MARSHALL

JUNE 30

Not a Disappointment

My command is this: Love each other as I have loved you. Greater love has no one than this, that one lay down his life for his friends. You are my friends if you do what I command (JOHN 15:12–14).

The Bible has a lot to say about friends. In Proverbs 18:24 it says, "A man of many companions may come to ruin, but there is a friend who sticks closer than a brother."

On a recent job interview, I was asked some very personal questions that started me thinking. I was instructed to think first of the strong points and then the weak points of my closest and dearest friend. My mind quickly turned to that special individual who listens so well and to whom I had confided so much. Those quiet times of sharing and laughter, joy and tears were always kept in the deepest part of the heart.

The difficult task came when I tried to enumerate the weak points of that "special friend." When we think of that certain person, though we are aware of shortcomings, we tend to overlook them just because we are friends. I began to think, however, of the times when even my best buddy had let me down.

Going home that day, I sensed in my heart that Jesus was talking to me. I was reminded that through all the trials in which His promises were tested, Jesus has remained my dearest and best Friend. There is no disappointment in Him.   JUDY FREELAND

The Everlasting Arms

The eternal God is your refuge, and underneath are the everlasting arms (DEUTERONOMY 33:27).

Most of us have had an "I'll do it myself" attitude all our lives. It is just human nature to want to be independent, but God desires that we become as little children in our complete trust in our Heavenly Father.

At age 35, I was a wife and the mother of five children. My husband became ill, and serious surgery was recommended. In those days, it was not common surgery nor was it highly successful. *Lord, how could I ever survive without Paul? How would I ever be able to provide for our children? Could I, through Christ's strength, be father and mother to them?* Hundreds of questions seemed to flood my mind.

I searched the Scriptures for promises that would apply in my situation. They had always met my heart's need, but at this particular time, it was a verse from Simpson's hymn, "The Everlasting Arms," that stilled my fears.

> Underneath us—oh, how easy!
> We have not to mount on high;
> But to sink into His fullness
> And in trustful weakness lie.

How refreshing! I did not have to be strong in this situation. He would be my strength as I rested in Him. Even though my legs felt rubbery, I knew for certain that my feet were planted on the rock. I did not need to have all the answers for the future; I only needed to trust Him and walk with Him in obedience.

Resting in Him is such a reassuring posture. How can we possibly fail? He takes full responsibility when we walk in simple obedience and trust.   JEAN BUBNA

Love Your Enemy

If your enemy is hungry, feed him; if he is thirsty, give him something to drink. In doing this, you will heap burning coals on his head (ROMANS 12:20).

As God's people, we should make friends instead of enemies. There are, however, those who want to make us their enemies. During the "Great Cultural Revolution" in China, my late father, an Alliance pastor in Kwongsi Province, was falsely accused because of the stand he took for his Christian faith. This false accusation cost him his basic human rights, and he was repeatedly and brutally beaten by the mob. Finally, on July 25, 1968, his attackers knocked him to the ground unconscious. Then they stomped on his stomach until he died.

The informant whose testimony led to my father's arrest was one of the deaconesses whom we had known for years. We could not believe such betrayal!

In 1981, my husband and I went back home for a visit. While there, we attended a banquet to celebrate my brother's wedding. We were amazed to find that my mother had invited the informant to the banquet. She harbored absolutely no hatred against her enemy.

In 1983, my father's citizenship was restored posthumously, for which we were thankful. My mother's example of loving her enemies was an effective witness to the unsaved world that Christians could really live up to what they professed.

Conviction is brought about by both our profession and our actual behavior. DORCAS LOH

Better Than Gold

These have come so that your faith—of greater worth than gold, which perishes even though refined by fire—may be proved genuine and may result in praise, glory and honor when Jesus Christ is revealed (1 PETER 1:7).

Just what is this thing called gold? It is something that is treasured, prized and sometimes presented as an award, as in the Olympic Games. Because of its value, gold is insured and carefully guarded. It is precious and is coveted by many.

The term *gold* is commonly used to indicate something of great beauty or value, for example: the golden rule of moral guidance, the pot of gold at the rainbow's end, the Golden Fleece of mythology or the Golden Gate Bridge in San Francisco.

Gold comes in many colors and types. It can be green, pink, white or yellow; it can be gilt, plate or leaf.

There are many references to gold in God's Word. But more precious and desirable than gold, we are told, are these—the proving of your faith (1 Peter 1:7), wisdom (Proverbs 16:16), knowledge (Proverbs 8:10) God's law (Psalm 119:72) and His commands (Psalm 119:127).

Just as there are many kinds of gold, many purposes for its use and many methods of acquiring it, so there are different processes by which God works in us to bring us to perfection. It may be testing (Job 23:10), refining (Proverbs 17:3) or purging (Isaiah 1:25). Whatever the method God uses, it is meant to separate the dross or worthless elements from our lives so that our faith "may be proved genuine and may result in praise, glory and honor when Jesus Christ is revealed."   ETHEL K. HUTTAR

JULY **4**

Never Lonely

A friend loves at all times, and a brother is born for adversity (PROVERBS 17:17).

When I retired five years ago, my one request was, "Lord, please don't let me be lonely." In answer, my loving, Heavenly Father sent a host of wonderful friends and many challenging avenues to explore.

My life has been filled with love. A necessary leavening, love is the agent without which we could never rise to any height. I praise the Lord for people who love and people who care.

Being loved is not something that happens without some effort on our part. We must be loving, caring people with a desire to reach out to others in need. Love is contagious. Each one reaches out to another. Then love covers a multitude of sins and makes everything beautiful.

I thank the Lord for my loving and caring family. My three daughters have families of their own; they now teach their children to always love one another. In ever-widening circles, love goes on and on, continuing to grow and to touch the lives of others.

Today, have you told someone you love him or her? Do not let time slip away from you. The day is coming when love will rule the world. Wonderful day!   EVELYN CUTRER

More Time with Him

The Lord will guide you always; he will satisfy your need in a sun-scorched land and will strengthen your frame (ISAIAH 58:11).

While I was still in elementary school, God let me know, through the lives of several missionaries, that He wanted me to serve Him in Africa. But just recently He gave me this verse in Isaiah with the renewed promise that even here in the African sun, He will guide me and those with whom I work and will give us daily strength.

He will also guide the women of this sun-scorched land to Himself that they too may know His love and presence in their lives — women like Esther.

Esther grew up close to a strong Christian church. She attended services regularly, gave herself to the Lord early in her life but remained weak and insecure in her attitude toward serving her God. She was willing to stand behind someone but fearful of leadership. When asked, "Will you teach a Bible class? Lead a women's group?" she replied, "No, I can't."

Through special courses, however, Esther became involved in studying the Word. As she would come with new ideas and plans for outreach, we told her, "Great! Go and do it!"

She began to study more of God's Word and to spend more time in His presence in prayer. Now she leads the largest women's group in the Libreville church. She counsels many women each week and is daily serving her God and His people here in Gabon. Esther is a woman who walks in His presence and knows that God is with her.

Do you have the assurance that the Lord is guiding you and daily strengthening your frame? You may if you spend daily time in His presence.   RUTH BOWMAN

Strength through Trials

But he knows the way that I take; when he has tested me, I will come forth as gold (JOB 23:10).

I had just listened to my friend Linda's sad story. A young man seemed to like her. They worked in the same office, and he often stopped by to visit, watched for her arrival and spent as much time as he could over lunch break and after hours talking with her.

Then suddenly it all stopped. She could not think of anything she had said to offend him. He did not act as though he disliked her; he just had excuses for leaving early and no longer sought out her company.

Most of us at some time have been on the receiving end of that kind of pain and have felt as Linda. Her pride prevented her from asking him what happened or from causing a scene. She probably wished she could throw herself at him, burst into tears and accusations and beg him to like her again. Instead, she waits in silence.

I doubt that this young man will come back to Linda. She has no claims on him. In a few weeks, she will recover from the hurt and shame and will go on with her life. But how sad if she does not grow from this bitter experience.

The other day I saw a poster of a winter scene. A bare, black tree stood alone in a canyon with icy white mountains behind it. The caption: "Do not pray for an easy life. Pray to be a strong person."

These wintry blasts can break us, or they can help to make us strong. Pray that God will make you a stronger person.   DEBBIE COWLES

The Weight Watcher

Therefore, since we are surrounded by such a great cloud of witnesses, let us throw off everything that hinders and the sin that so easily entangles, and let us run with perseverance the race marked out for us (HEBREWS 12:1).

The other day as I stood in line for my "weigh-in" at the Weight Watchers' meeting, my attention was focused on a mother and daughter who were standing in front of me. As it came time for the daughter to be weighed, she turned to her mother and said, "Here, Mom. Hold my heavy purse while I get on the scale."

Immediately my mind flashed to the verse in Hebrews where we are cautioned to "throw off everything that hinders." Just as this daughter handed her purse to her mother, we are to turn over to another those things that hold us back spiritually. And who better to hand them to than the One who is the "author and perfecter of our faith" (verse 2).

This takes action on our part. We are to say, "Here, Lord. I am tired and weary of carrying around this excess baggage. I give it to You to be put under Your blood." The Lord has assured us in His Word that His blood will cleanse us and remove those hindrances that are preventing us from living a victorious Christian life.

We are not, however, to be like the daughter who took back her purse after being weighed. Once we hand those weights over to the Lord, we are to leave them with Him. We are to forget and forsake them.

Today, as we step on His scale for our "weigh-in," we need not despair. Jesus is right there beside us, just as this mother was beside her daughter, to receive those things that are impeding our progress. As we lay them aside, we can get back on God's scale with confidence.   MARIE HINEMAN

The Way Out

But I will rescue you on that day, declares the Lord; you will not be handed over to those you fear (JEREMIAH 39:17).

When I visited my sister and her family in Berlin, Germany, we made several trips through Checkpoint Charlie into East Berlin to shop and to eat lunch in the little cafes. The highlight of the trip, however, was a visit to the unusual little village of Stienstuken.

When the Communists built the Berlin Wall, they somehow left inside their territory 20 homes that should have been on the West Berlin side of the wall. As a result, this village was bordered on one side by no man's land and on the other three sides by the wall. For 17 years these people could not get in or out except by helicopter. Groceries were airlifted in, the sick were airlifted out and relatives were brought to visit by this "Stienstuken Bird." Steadfastly, these people refused to permit an opening in the wall with access into the East Communist sector. Instead, they held out for freedom.

After years of negotiations, the East Germans agreed to open a road through the wall to the free West Berlin side. Though the corridor was just wide enough for one vehicle to go through, to the folks in Stienstuken, it was as good as any six-lane highway.

I thought of the many situations that must have arisen during those 17 years. In the middle of the village sat the helicopter that had been their lifeline, certainly a constant reminder of the price of freedom.

In the same sense, Satan had walled us in and would not relinquish his control. We were cut off from God, but one day He paid sin's price for our freedom, and the way "out" was made through the cross.   DELORES TAYLOR

JULY 9

God's Economy

The priests who carried the ark of the covenant of the Lord stood firm on dry ground in the middle of the Jordan, while all Israel passed by until the whole nation had completed the crossing on dry ground (JOSHUA 3:17).

Our world is influenced by the production, distribution and consumption of goods and services. We watch the evening news for the slightest fluctuation in the Dow-Jones average. God's Word repeatedly tells us to trust Him, yet we fear a future of deprivation.

Elisha lived in God's economy. When the widow of Second Kings 4 approached him, she saw only one small jar of oil. Elisha saw God's supply of oil, and he called for her to demonstrate her faith. God filled every jar that she brought.

Second Kings 3:17 gives to us another of Elisha's lessons in economics. As the kings dug ditches in the dry valley, the Lord amply supplied their need for water.

In Second Kings 5, we see Naaman brought into the economy of God. Naaman responded in his basic sense economy. He trusted in his gold and silver to deliver him. But there was no healing until he went God's way. He had to go to the *right* river and to immerse himself the *exact* number of times.

Joshua and the people of Israel had to cross the Jordan at floodtide, impossible under a fleshly economy. But as the priests stepped into the river, it stopped flowing. By faith, the people crossed on dry ground.

Today, let us not look at our needs but at God's supply. Let us dare to set out our jars, dig in a dry valley, dip seven times in the right river and thank God for the blessing obtained by doing it His way.   MARGARET A. CUMMINGS

JULY 10

Deny and Follow

Then he called the crowd to him along with his disciples and said: "If anyone would come after me, he must deny himself and take up his cross and follow me" (MARK 8:34).

There is no worthwhile undertaking that does not require denial in one form or another. Someone has said, "There are no crown-wearers in heaven above who were not cross-bearers here below." Can we not assume, then, that self-denial and cross bearing for His sake will bring reward?

It requires self-denial to regularly spend time alone with God. But nothing can compare with the blessing of "getting up before daybreak" to have fellowship and communion with God. The Lord Himself set that example (Mark 1:35). There at His feet, where we learn how holy He is, we may also understand how holy He expects us to be. How refreshed and strengthened we come away after having denied ourselves those few extra hours of sleep that we might wait in His very presence.

Where else can we learn sorrow for sin and patience in suffering? Where could I have received strength in my times of need, had I not learned that I must walk with Him on the mountaintop if I expect to find His help in the valley of suffering and anguish?

And anyone who does not take his cross and follow me is not worthy of me (Matthew 10:38).   MAY S. BROWN

Standing by the Gate

When Peter saw this, he said to them: "Men of Israel, why does this surprise you? Why do you stare at us as if by our own power or godliness we have made this man walk?" (ACTS 3:12).

I t is three o'clock in the afternoon in Jerusalem — the hour of prayer. As I stand by the Temple gate called Beautiful, I see a man being carried by several of his friends. I step back into the shadows to watch. They bring their burden close to the gate, set him down, then turn and leave. In the crippled beggar's hand he holds a small bowl which he extends toward the worshipers as they enter the Temple.

He begins his pitiful wail: "Alms, alms." Some people totally ignore the man; others stop to drop a coin into the bowl.

Then I notice two men approaching. The beggar looks up and speaks directly to them, "Alms, alms." They stop and look into his face. The older one speaks: "Look at us! We do not have any money, but what we have we gladly give to you. In the name of Jesus Christ of Nazareth, walk!"

I watch as the drama unfolds. The beggar takes the man's hand, stands to his feet and begins to walk. Now he is shouting and praising God. A crowd is gathering, and it is difficult for me to see what is happening.

Someone identifies the men as Peter and John, disciples of Jesus Christ. Peter steps into Solomon's Hall and begins to speak. The crowd is silent as he talks of all that is available through faith in the resurrected Lord.

Lives were changed today at the Beautiful Gate. Two men, eager to serve their Lord, stopped to help a man in need. Perhaps today your path may cross that of someone who is in need. Will you be able to say, "What I have I gladly give to you, in the name of Jesus . . ."?

BETTY GANGEL

JULY 12
Such Simple Words

As long as Moses held up his hands, the Israelites were winning, but whenever he lowered his hands, the Amalekites were winning (EXODUS 17:11).

L et me know if there is anything I can do!" They are such common, simple words. People say them to others who are going through some difficult experience. But when we say them, do we expect to get involved, to hurt as they hurt and to stand by until victory comes?

Think for a moment of Moses as he led the Israelites toward the Promised Land. When Amalek came to attack them, Joshua was told to choose men to go out and fight. What did Moses do? He took his place on the top of the hill with the rod of God in his hand. There was power in that rod. Miracles had been accomplished through its use.

Aaron and Hur climbed the hill with Moses. Why? Moses had already said that *he* would stand on the hill and hold out the rod during the battle. As he held out the rod, Israel was winning, but when he became weary and his hands drooped, the enemy prevailed.

Aaron and Hur then took a stone and placed it so that Moses could sit down. Was that not what he needed — rest for his weary body? Yes, but more than that! The two men *held up* his hands — Aaron on one side and Hur on the other. And victory came.

Why did they not relieve Moses of the rod and "take turns" holding it up? This was not a time for self-glory. God was to be glorified.

Someone you know may be in the throes of difficulty or anguish. Finding a stone for him to sit on may provide some degree of rest, but remember, it takes the personal touch to assure victory.   DORIS HADLEY

JULY 13

God's Plan for You

"For I know the plans I have for you," declares the Lord, "plans to prosper you and not to harm you, plans to give you hope and a future" (JEREMIAH 29:11).

Our finite minds are able to capture only the present. We make plans by pondering current circumstances and remembering past experiences. No human plans can ever be perfect. In contrast, our infinite, all-wise God has His perfect plans for us. He is not only aware of our past and present but all of our tomorrows, too!

The Israelites were exiled in Babylon — a people without a home. Insecurity about their future plagued them. False prophets invented spurious dreams and hopes, instilling apprehension about an imminent return to Jerusalem. Yet God, through Jeremiah, assured them of His plans to give them "hope and a future."

We can likewise trust our Lord with the plans that He has for us. You may be facing some uncertainty about your future, or you may be unsettled by the thought of change. In the midst of your darkness, forget all outside voices and rest in the assurance of God's unfailing love. As He did with the Israelites, He will set you free from your bondage of fear, anxiety or insecurity.

Fully trusting and obeying our Lord may be a difficult exercise. Take comfort during challenging times in knowing that God's ways and thoughts are higher than ours (Isaiah 55:9). Dwell on the faithfulness of His Word and give thanks to Him for the plans He reveals. ARLISS M. ALLEN

JULY 14

Separate the Circles

For our struggle is not against flesh and blood, but against the rulers, against the authorities, against the powers of this dark world and against the spiritual forces of evil in the heavenly realms (EPHESIANS 6:12).

As the anxious bride of a dedicated, talented young minister, I wanted to be the best preacher's wife that this world had ever known. This high ideal, however, was soon to be dimmed, shaken and then almost shattered, as I faced the reality of dealing with well-meaning saints who are exceptionally gifted in "ideal shattering."

But God, in His loving, faithful way, taught me a beautiful and long-lasting lesson from this verse in Ephesians.

First, we must place all of the people among whom we minister into one circle called "flesh and blood"; then, into another circle, place Satan and his destructive ways. Now, *separate the circles!* Put Satan into one circle and the one whom Satan is using at the moment into the other. When the trials begin to come from whomever, we recognize them for what they actually are, the works of Satan, *not* people.

Now we can understand that our warfare is not with "Sister Long-nose" but with the critical, inquisitive, destructive power of Satan within her. Our battle is not with "Mr. Know-it-all" but with the proud and arrogant spirit of Satan governing him at the moment. It is not the brash, overbearing board member but a divisive devil who desires to disrupt the harmonious flow of God's unity in the body of believers.

Once we are able to assess our relationships in this light, we are able to pray sincerely and honestly for those who sometimes make our lives unpleasant.   JEANETTE HENLEY

New Shoes

Delight yourself in the Lord and he will give you the desires of your heart (PSALM 37:4).

My five-year-old daughter loves new shoes. All day yesterday she wore her brand-new white patent leather shoes around the house; last night, she fell asleep wearing them. This morning she wanted to wear them to school. When I told her she had to wait until Sunday, her happy attitude became one of grumbling and complaining. "I don't even want to go to school! I am going to cry all day!" She laid back down on her bed, sulking. When her brother came in all dressed for school and wearing his new sneakers, she said, "You're lucky! It's just not fair."

I could see in my daughter a mirror of myself. I thought of how easily my happy attitude can change into one of complaining and grumbling.

We all have expectations as we face each new day. Circumstances often change, and our plans must be put aside. Have you ever intended to spend the day baking, only to receive a call from an elderly church member who needs a ride to her doctor—now? Or how many times in the middle of laundry have my kids asked me to read a book, take a walk, play with dolls or puzzles or who knows what else?

Our attitude ought not to be, "What do *I* want to do?" Rather, we should pray, "Lord, I'm Yours; *You* lead the way." If we automatically say no to elderly women, little children or other unscheduled interruptions, we may get all our work accomplished, but we may also miss the Lord's blessing in the process.

If we give every day's plans to God, each intrusion or disappointment becomes a part of His plan in molding us into the person He wants us to be.   SHERRY HARTLEY

To Know Him

If I have found favor in your eyes, teach me your ways so I may know you and continue to find favor with you (EXODUS 33:13).

Nothing in the Christian life, and certainly nothing in the world, is as wonderful as knowing God intimately. In Solomon's Song, the Shulamite maiden cries out, "Take me away with you—let us hurry!" (1:4).

No longer was the Shulamite satisfied with a knowledge of things *about* her companion. She wanted to really *know* him. She was consumed by a deep and intense longing for a more intimate relationship with him.

Like the Shulamite maiden and her companion, let us press on to know the Lord, not for anything He has done or will do for us but simply because we love Him for Himself.

Moses longed for a deeper knowing: His heart cry was "Teach me your ways so I may know you."

Paul said, "I want to know Christ and the Power of his resurrection and the fellowship of sharing in his sufferings, . . ." (Philippians 3:10).

God's desire has always been to have intimate fellowship with mankind. When He gave Moses the pattern for the Tabernacle in the wilderness, He said: "Then have them make a sanctuary for me, and I will dwell among them" (Exodus 25:8).

Today, all who by faith in the Lord Jesus have entered the door of salvation are "in Christ." But God never wanted us to remain in the Outer Court, or even in the Inner Court. His is the call of the Bridegroom to His bride. He calls us to enter the Holy of Holies, the place of intimacy, of perfect peace and rest.   BETSY PHILLIPS

The Lord Knows Best

As obedient children, do not conform to the evil desires you had when you lived in ignorance. But just as he who called you is holy, so be holy in all you do (1 PETER 1:14–15).

Have you learned lessons from your children? I certainly have! Though their disobedience grieves my heart, they are still my children. The Lord reminds me that this is how He feels when I resist what He has planned for me. I thank the Lord for our four sons and for the lessons God has taught and is teaching me through them.

Having sons in the home provides many opportunities to share God's Word with young men. The easiest way to begin such counsel is to talk about their homes. If their parents are Christians and have prayed for them, though young people may be rebelling and trying to "make it on their own," their hearts will be touched by thoughts of home.

If today your children are in rebellion, take heart. They are not resisting you; rather, they are rebelling against the will of God for their lives. Continue to pray for them. Ask the Lord to send across their pathway one who will share the claims of Christ upon his own life.

It is the Lord's desire that all of His children obey and quickly answer yes to all He commands us to do. But is it not encouraging to know that He never gives up on us? While we may find ourselves in deep difficulty as a result of disobedience, He picks up the broken pieces and puts everything back in order. Through this display of grace, we learn to lean on Him for wisdom, understanding and all that we need in our lives. YVONNE DAVEY

Only Believe

So the man went away and began to tell in the Decapolis how much Jesus had done for him. And all the people were amazed (MARK 5:20).

Consider what the Bible says about how God deals with His children. Where could you find anything more exciting? The world might understandably say, "I've never heard of such a thing!"

Think of Noah building a boat, something never before heard of—and on dry land! Imagine him preaching to the people of his day that the rain of God's judgment was coming and that unless they came into the ark, they would all drown. Noah, how ridiculous! Though a safe refuge was provided, only a handful were saved.

Think of baby Moses being placed in a basket and left by the side of the river in hope that he might escape Pharaoh's fatal decree. Foolish! Yet the princess saw him and took pity on him. Moses survived to lead thousands of his people out of Egypt.

Then there was Abraham, who left his country and clan in obedience to God's instructions. Because he obeyed, God used his faith to bless believers through the ages.

Three Jewish young men, believing they should obey God rather than the decree from the king of Babylon, found themselves in a burning, red hot furnace. Imagine the surprise of the onlookers when they saw a fourth man in there walking around!

Judgment is coming on our land. If rain begins and pelts our little vessel, we are safe inside because He has control. Does our furnace grow hotter? As the world observes, may they see the "fourth man" and recognize Him as the Son of God who works in our lives.   DELORES TAYLOR

Determination, Desertion, Devotion

Then Jesus told them, "This very night you will all fall away on account of me" (MATTHEW 26:31).

In Matthew 26:30 we read, "They went out." The disciples went with Jesus out to the Mount of Olives knowing something was going to happen. They had been through a great deal together, and they were determined to stay together to the end.

Then in verse 43 we read, "He found them sleeping." Not only once, but twice, Jesus came to them seeking prayer support in His desperate hour. When weariness overcame them, however, their determination gave way. Later we read that "all the disciples deserted him and fled."

We do not read anything more about the disciples, as a group, until after the Lord arose from the grave. They must have had much to talk about. Why had they fled? Was He coming back? When? Then in 28:17, we read that "they worshiped him; but some doubted."

Our spiritual lives are often just like the disciples'. We start out on fire for the Lord. But then we are lulled to sleep by pleasures and the things of the world. We neglect our devotions and become careless about attendance at the house of the Lord. Some even draw away from the things of God completely — that is, until a catastrophe strikes. Then we want to worship Him and ask for His help.

Why not learn from these experiences, so that when troubles do come our way, we will be in communion with Him and He will see us through.   ELSIE J. MCILRATH

His Presence

You did not recognize the time of God's coming to you (LUKE 19:44).

J esus comes to us in many ways and at unsuspecting moments. The conversation on the Emmaus road led to closer fellowship as the travelers responded to Jesus' words and invited Him into their home. It is as we spend time actively seeking fellowship with Jesus, that we really learn to know Him and become a partaker of His life and ministry. Only when we have met Him on this intimate level can we effectively tell others about Him.

Often He comes to us in unexpected ways. Sickness, if rightly accepted, often reveals Him to us. In the quietness of a feverish night, we sense His nearness and are reminded of His constant care. He gives us assurance that nothing can touch us apart from His loving permission.

Dengue fever was an unwelcome interruption of my routine in Mali, Africa. My feverish, aching head could not concentrate on praying. I heard the sound of singing coming from the church as the Christians met for their weekly prayer meeting. Their promise to pray for me had comforted me. The aching seemed to worsen and then, in response to their prayers, the fever broke.

Although separated by walls and yards, I had experienced the healing hand of Jesus as I fellowshiped in the Spirit with my African family. In a few days I was able to witness publicly about what Jesus had done. Those days of sickness were not pleasant, but they were precious because of His nearness.

We need to learn to look for Him in all our experiences. Recognizing His presence will make those experiences all that He intends them to be.   LINDA MCKELVEY

Esteem One Another

I pray that out of his glorious riches he may strengthen you with power through his Spirit in your inner being (EPHESIANS 3:16).

Lately I have read several things dealing with our tendency to wear "masks." We put up fronts, even when we do not mean to. Of course, this can make the command to "carry each other's burdens" difficult to do (Galatians 6:2). Few of us are able to first reveal our burdens. Perhaps we could remedy this by learning to view others from the same vantage point from which we view ourselves.

Not long ago, my husband delivered what I considered to be a particularly eloquent sermon. When he seemed to need affirmation, I thought, "How can he be needing so much encouragement when he is such an encouragement to others?" But suddenly the light dawned, and I understood that inside this pastor-leader lives a "little ole me" just like the one inside me and inside everyone else. I remembered then how much I need to know that it is "okay" when I teach a lesson, serve a dinner or write an article. I am not looking for accolades but rather for a sense of security and of rightness. No wonder Paul wrote that we need to be made stronger down inside the "little ole me" — the inner man.

How wonderful to learn that this can happen from the inside, through the work of the Holy Spirit. But we must tune our hearts to listen to His voice. Then we will no longer be so dependent upon the external voices of encouragement — as important as they are.

We must first of all depend on the Lord for guidance. Then, as we obey, He will give us the calm assurance that what we have done is not only "okay" but is perfect and right because it was done to please Him.   CAROLYN BUSH

God's Plan for Prisoners

The spirit of the Lord is on me, because he has anointed me to preach good news to the poor. He has sent me to proclaim freedom for the prisoners and recovery of sight for the blind (LUKE 4:18).

Have you ever felt imprisoned by some problem, attitude or relationship in your life? Whether it is a financial problem, a critical attitude or an inability to get along with others, we want to blame the situation on someone else. Such a prison, however, is frequently self-made. Despite that fact, a prison is a prison — and we just want out!

In Acts 16:25–33, God provides an example for dealing with imprisonment. We are to pray and sing praises to God so that others can hear us, for they also live in some kind of prison. When we accept our lot in life with joy, no matter what happens, then the great earthquake mentioned in verse 26 can occur, the prison doors will be opened and we shall be set free. We cannot plan this release. Only God can direct it. Even if it takes years to happen, we are to serve Him with a joyful heart.

Paul and Silas had been thrown into jail for obeying God. They were beaten and their feet were fastened with stocks. Even that could not stifle the joy in their hearts.

Our jailor is the person we associate with or blame for our problem — our spouse when marital problems arise; our child in adolescent or discipline problems; our opponent in any disagreement.

If we live in verse 25, if we dare to pray and praise in our situation, we will see the kind of complete turning that occurred for Paul and Silas.   LAURA MARSHALL

Desert Places

The Lord your God has blessed you in all the work of your hands. He has watched over your journey through this vast desert (DEUTERONOMY 2:7).

It was early morning. The children of Israel had gathered to hear their leader speak. Centuries later, as I sit in the cool morning of a similar day, I read from my Bible the story of Moses as he spoke to his people for the last time. I think of their miraculous rescue from Egypt and of God's continual care through the desert. I review the bitter lesson of their terrible idolatry when Moses went to the mountain to receive the Law, of God's anger, forgiveness and restoration.

In many ways, the Israelites' odyssey from Egypt to the Promised Land parallels our own deliverance from the bondage of sin to the kingdom of God. By observing His dealings with Israel, we learn a lot about God's relationship to us.

But why was there a desert experience at all? Why are there those lonely times when we lack the abundant joy we were led to expect in our Christian life?

There come times in our Christian walk when we must go on knowing only the sense of holding on to God's hand. Because we are "growing in Christ," God's commands to us will involve stretching and reaching out beyond ourselves. Our willingness to obey will determine our spiritual growth.

Today let us take our eyes off our problems and gaze steadfastly at our Savior. Let our prayer be that we may know the victorious Christian walk, not the aimless plodding through the desert.   SUSAN BLISS

JULY 24
Salt and Light

You are the salt of the earth. . . . You are the light of the world. . . .
Let your light shine before men, that they may see your good deeds and
praise your Father in heaven (MATTHEW 5:13–14, 16).

Anyone who has had to go on a no-salt diet knows how miserable it is to eat salt-free food. One who has been locked in a dark chamber understands the longing for light.

There are many people around us who live in a world of "no light" and "no salt." They cannot see real truth, nor can they taste the joy and happiness that is the possession of God's children. To find some meaning in life, many plunge into various illicit pleasures only to find that they bring nothing but darkness and self-reproach.

We meet these people every day in our offices, in the marketplace and even in our homes. Light has never reached them; they have never tasted of the goodness of Christ. Often it is the Christians who have failed them. We fail them while we are busy with our church activities. We fail them while we enjoy our own group fellowship.

The cry for light and for some meaning to life has never been louder. We hear it everywhere—when we go about our routine, turn on our television or scan the magazines in the supermarket. Beneath those happy smiles are many broken hearts and empty, ruined lives.

Some have reached out in Christ's love to offer His light, joy, healing and hope. But *some* is not enough. Our Lord would not command us to be the world's salt and light if He had not equipped us to obey. Through His indwelling Holy Spirit, we possess the truth of the gospel that is both salt and light. It is up to us to share it. In all our daily activities and contacts, let us diligently lift up Jesus as the Light of the World and the only Savior from sin. HOANG B. NGUYEN

Give Thanks

Give thanks in all circumstances, for this is God's will for you in Christ Jesus (1 THESSALONIANS 5:18).

"All circumstances? That's asking a bit too much, isn't it, Lord? Good things — of course. But bad things? — well, I'm not so sure."

One of the most dreaded words in our language is "cancer." I have been one of its victims. Why? Why does the Lord permit His own to suffer? Why does He not always miraculously heal? In my case, it may be because of the many things He has taught me.

Though I have loved His Word from my childhood, my suffering has given me a much greater appreciation for it. Never before did it afford such comfort. Never did I realize how important it is to have the Word in my heart.

I believe the Lord also permitted this suffering so that I might better appreciate the body of believers. I received so many cards that the girl who brought them to me said, "You have to be the most popular patient in this hospital."

God taught me anew, through these expressions of love and concern, the importance of remembering others in their need. I was reminded, too, of the importance of prayer. Acute pain renders it difficult to pray for yourself. Someone else must do the praying.

One who has suffered is better able to empathize with others who are going through painful experiences. I had the opportunity to talk with a woman who was facing the same surgery I had had. Mostly for that reason, she listened to my testimony. Later she accepted Christ, attended a church and, one year later, went to be with the Lord.

Truly, God is working out His will through *all* our circumstances. BETTY PEACE

Maggie's Gift

"I tell you the truth," he said, "this poor widow has put in more than all the others" (LUKE 21:3).

I can still see the pristine beauty of the rich, green valley. Bouquets of summer flowers dotted the well-worn path from Maggie's house to the old frame church deep in the heart of the mountains.

Maggie, her calico apron freshly ironed and her bonnet tied beneath her chin, picked up the covered basket and ran barefoot along the trail toward the weathered church building. Inside, the song service had already begun. I played the piano while my husband, a young ministerial student, led the singing.

Following God's direction, we were conducting services in remote churches scattered throughout the mountain region. Although most of the congregation were poor, they were rich in a proud heritage and bound by a spirit of love.

It was the last night of our meetings in the area. In their effort to show their appreciation, the people had decided to collect a love offering to help defray our expenses. The wooden plate passed from hand to hand as each person contributed what he or she could. As the plate approached Maggie, she took from her basket a jar of freshly canned, home-grown green beans. Having nothing else to offer, she placed it unabashedly in the offering plate.

I recalled the story in Luke concerning the poor widow who put in her two mites into the offering box as a gift to God. Her faith and love must have pleased the Lord, for He used her sacrifice to emphasize a truth.

I would like my life to reflect the joy of giving as evidenced by Maggie's offering. To me, her sacrifice will always be a lesson in sharing and giving.   VIVIAN WYATT

Well-laid Plans

Now listen, you who say, "Today or tomorrow we will go to this or that city, spend a year there, carry on business and make money." Why, you do not even know that will happen tomorrow. What is your life? You are a mist that appears for a little while and then vanishes (JAMES 4:13–14).

I had come home after being away five days attending a committee meeting. My mind was full of plans and projects that I determined would be top priority for the days and weeks ahead.

The next morning as my husband lay in the hospital in the throes of a heart attack, I realized that the priorities I had been so neatly organizing were "going down the drain." What had happened? Had God changed His plans? No. God in His sovereign will knew all about this day. His plans had not changed, but mine certainly had. I had set my priorities and plans according to the knowledge I had at the time. Now they no longer seemed important. Top priority had now become *life* — the life of my husband!

Plans, projects and priorities are not wrong. But James reminds us that this life is but a mist — appearing for a brief moment only to vanish. For that reason, I believe God wants us to plan and use our time wisely. Proverbs 16:9 indicates that an individual may plan his course, but God is in control. He is sovereign, wise and full of knowledge. He is the one who determines the course of our days. To Him be the glory!   JEAN WOLTERS

Tender, Loving Care

I tell you the truth, unless a kernel of wheat falls to the ground and dies, it remains only a single seed. But if it dies, it produces many seeds (JOHN 12:24).

Once again this summer, the flowers in my window boxes have outdone themselves. The big, red geranium blossoms are like individual bouquets with deep, green foliage for a background. The red, pink and white begonias were not to be eclipsed by the geraniums and are just as lovely in their delicate beauty.

Passers-by on our back country road have admired the flowers and given credit to my tender, loving care. Tender, loving care? Yes, but not mine. If they could have seen the dry, brown, ugly-looking geranium stalks that came out of my cellar this spring, they would have despaired, as I do each spring. Only God's tender, loving care can bring such beauty from those lifeless, unpromising stalks.

And so it is with us! All we have to offer Him is our sinful, unpromising selves, but He can make something beautiful of our lives if we allow Him.   RUBY WATROUS

The King's Children

Delight yourself in the Lord and he will give you the desires of your heart (PSALM 37:4).

Why do we have such a difficult time believing the promises of God's Word? Why do we feel that these promises are for someone else but surely not for us? Why should we feel that God will supply our *needs* but not our *desires*?

As committed Christians, we are asked to surrender our *all* to Jesus. If we are faithful to Him, we can expect that He will, indeed, be faithful in His promises to us. Jesus states "Truly I say to you, there is no one who has left house or wife or brothers or parents or children, for the sake of the kingdom of God, who will fail to receive many times as much in this age and, in the age to come, eternal life" (Luke 18:29–30).

Five years ago, my husband and I left family, home and a business to become full-time missionaries. For years, my husband has teased me that he was taking me to Hawaii on our 20th anniversary. This was the year, but as the date approached the trip to Hawaii was out of the question. Our "faith salary" just did not stretch for such an extravagance, especially with our family of eight.

Three weeks before our anniversary, a very dear friend called and asked if we would consider joining him and his wife on a 10-day vacation to Hawaii. Our dream unfolded before us, and we were soon packing our bags for this miracle trip.

This entire experience proved once again that we do serve a first-class God. We are a royal priesthood and children of the King! The world needs to witness this inheritance we claim.   SALLY KNIPE

God's Plan Is Perfect

"For I know the plans I have for you," declares the Lord, "plans to prosper you and not to harm you, plans to give you hope and a future" (Jeremiah 29:11).

I lay in my hospital bed very ill and not expected to live. One of the nursing staff quietly talked to me about my condition. "Was I bitter against God?" she asked.

"No, God makes no mistakes," I replied. "He has an overall plan for my life. Of course I have goals and objectives I would like to see accomplished. I have children that I would like to raise. I have a husband who needs me. But why should I insist on my own way for such a small time slot in God's grand and sovereign design?"

My husband and I were missionaries in Mali. The tribe with whom we worked were very responsive, and our ministry was both satisfying and rewarding.

When it became apparent that I had a life-threatening blood problem, I was rushed back to the States. The Lord repeatedly brought to my mind Romans 8:28, "And we know that in all things God works for the good of those who love him, who have been called according to his purpose."

During our trials, we fail to see how these words apply to our situation. But God has revealed to me many things that He is working for the good of those who love Him.

Without the comfort of the Holy Spirit and the encouragement of God's Word, we are helpless to confront the hardships of human living. It does not take a super saint to live above adverse circumstances. It just takes a born-again believer who chooses to rely on the grace of God that is available for the asking.

Some day our questions will all be answered, and we will understand His plan.   DONNA R. ALBRIGHT

Jesus and Women

He will be great and will be called the Son of the Most High. The Lord God will give him the throne of his father David (LUKE 1:32).

Much controversy has arisen around the relationship of Jesus and His mother. Jesus was conceived by the Holy Spirit and was the only begotten Son of God, but he received all His human characteristics through His mother, Mary.

Though Mary was Jesus' human mother, she, like us, came to realize that the only way it is possible to become a child of God is to be born into the family of God. Through this new birth, we take on the "family traits" that mark us as Christians.

The compassion and tenderness of Jesus is much in evidence in the story of the woman caught in the act of adultery (John 8:3–11). The men who brought her to Him were authorities on the sacred law. They had observed her guilt, and they knew the prescribed punishment. Now, they were insisting that Jesus stand by the law and direct execution.

The accusers had not reckoned with the perfect insight of the One to whom they had appealed. "If any one of you is without sin, let him be the first to throw a stone at her" (verse 2). All were condemned by the knowledge of their guilt, so, without pressing the charge any further, they quietly left the scene.

Jesus' solemn and gracious words, "Neither do I condemn you, go now and leave your life of sin" (verse 11), are a message to us, as they were to her, that grace with mercy is superior to law.   CORA E. STAUB

Lessons from Miriam

So Miriam was confined outside the camp for seven days, and the people did not move on till she was brought back (NUMBERS 12:15).

Miriam's story is a familiar one. What woman does not admire her boldness and courage? After the children of Israel crossed the Red Sea, Miriam led the women in a dance of victory. Not only did they dance, they sang praises to the Lord.

Miriam prophesied among the Israelites. Evidently, her life was spent in pointing others to God. Few women were blessed in this way.

In Numbers 12, we read about Miriam and Aaron and their criticism of Moses' choice of a wife. As if this were not enough, they spoke with contempt of his ministry.

The Lord dealt harshly with Miriam, and she was smitten with leprosy. What if the Lord were to judge us in similar fashion when we criticize our Christian brothers? We wonder why Aaron did not receive the same punishment. Could it have been because it hurt him as much to see her in this condition as it would have had God stricken him? Or was it perhaps because such punishment would have prevented him from performing his priestly function?

Their sin and God's discipline halted the forward progress of the children of Israel. "The people did not move on till she was brought back." Sin in any member affects the entire body of Christ. But the children of Israel waited until she could come back into the camp.

Do busy schedules prevent us from slowing our steps to help a brother or sister back into his or her right relationship with God? Until they are "brought back," do we pray for them?   DELORES TAYLOR

God's Umbrella

Peace I leave with you; my peace I give you. I do not give to you as the world gives. Do not let your hearts be troubled and do not be afraid (JOHN 14:27).

They say that into each life some rain must fall. I prefer the sunshine, but several years ago, I had an unexpected rainfall. I discovered a small lump. The following Sunday I was anointed and that evening I called my parents. My dad prayed with me over the phone. From that point on, I was convinced that everything was all right. I awakened in the night and immediately checked to see if the lump was gone. I would not have been surprised if it had been, but it was still there.

I told the Lord that I knew He could make it disappear before any surgery was needed, but if not, I still believed He was working. The next day the doctor scheduled me for a biopsy. Having never had surgery, I admit I was somewhat frightened. Jesus gave me peace, however, and I went into surgery knowing that God was with me. I felt relieved when I was told the tumor was benign. Later the doctor said, "I'm sorry, but I must tell you something." He went on to say that it happened very rarely, but further tests had revealed that there was a malignancy.

I had been so convinced that everything was all right, and the people of God had believed with me. I had heard of other amazing healings. Why not me? The Lord had to remind me that His plan for one of His children may not be the same as for another. But when we love Him enough to trust Him to work in our lives, "He doeth all things well."

This time I went into surgery knowing I had a malignancy. Would I still know His peace? Yes, I did. And it was truly the "peace of God" (Philippians 4:7).   BETTY PEACE

I Stopped This Morning

O Lord, our Lord, how majestic is your name in all the earth! You have set your glory above the heavens (PSALM 8:1).

I stopped this morning, Lord; I stopped and listened. What did I hear? I heard You, the Creator, the Great One who designs. I stopped. I touched. I felt. What did I touch and feel, Lord? I felt Your clean, cool air. It made the pine cones snap and little seeds come floating down to earth to die and to live again.

"I stopped this morning, Lord, to enjoy Your warm sunshine. It warmed my face. It felt good wherever it touched. You are the Sunshine of life, and whenever we stop and let You touch our hearts and lives, we are like the pine cones. We leave seeds all around us. Some will die, but many others will float out to who knows where and take on life as only You can give it.

"When the world seems cold, You are warmth and comfort. You give us rich, lush shade in the heat of life. You give life and hope. Thank You, Lord Jesus." HELEN CRIMM

Where Is Our Faith?

He got up and rebuked the wind and the raging waters; the storm subsided, and all was calm. "Where is your faith?" he asked his disciples (LUKE 8:24–25a).

W*here is our faith* when the things we want most in life seem always to elude us? Where is our faith when a loved one is snatched away, when sorrow comes and tears fill our eyes?

Where is our faith when our world seems to be tumbling in? Where is our faith when others look to us for strength, and we are weak? Where is our faith when we cannot see beyond our trials to know the whys and wherefores?

Where is our faith when doubts come, and we feel that God has forsaken us? Where is our faith when our hearts break with the realization that our dreams are not coming true? Where is our faith when we have prayed and our answers seem so long in coming?

Is it in the One who holds the future in His hands, the One who can calm the mighty winds? Do we trust Him when we cannot see or do we walk about blindly as others do? *Help us, Lord, when our faith is weak. Take our hands and lead us gently.*

When trying days come our way, let us cling to the only thing in life that is steadfast and sure. He will dry the tears from our eyes, set our hearts aglow and fill us with His joy.   JUDY FREELAND

I Have Been There!

I consider that our present sufferings are not worth comparing with the glory that will be revealed in us (ROMANS 8:18).

Several years ago, I went through a time of deep depression. I remember thinking that I would never be free of this life of darkness and despair. I would cry out, "Oh, Lord, have You deserted me? Why, Lord, must I suffer this?" Through much prayer and a slow process of inner healing, however, I was totally freed from my dependence on all medication.

For the last five years, my family and I have been on the mission field where we work with abused and neglected children of all ages. More than 30 of these children have lived in our home, all of them having experienced unusual emotional trauma. Now I see why the Lord allowed me to feel that loneliness, depression and rejection.

When, as children, our self-esteem is damaged, it is only through the love of our Lord that we can begin to discover those gifts and qualities that make us special. Because of the "unconditional love" I received as part of my healing, I can, in turn, give that love to these hurting ones.

Since it is true that we can only lead others on paths we have walked, the trials and suffering we experience may well serve as the training we need in order to reach out to others. With Christlike compassion, we can share with others the lessons we have learned. We can assure them that our sufferings are only temporary and that the glory to follow always makes them worthwhile.

"Yes, I know what you are going through; I've been there"!   SALLY KNIPE

Light upon Our Way

What you decide on will be done, and light will shine on your ways. (JOB 22:28).

My aged parents had sold their home in order to pay delinquent bills and had to live with us. Mother, a severe arthritic, had little use of either hands or body. Her memory was also affected. My father, troubled with heart disease and emphysema, was filled with anger at Mother's limitations and his apparent failure. His depression and embarrassment caused his behavior to be unpredictable and explosive.

What should we do? After three months, I was exhausted from caring for my mother, monitoring my father's behavior, maintaining our home, helping my husband and sons adjust and trying to find some financial assistance. We had only $1,000 remaining. Burial arrangements had been made in a midwestern state 1,300 miles away. We felt the heavy hand of our enemy upon us!

One morning as I rushed through my chores, the thought flashed through my mind, "Go! Read the book of Job." I had heard of Job, a man of patience, but I had never sat down and read that particular book. I opened my Bible to chapter 1. Quickly I read through the book, realizing in it a pattern for successful living. Answers would come—and they did!

Within the next months I found a source of financial help. We were able to celebrate the holidays together, and then I accompanied my parents to a long-term care residence in California. Later, as I stood by their graves, I thanked God for the lessons from Job and for the light that He had shown on our path.   ERNESTINE M. SCHINDLER

AUGUST 7

Love's Price

For you know that it was not with perishable things such as silver or gold that you were redeemed . . . but with the precious blood of Christ, a lamb without blemish or defect (1 PETER 1:18–19).

When a university student was teased because he did not have a girlfriend, his response was, "I cannot afford to love; I have neither time nor money." Love has a price. It may cost not only in time and money but in loved ones, friends, job and possibly your very life. And love can be very painful if it is not reciprocated.

John 3:16 tells us that God gave because he "so loved." Love constrained Him to give. The object of His love was "the world," mankind whom He had created in His own image so that He might have the joy of fellowship with them. Then, by a willful act of disobedience, man broke that relationship and brought sorrow and death upon the entire race.

Why did God give? He is not willing that any should perish but that each one should repent of his sin (2 Peter 3:9). When did God give? While all of us were not only sinners but also enemies of God (Romans 5:8, 10). What did God give? He gave His only begotten Son—His very best. How did He do it? He sent Jesus, our sacrificial Lamb, to the cross to pay the price of our sin. What love! Jesus, the sinless One, was made sin for us that through His obedience many might be made righteous (2 Corinthians 5:21).

Now He asks us to reciprocate that love by believing in Christ and receiving Him as Savior. We follow this by living for Him and showing others the way to life eternal.

Love costs. It cost God His Son. It cost Jesus His life. What is it costing us? PEARL FUSTEY

AUGUST 8

The Great Provider

And my God will meet all your needs according to his glorious riches in Christ Jesus (PHILIPPIANS 4:19).

We were a large family and did not have much money. Our family "happening" was a ride out into the country to visit my dad's brother and his family.

I was about eight years old, and I enjoyed listening to the older folks' conversation. Some of the things they said worried me, though. I remember my dad saying that the oncoming car lights blinded him. They talked about my grandmother's sickness and their concern about whether the old car would make the trip, in case she died.

Later on, I put a lot of stock in Dad's interpretation of the news from the European war front. He was a faithful listener to Gabriel Heater, noted news reporter of the 1930s. My measure of security rose and fell as my parents discussed the things that touched our family.

One night I heard my mother and father talking about food for the coming week. Work was scarce, and money was getting low. The cupboard was bare except for a small amount of flour.

We were on our way back from a visit with relatives. As we rounded a curve in the lonely road, I heard Mother say, "What's that?" As my dad brought the car to a halt, the lights shone on a crate in the middle of the road. In that crate were six live chickens. We could not believe our eyes. Getting those cackling chickens home was a real feat, but before they could sneeze, my mother had those fellows killed, plucked, cut up and ready to fry.

God provides for His children in many strange ways. He knows when there is only a little flour in the cupboard. He will be our sufficiency through all of life.   DELORES TAYLOR

Cruising with the Lord

You guide me with your counsel, and afterward you will take me into glory (PSALM 73:24).

Recently, while driving down the interstate, instead of putting the "pedal to the metal," I just sat back, enjoyed the scenery and let our cruisematic do all the work. I had never realized just how easy it is to be an inconsistent driver, but the cruisematic has taught me some lessons.

With the cruisematic in control, there is no slowing down when going up a hill or rounding a curve; no speeding up when passing another vehicle, no slowing down when passing a radar detector! You no longer slow down when talking or speed up when singing, or whatever else you do when you drive. All you have to do when the cruisematic is functioning is steer.

I thought about the cruisematic in relation to the Christian life. The Holy Spirit in us wants full control so that He can steer us around, over or through every circumstance in a way that will bring glory to God. Our will is like the steering wheel. We aim the car in the direction we want it to go. Sometimes we get into difficulty and wish we were somewhere else.

If we will only let the Holy Spirit, our "cruisematic," take full control and determine in our hearts to allow Him to take over our will or "steering wheel," we will have joy and peace in our circumstances. We will also find our lives becoming more consistent and disciplined. YVONNE DAVEY

AUGUST **10**

Surrender Attachments

Then take them . . . for a pleasing aroma to the Lord, an offering made to the Lord by fire (EXODUS 29:25).

As a missionary mother, one of the struggles that had to be dealt with was sending our children away to missionary school. I knew I had become completely attached to them, and the periodic separations would be a tremendous trial.

Each time our children left us, a cloud of loneliness settled down. As I sought to learn the Lord's thoughts on the matter, He gently began to teach me about the word "attachment."

Attachments — especially to loved ones and children — are considered normal. Even though we verbally dedicate our children to the Lord, to actually release them into His care is very difficult.

Attachment is quite different from love. Attachment can be selfish and clingy; love is service and sacrifice. Love is surrendering all our "loves" to Jesus who masters them well. If our dear ones are suddenly taken from our sight and if they have truly been released to Jesus, they are completely safe in His care.

But "surrender" and "worry" cannot be companions. If we worry about what we have just surrendered, we have not truly surrendered it. There cannot be two options: either God takes the burden or we struggle with it.

BEVERLY ALBRECHT

AUGUST 11

Greatly Blessed

His compassions never fail. They are new every morning; great is your faithfulness (LAMENTATIONS 3:22–23).

This morning as I awoke, I remembered that today was my birthday. Alone in my room, as I had been every morning since the death of my husband, I felt suddenly sad. I was getting older than I cared to admit!

I rushed to answer the phone. My daughter was calling from Texas to sing "Happy Birthday." Then she said, "Mother, I hope we have you around for many more years to come. Have a good day. I love you."

Again the phone rang. This time a daughter who lives in the area also sang "Happy Birthday," and added, "Have a good day; I'll see you tonight."

Before I could finish making my bed, the phone rang again. My other daughter called to tell me that they would be taking me out for dinner that night. By this time, the feeling of sadness was gone.

Later, a friend dropped by. Her mother is failing fast, and she just felt that she wanted to come and talk with me for a while. We walked out to my garden so that I could give her some beets, and we talked about how good God is.

The mailman brought some birthday cards. Later, after I had picked up my grandson at school, I returned home to find that a dear friend had left a gift on my porch.

I just had to take time to praise the Lord. My blessings had been so many and so wonderful that the day had flown by and it was time to dress for dinner with my family.

Our God is so faithful. At the very time when our feelings are at a low ebb, God sends His "ministers" to offer tokens of His love. Let us be at His disposal that we might be able to encourage someone today.   EVELYN CUTRER

Stretch!

Then he said to the man "Stretch out your hand." So he stretched it out and it was completely restored, just as sound as the other (MATTHEW 12:13).

Before you left the comfort of your bed, did you reach your arms high in a long, luxurious stretch?

"Stretch!" Richard Simmons, one of today's many diet specialists, tells his followers. "There," he says enthusiastically, "doesn't that feel great!" I like stretching. It helps us get everything moving together. Watch how an infant wiggles and arches his or her back in a delicious awakening stretch. "A baby is growing when he stretches," is an old adage. This kind of stretching benefits us physically.

The virtuous woman, mentioned in Proverbs 31, stretches or extends her hand. This stretching describes her ministry to others. When Jesus faced the crippled man in Matthew 12:13, His instruction was "Stretch out your hand." This stretch involved healing.

While Moses was leading the Israelites on their journey, there were many occasions when God commanded him to stretch out his hand. In this stretching, God displayed His approval of Moses' leadership. These examples seem to indicate that God deals best with open, outstretched hands.

Minds also need to be stretched. A friend told me that she is memorizing to stretch her mind, and on the same day, I read in a current magazine that a young mother has adopted a project of Scripture memorizing for her children to prevent the summer doldrums.

Each of us needs to stretch in order to grow, to minister, to heal and to be open to God. It seems the perfect way not only to beat the doldrums but to prepare us for ministry. Come, then. Let us stretch together!   ROSALIND MCNAIR

AUGUST 13
God's Priorities

But seek first his kingdom and his righteousness, and all these things will be given to you as well (MATTHEW 6:33).

What are you trying to accomplish in your life? Has what you are doing brought peace and satisfaction?

As a student nurse, I felt that I wanted to become another Florence Nightingale, someone who "stood out." I wanted fame, but I also wanted fortune—money to buy clothing, house, car. Of course, I also wanted loads of boyfriends. I praise the Lord, however, that early in my schooling, I was amazed and impressed by the unselfish, loving spirit shown by some of the student nurses. They had something I wanted, and that Something was Jesus. I began to seek Him daily, and the better I knew Him, the more I loved Him and wanted His way, not mine, for my life.

Through Christ I received all the desires of my heart. He gave me a dedicated Christian doctor husband and four children. Our two boys and two girls all know and love the Lord. Each one is a college graduate, married to a Christian spouse. Each puts the Lord first and is in the center of God's will.

To keep Him first in my life, I found that I had to meet Him in the morning.

I met God in the morning
When my day was at its best,
And His presence came like sunrise,
Like a glory in my breast.

Now I think I know the secret
Learned from many a troubled way.
You must meet Him in the morning,
If you want Him through the day.   JEAN SHAMBURGER

God Is Enough

And God is able to make all grace abound to you, so that in all things at all times, having all you need, you will abound in every good work (2 CORINTHIANS 9:8).

God is enough. He is our all-sufficient One. He is able to make all things possible for us through His grace. The original word for this grace is "charis" or "free blessing." It is spontaneous and universal. So it is in God's adequacy that we find the provision which abounds with every blessing we need. He will keep nothing from us to fulfill His glorious purpose.

For what reason are these wonderful gifts supplied? "So that in all things at all times, having all you need, you will abound in every good work." Or, as one writer put it, you will have ample means in yourself to meet each and every situation with enough and more to spare for every good cause!

As we abound in all the lovely gifts of our Almighty God, there should be a natural overflow of grace from our lives. This overflow can touch those around us who are in need.

We need to ask God to make our service for Him more abounding. Remember, He is able to equip us with the abilities to meet the task.

> Daily WAIT upon Him for His grace.
> Be WILLING to be emptied of your own desires and to follow His direction for your life.
> Seek WISDOM from Him for each day.
> Work WORTHILY of God's high calling through diligence and faithfulness.

ARLISS M. ALLEN

Set the Standard

But set an example for the believers in speech, in life, in love, in faith and in purity (1 TIMOTHY 4:12).

It is Sunday morning in Zaire. The little church is mud-brick, the pews are backless wooden benches, the roof is thatch. People begin coming early, by twos and threes. As each one sits down, something remarkable happens. Nearly every person bows his head and spends time in silent prayer.

Long ago, some missionaries taught the members of this church the good habit of taking a moment to pray silently before the worship service begins. Today, many years after those first missionaries, the church is still following the training it received.

In Proverbs 22:6 we read, "Train a child in the way he should go, and when he is old he will not turn from it." We usually apply this word to parents—and rightly so. But have you ever thought of it in terms of your relationship with a new Christian?

Most of us have new converts somewhere within our sphere of influence. Are we, by our example, words and habits, helping those new Christians develop the good spiritual habits that produce strong Christians?

Without saying one word, we can teach a new Christian the value of personal Bible study, the importance of meeting together for public worship and the necessity of having our lives in line with the teachings of Scripture.

Someone was a conscientious parent to the church in Zaire, and that training is still in evidence. We, too, should take seriously our job of training new Christians so they will grow to be the mature believers God wants them to be. MYRA BROWN

AUGUST 16

Give Christ Your Trust

In him we were also chosen, having been predestined according to the plan of him who works out everything in conformity with the purpose of his will (EPHESIANS 1:11).

While listening to a Sunday school lesson recently, I learned something about myself that was quite unexpected.

The question put to me was, "Do you want a binding contract in your relationship with the Lord?" If I had been asked that question on a one-to-one basis, I would have answered, "Of course not, contracts do away with trust." Yet as I listened to the teacher, a very dear friend of mine, I realized that my attitude had been saying something quite different.

I had been praying for certain personal needs and asking God to take care of them, according to His promises, and reminding Him of those promises. When I felt I was being treated unfairly, or when justice did not come to me, I would cry out, thus endeavoring to bind God to a contractual agreement.

As I listened to the lesson, I had to be honest—I was guilty. I began to pray and confess my guilt to my Heavenly Father. I recognized that I must learn to trust with my whole heart, without any bond or agreement.

Acknowledging that He must be Lord of everything or He is not Lord of anything, was a definite milestone for me. If we believe that He is the "only wise God," do we trust Him implicitly to work out everything in our lives for our good and for His glory?   VIRGINIA CUTHRIELL

A Woman's Version

Now these three remain: faith, hope and love. But the greatest of these is love (1 CORINTHIANS 13:13).

If I can speak eloquently before a large Bible study, amazing others with my wit and wisdom, but do not have love for those to whom I speak, I am just another babbler.

If I have great insight and understanding, if I am a prayer warrior with a long list of answered prayers, but do not love my mother-in-law, I am useless.

If I give away all I own and if I burn out for God with my dedication to church organizations and groups but do not love my neighbor, I have not pleased God.

True love is patient, even when waiting two hours for the Salvation Army truck to pick up my donations. Love is kind, even to the clerk who says I cannot get a refund without a receipt—even though it was a gift! Love does not envy, not even my neighbor who has new carpet while my ancient rug gets shabbier and shabbier. Love does not boast nor is it proud of my organization, my accomplishments and my strengths that are all from Him.

Love is not rude, not even to the fifth telephone salesman this week offering free carpet cleaning. Love is not self-seeking, even if it means giving up my scheduled day for toys, games or chitchat.

Love always protects, even the one who seems to deserve what is coming. Love always trusts, even when the good is harder and harder to find. It always hopes, even when all odds are against it. It always perseveres, even when the rest of the world says, "Give in—*quit!*"

It is great to be a super Christian—a paragon of faith and hope. But the thing that matters most to God is *love*.

DENISE S. HAMMER

A Proper Response

So Eli told Samuel, "Go and lie down, and if he calls you, say, 'Speak Lord, for your servant is listening.'" So Samuel went and lay down in his place (1 SAMUEL 3:9).

God's call demands a response. There are, however, many possible reactions to that call. One individual will say no to God, then will reverse his decision and act in obedience. Another person will respond with an immediate yes, yet harbor the feeling that he has been forced to make the response because of his fear of angering God.

Another responds with an eager readiness to serve the Lord he loves, and still another responds in his heart to the call of God, yet is unable, because of circumstances beyond his control, to take his place in full-time service.

What constitutes a proper response to God? It is not our ability to follow through on our call; it is our willingness to say yes that counts. It is the surrender of our will to His divine purpose that touches the heart of God.

In my teenage years, I had a tremendous desire to go into full-time Christian service. Doors closed, and for years I felt frustration and failure. I could not say an unconditional yes to God, because it meant being left behind while others went to foreign fields. Yet some struggle with the fear that God might call them to serve overseas.

Today God may be speaking to us about a special ministry. He may want us to cross the street to talk with a neighbor or to right a wrong. He may simply be asking us to be faithful in our homes, to get those dishes done and to be the wife and mother He intended us to be. Whatever God lays on our hearts, we need not be afraid, for He will not send us where He cannot keep us nor will He call us and then not equip us.   LOIS M. OSTER

Greet the Day

But I will sing of your strength, in the morning I will sing of your love (PSALM 59:16).

I am a morning person. I love each new day. Often waking early, I do some housework, then hurry off to jog before the sun rises high enough to burn off the cool summer mist that lies on the field and in the dips of the road.

It has always been easier for me to pray at the beginning of the new day. I am clear-headed, alert and rarely sleepy or exhausted. I have learned that these are my precious few hours of peak energy. I must use them to maximum efficiency. By noon, I am starting to sag, so the afternoon is good for quiet pastimes — a nap, a book or desk work.

Most of us have forgotten how to greet the day. We have lost the consciousness that a new day is sacred. Each one is a rare and precious gift from the hand of God. It is another opportunity to start all over, to raise one's head from the pillow with a glad heart, to watch the clouds roll across the grey sky, now stained with pink, and breathe a prayer of gratitude, "Oh, God, life again. Again, life."

That is the secret in the awesome moment as dawn comes again. God is a God of starting again, of wiping away all that has become weary and sour and haggard and worn.

So come, Christian. Choose to rise and choose to have a heart that greets the great gift, Day — this symbol of a rising-again God who holds everything in His power and who will not allow our spinning world to veer off course. Find the magic of the morning. Form a morning prayer. Let it be one of utter gratitude for this rare life. Know the silent secret in the streak of pearl light against the night. Day starts again, and so can we, filled with the God of the day who makes all things new.   KAREN MAINS

Not Always Roses

I have told you these things, so that in me you may have peace. In this world you will have trouble. But take heart! I have overcome the world (JOHN 16:33).

As Christians, we are not exempt from problems that are common to all of mankind. Such things as poverty, sickness, old age and tragedy are part of the business of living.

Christ knows about our needs and troubles. He is aware of our struggles with personal sin and of our relationships in the sinful world in which we live.

In spite of all He knows, He commands us believers to be cheerful. We have experienced forgiveness through the cross, and that should fill us with joy.

Christ told us that we will have problems in this life. His command to "take heart" is based on our being united with Him through faith. His person and work are the grounds of joy for every believer.

Obedience to the commands of Christ will bring many surprise blessings to our lives. Through our joy we can strengthen the weak, encourage the downcast and comfort the dying. Through our good cheer, we can give light to a dying world in need of the joy and radiance that come from the cross of our Savior, Jesus Christ.

"But rejoice that you participate in the sufferings of Christ, so that you may be overjoyed when his glory is revealed" (1 Peter 4:13).   CAROL MCSPADDEN

Plugged In

His divine power has given us everything we need for life and godliness through our knowledge of him who called us by his own glory and goodness. (2 PETER 1:3).

A few months ago, my husband and I decided that our old vacuum cleaner needed help. After a lengthy discussion, we drove to the shopping center and bought a powerhead attachment.

When I brought my new "toy" home, I was anxious to try it out. After unpacking the powerhead, I took my vacuum cleaner out of the closet and went to work.

About 15 minutes later, I stopped pushing the powerhead back and forth. I was greatly disappointed, for the cleaner was performing no better than before I had spent a small fortune for the attachment. What a letdown!

Suddenly, I realized that the powerhead was not receiving any power. I had forgotten to plug it in! I had worked hard, going through all the right motions, but without the flow of power, I had achieved little.

This same principle holds true for our spiritual endeavors. We can go through all the right motions, say the right words and do the right things without achieving the desired results. Have you ever wondered why?

The disciples of Jesus knew the source of His power. On one occasion, they asked Him, "Lord, teach us to pray." The Lord drew strength and wisdom from the Father—and so can we!

In the morning, we can ask Him for direction and strength for that day. In the evening, we can thank Him for being with us. JOYCE STRECKER

A Mother's Question

Sons are a heritage from the Lord, children a reward from him (PSALM 127:3).

You just washed yesterday and now the laundry hamper is overflowing with dirty clothes. Where do they come from? They seem to have a "life" of their own.

My children have a real talent for filling up the hamper as soon as I empty it. They are excellent examples of the "Laundry Principle" that dirty clothes will expand to fill the available hamper space (and then some). The two boys never seem to miss stepping into a mud puddle or rolling in the dirt at a ball game! My darling daughter cannot bear to wear a single outfit for more than eight hours at a time. Her apparel may stay on the floor for a week before hitting the hamper, but when it hits, the hamper is suddenly overflowing—usually on the same day it was emptied (another Laundry Principle).

What to do? Believe and claim Psalm 127:3 that children are a gift from God. The laundry that comes off their little (or big) bodies is *gift wrapping*! When we care for the gift wrapping, we have a special opportunity to pray for the child who wears the clothing. As we commit each gift-child back to God and pray for him or her, our washers and dryers can become altars to God and laundry can become a blessing.

What better way can be found in which to spend this time than in singing, praying and praising the One who died to wash us from our sin.   LAURA MARSHALL

Obey His Call

The Lord had said to Abram, "Leave your country, your people and your father's household and go to the land I will show you." So Abram left, as the Lord had told him; and Lot went with him. Abram was seventy-five years old when he set out from Haran (GENESIS 12:1, 4).

The "call" of Abraham is a vital portion of Scripture. God asked him to make what could, both then and now, be considered a large sacrifice. He was to leave everything, including his country, his people, his father's household — even his cultural identity — to find a new identity in God.

It is encouraging that God did not lead him to a new land and then leave him; rather, his call was beautifully given with seven promises of what God would do because of Abraham's obedience. God promised to make of him a great nation and to make his name great. That nation was to be God's witness to other nations. God blessed Abraham with the intention that he would be God's agent of blessing to the nations and that through his descendents would come Jesus Christ, the world's greatest blessing.

Abraham is a model of obedience to the call of God and forms a pattern for missionary activity throughout the world. God said, "Go" and Abraham in obedience went, even though he was 75 years old.

What is God calling you to do or be? Where is He calling you to go? What is He asking you to leave behind so that you can follow Him? God fulfills His plan for the world through His people; therefore, your obedience can have worldwide implications. He blesses you in order that you might be a blessing. Are you a channel of God's blessing?

DONA SCHEPENS

A Confession

As for God, his way is perfect; the word of the Lord is flawless. He is a shield for all who take refuge in him (PSALM 18:30).

How little I have claimed
   Of what I could have owned.
I've minimized God's power to do,
   And struggled on alone!

I've done without the blessing
   God wanted to bestow,
And failed to be a blessing
   To those about, I know.

How little I have prayed
   And talked with Him above.
I've labored on in dull routine
   And lacked God's fire of love.

I've worried, schemed and planned
   And, oh, so anxious been,
When all would have come out just right
   Had I left it up to Him!

CORABELLE SPIER

Vessels of Value

But we have this treasure in jars of clay to show that this all-surpassing power is from God and not from us (2 CORINTHIANS 4:7).

We see all sizes and shapes of clay pottery here in our rural African culture. Large pots, small pots—all have a purpose, but none of them are really attractive.

I have discovered that some of the most ugly, chipped and misshapen pots can contain the most delicious concoctions. On the other hand, some expensive, shiny pots often offer something quite unappetizing.

Paul spoke to Timothy about an instrument for noble use, set apart and useful for the Master, prepared for good service of every sort (2 Timothy 2:21). It is God's plan that every believer be set apart and made useful to the Master, serving Him in many diverse ways.

There have been days when, as I treated patients, I have hidden rather than glorified the Treasure I contained. The vessel was all that showed, and it was weak and ugly. I have had to ask forgiveness for these times as well as for the times I have wished I were something other than a simple clay pot.

The above verse is one of my favorites. How often God has brought it to my attention to challenge and encourage me. Think of it! God desires to fill simple clay vessels with His power. This Treasure, the Light of the World, the Water of Life, abides in *us*. What a privilege is ours! The frailty of these human containers can magnify God's power. The vessels have nothing of which to boast except that which they contain.   JESSIE NEHLSEN

Walk with Him

But if we walk in the light, as he is in the light, we have fellowship with one another, and the blood of Jesus, his Son, purifies us from all sin (1 JOHN 1:7).

Our first need is to receive His salvation by being forgiven and cleansed by His blood. What a wonderful Savior, to provide such a marvelous salvation for us!

Once we have been saved, we can begin to walk in His light. It is never dark where Jesus is, because He is the Light. He said of Himself, "I am the light of the world. Whoever follows me will never walk in darkness, but will have the light of life" (John 8:12). If we obey God's Word and seek to please Him in our behavior, we can be certain we are walking in the light. We can also have real fellowship with Him. This walk of companionship with God will make it easy to have good fellowship with His people.

At some time we may walk in the valley of sorrow, but it will be light because Jesus is with us. His promise is that He will be with us *always* (Matthew 28:20). So since He is with us and He is the Light, we do not need to fear that the darkness will overwhelm us.   ERMA POSEY

AUGUST 27

Stand Firm

Therefore, my dear brothers, stand firm. Let nothing move you. Always give yourselves fully to the work of the Lord, because you know that your labor in the Lord is not in vain (1 CORINTHIANS 15:58).

The Apostle Paul has just completed his review of the gospel: Jesus lived, died according to the Scriptures and is alive. Now he bursts into the theme of the mystery, that those who believe this gospel will be changed. Those who died in Christ will rise first, then those who are alive will be caught up to be with Christ. He climaxes his explanation with a shout of victory over our enemy, death. "But thanks be to God! He gives us the victory through our Lord Jesus Christ" (1 Corinthians 15:57).

The Holy Spirit knew that this truth could very easily become commonplace. In the stress and grind of life, its importance might grow dim. In concluding this portion, He reminds us that we will only experience this "change" if we are faithful.

The words *steadfast, immovable* and *abounding* found in the King James Version, can be the key to our faithfulness. These words apply to our involvement in the work of the Lord. In this "occupation" we are to be fixed, unyielding and overflowing.

What a clear picture of God's design for the believer's works. We are to guard against being moved away from our responsibilities in the work of the kingdom. We also need to be involved in the lives of those around us as an overflow of our faith in Christ.

Another translation (Beck) of this verse reads: "Always keep on doing a great work for the Lord, since you know in the Lord your hard work isn't wasted."   RUTH THOMAS

In His Likeness

For those God foreknew he also predestined to be conformed to the likeness of his Son, that he might be the firstborn among many brothers. (ROMANS 8:29).

Just after telling us that He works for the good of those who love Him, God gives us this incredible promise. He tells us that part of this "good" is that we are being conformed to the likeness of His Son. This is both a present and future promise. He begins the moment we believe and continues until His goal is accomplished.

When I first began to appreciate what God was trying to do in the lives of His children, it was enough to simply believe that He is committed to making us like His Son. As the experiences of life multiplied in variety and intensity — happiness and heartbreak, achievement and disappointment, health and sickness — I became aware of the pattern of God's disciplining. Those things He sends or allows are what He decides are best suited to each of us.

Our problem is that we become engulfed by how we feel about our circumstances. God does not label things good or bad the way we do. In Psalm 139 it says that the darkness is as light to Him (verse 12). His motives are pure; His goal is clear. He wants us to be like His Son; however, our response to His provisions is our own.

Since God will never violate our will, what can we do to increase the value of the disciplines He provides? We can be thankful in and for each circumstance. We can also be continually forgiving. These responses often do not come easily, especially when our suffering or outrage are starkly real. If we lean on God's sovereignty and yield to His will, then He can perfect in us His original design — the likeness of His Son.   ELOIS R. FIELD

Lest We Forget

The prayer of a righteous man is powerful and effective (JAMES 5:16).

One thing that has meant a lot to me since my retirement is being able to look back in my little prayer book and see how God has really answered.

My working years were so filled with demands that I did not take the time to keep records. I did learn one thing, however, and that is that God does things in His own time. Even when the answer was delayed, I knew that God had not forgotten.

Through the years I have marvelled at the way God works. He wants only good for us and would do more, but as the Scripture says, "You do not have, because you do not ask God" (James 4:2).

How many times in our busy lives have we forgotten to thank the Lord for our blessings? Perhaps we have even failed to acknowledge answers to prayer when they come. Just a backward glance through my prayer book brings great satisfaction. There are the requests and here, the answers. Amazing! God knew my every need and met each one just in time.

Our Lord works in mysterious and wonderful ways. At times, He uses others to be the bearers of our gifts and answers. If we allow God to work in us, He may answer another's prayer through us and enable us to demonstrate our loving concern in a tangible way.

Keeping a journal in which you record your requests and answers will enrich your prayer life. We are such children — always asking and wanting to receive. Ask in faith, adding your praise. Make a record of each request. Take time, lest you forget!   EVELYN CUTRER

Water — Source of Life

Come, all you who are thirsty, come to the waters (ISAIAH 55:1).

Water is vital to life. A powerful force, it can be flowing, spurting or gushing. Water has many important functions. It satisfies, cleanses, refreshes and energizes. It can heal hurts, cool fever and quench thirst.

In the spiritual context, each of us has a critical need for water. While God may send showers of blessing and glorious rivers of peace as His gifts and bonuses, there is another form of water that is accessible only when we become the drawer or participant. God Himself is the Fountain of Life — a source of supply from which water must be *drawn*. In order to experience Christ's blessing and fullness in our lives, we must be the seeker; we must come to the Fountain and draw from Him to satisfy spiritual thirst.

- Is there a burden you need to surrender in order to know His fullness in your life? (John 4:28)
- Do you need His cleansing to flow through you so that He can use you? (Ephesians 5:26)
- Are you experiencing spiritual dryness, and do you feel the need of having His life springing up in your soul? (John 4:14)
- In a time of turmoil, distress or depression, do you need the healing and calm found in the Living Water? (Psalm 42:2)
- Do you feel a thirst in your soul, a thirst that cannot be satisfied with earthly remedies? (John 6:35)

Everyone who has a thirst is invited to come to the waters. We must act on that invitation to receive the water that is so vital to our spiritual life.   ETHEL K. HUTTAR

Learning Takes Time

But we had hoped that he was the one who was going to redeem Israel. And what is more, it is the third day since all this took place (LUKE 24:21).

As they walked along, the men had many questions on their minds. They had left Jerusalem and the fellowship of the apostles and were now journeying toward Emmaus. With all their doubts, there was still a spark of hope in them as they puzzled over the events of the Crucifixion. When Jesus joined them, He fanned that spark by quoting the Scriptures. Although their doubts kept them from recognizing Him, there was something about Him that made them desire His company.

When we have doubts or discouragements, do we turn to His Word for the comfort and assurance provided there? Do we allow Him to come to us through that Word?

We are too often satisfied with a few uplifting words from Scripture or from a friend, when we need to press on to Jesus Himself. If something from God's Word or some word from one of His servants causes our heart to burn, let us not turn to people or to other writings and miss an opportunity to deepen our relationship with Christ.

Do we take time to urge Him to stay and fellowship with us? It was only as they ate together in intimate, unhurried companionship, that their eyes were opened and they knew Him. It is only when we have actually seen and recognized Him that we have something to share — a reason to go back to Jerusalem and tell others.

It was while they were relating their experience to the group that Jesus appeared in their midst. Have we had this privilege of encouraging others to see Him because we have truly seen Him ourselves? LINDA MCKELVEY

My Constant Companion

As obedient children, do not conform to the evil desires you had when you lived in ignorance. But just as he who called you is holy, so be holy in all you do (1 PETER 1:14–15).

Our family had no contact with the gospel until I was 12. Then we began to attend a Sunday school that had been started in the country schoolhouse. A year later I accepted Christ as my personal Savior, and my life was changed. As years passed, I longed to know God better and to tell others about Him. Then opportunity came to attend Bible college.

During a chapel service, I felt a desperate need for the Holy Spirit. I hurried down to the musty old basement and found a vacant music room. There, as the Lord revealed my real self, I surrendered to Him, and His joy filled my soul.

Years later on the mission field, I had allowed my busyness to dull my spiritual life. I struggled. I was frustrated. Why were the Indians of Ecuador indifferent to God's Word?

While I was home on furlough, the Holy Spirit dealt with me. As I acknowledged my faults, God cleansed, and His Spirit again controlled my life.

Once more on the field, the Otavalan Indian work beckoned me. The Mission offered me a more fruitful area of ministry, but I would not be deferred. The Mission told me Indian work was too hard for a single woman alone. But I was not alone. The Holy Spirit was my constant Companion. *He* would work.   EVELYN RYCHNER

Contentment Is Gain

Keep your lives free from the love of money and be content with what you have (HEBREWS 13:5).

As a missionary in Burkina Faso, I was surprised to find that many Africans in our adopted country seemed contented. Paul said that contentment, when coupled with godliness, was "great gain" (1 Timothy 6:6).

As missionaries, we have hurt with the Africans through years of famine, crop failures, dry wells and dead livestock. What a test of one's faith. Often I have asked myself, *How would I score? Could I pass the test?*

I have observed Rebecca, a pastor's godly wife, as she cooks over an open fire, scrubs her clothes by hand and farms with a hoe. I have seen in her life a submissive, joyful acceptance of the will of God, a contentment with what she has. I marvel at her calmness in turmoil, as she supervises the 35 children under her dormitory roof. I remember her complete trust when food and money were gone. I marveled at how God's grace was her strength the day she rode in the ambulance with her sick husband. She had brought her precious Bible with her, hoping she would be able to witness to the driver during the long ride. This godly woman, so poor in this world's goods, is completely absorbed in telling those who cross her path about Jesus, her dearest Friend.

God makes these two priceless characteristics — godliness and contentment — available to each of His children. But they seem to reside only in the lives of those who are walking close to God and whose treasures are in heaven.

What would an examination of our hearts reveal? Do we desire godliness and contentment in our lives?

JESSIE NEHLSEN

Are You an Abraham?

I press on toward the goal to win the prize for which God has called me heavenward in Christ Jesus (PHILIPPIANS 3:14).

Most of us easily recognize the names Abraham, Isaac and Jacob as patriarchs and men of faith. They were among the first to set out on the walk of faith, and we measure our spiritual progress by theirs.

Closely related to these men was Terah, Abraham's father. Not much is said about him, but what we do know stimulates our imaginations. Toward the end of Genesis 11, there seem to be clues as to why Terah is forgotten while Abraham is remembered.

Terah had three sons in Ur: Abraham, the eldest; Nahor, the middle son and Haran, the youngest. Haran, Lot's father, died in the land of Ur. Following this tragedy, Scripture tells us that Terah set out from Ur and headed toward Canaan with his family. He only went as far as Haran (roughly 600 miles) a town he named after his second son.

It is at this point that we begin to speculate. Did God call Terah to leave Ur and move toward Canaan even before he called Abraham? If so, we wonder why he did not complete his journey.

Was Terah like many of us who, when we hear God speak, start out with good intentions, complete part of a task and then lose our motivation? Or was he like others of us who, after the pain of a crisis has passed, become comfortable and lose our vision to move on in faith?

We need to be like Abraham, whom we remember for his obedience to God. We need the motivation to go on beyond Haran. We need to pursue God's goal for our lives in times of ease as well as in times of tragedy.   RUTH DAVIS

Rooted in Him

The Lord will fulfill his purpose for me; your love, O Lord, endures forever — do not abandon the works of your hands (PSALM 138:8).

I live in an apartment in a "bedtown" 33 minutes by express train from downtown Tokyo. For the first time in 15 years, I have no yard to care for. I decided to rent a small plot from a nearby Japanese farmer. This makes me a closer friend than just exchanging daily greetings. Perhaps in the future he will sell us land to build a church.

One day while tending my garden, I looked at my Mexican sunflowers. Unlike the common, one-flower variety, these had a number of lovely orange blooms. I noticed that the strong winds for which our prefecture is known had blown the plants over. Even though the stems were bent or broken, my flowers were still blooming. I propped these up as well as I could with plastic poles and string.

I thought of how the Lord, who sees our doubts, problems and failures, "props us up." These supports may be Scripture verses, the example of friends or answers to prayer. If the root is still intact — if we believe in Jesus as our Savior — we can still bloom and bear fruit for Him.

When the world looks at Christians, they might wonder if we are any good at all. We should try to look at one another as Jesus looks at us and believe that God is still tending His garden. As long as we are grounded in Him and His Word, we will continue to produce spiritual fruit.

LOIS J. LONG

Learning My Role

The share of the man who stayed with the supplies is to be the same as that of him who went down to the battle. All will share alike (1 SAMUEL 30:24).

In the West, it seems essential for a woman to have a role and to know what that role is. As a pastor's wife, I had given that idea much thought and had written and taught a course on the creative role of a woman. As a new missionary, it was a shock to find that my role as mother, housekeeper, cook and pastor's wife had been taken from me. The children were sent off to missionary school, the servants did the housecleaning and cooking and we were no longer involved in pastoral ministries. What was my role now? As a woman, was it important that I have a role?

I had many hurts and struggles within and was extremely confused about my calling. I had a desire to minister for God in my adopted country, but what was my role? I had always felt it important to be a good wife, mother and homemaker, but now all that had been cut away. I felt bare and useless. I flew to my refuge, the Lord. I felt that He had lessons to teach me, and I wanted to learn.

A tree must be stripped of its leaves and bark before it can be effectively used by the builder. After all, does it matter whether or not we have a job description, a role or title? Surely, if our lives are spent in humble service for our King, if we are always ready to obey His Word—regardless of the cost or lack of recognition—this too will bring its reward.   BEVERLY ALBRECHT

In His Time

The Lord is not slow in keeping his promise, as some understand slowness. He is patient with you, not wanting anyone to perish, but everyone to come to repentance. (2 PETER 3:9).

The answers to our prayers are timed. When it is fair to all involved, God will answer! His answers are so much wiser than our requests. They will not only benefit us or teach us some valuable lessons, they will also be a light and help to others. When God delays the answer, this test of our faith teaches us patience. We learn that He makes no mistakes.

Do we know when He answers? Perhaps that answer has come, but because it was not what we were hoping for, we did not recognize it as an answer. God's ways are past our finding out. We may have one thing in our mind, but God has quite another.

One morning, as I was getting out of bed, I was impressed with the thought that God is doing more than we think! Even though we do not observe any change in a situation, knowing God is at work should be an encouragement to us, especially to those of us who are trusting for the salvation of loved ones. "I am the Lord; in its time I will do this swiftly" (Isaiah 60:22).   CORABELLE SPIER

Goodbyes

Now I know that you fear God, because you have not withheld from me your son, your only son (GENESIS 22:12b).

They left today. My two precious children got on the plane and went to school for the first time. How excited we were when we first spotted the plane. Our excitement waned a bit as the plane landed and reality took hold. We all hugged and kissed while the pilot waited patiently. They looked so brave climbing into the plane.

As the doors closed, four tiny eyes peered through the window, and two little hands waved furiously. The plane taxied down the runway, and I kept waving and smiling, knowing they were too far away to see my tears.

Oh, Lord, even though I hurt inside, I know these children are Yours. We gave them back to you when they were born. You have given them health, happiness and love. What more could we ask? Through the separation, Your arms still encircle us as a family. Knowing our children have received You as their Savior gives us real peace.

All over this island today, parents and children were hurting as they left one another. There was only one thing that could justify the hurt, and that is the redemption of lost men and women.

This was written the day we sent our two first graders to school. Since then we have sent two others. It does not get any easier, but God never calls us to a task to desert us. Our children are very happy. And though the goodbyes are hard, our family times are more meaningful than that of many families in the States. We would not trade places with anyone.   CAROL MCDONALD

No Mistakes

Trust in the Lord with all your heart and lean not on your own understanding (PROVERBS 3:5).

My Father's way may twist and turn,
  My heart may throb and ache;
But in my soul I'm glad to know
  He maketh no mistake.

My cherished plans may go astray,
  My hopes may fade away;
But still I'll trust my Lord to lead,
  For He doth know the way.

Though night be dark and it may seem
  That day will never break,
I'll pin my faith, my all, on Him;
  He maketh no mistake.

There's so much now I cannot see,
  My eyesight's far too dim;
But come what may, I'll simply trust
  And leave it all to Him.

For by and by the mist will lift,
  And plain it all He'll make;
Through all the way, though dark to me
  He made not one mistake.

A.M. Overton
PEARL FUSTEY

Pride

A man's pride brings him low, but a man of lowly spirit gains honor (PROVERBS 29:23).

When did you wage your latest battle with pride? What form did it take? Was it easy to identify — so obvious and blatant that you immediately knew what you were up against? Perhaps it was deceptive and foxy, only recognizable after a regrettable fall. For every personal encounter with this dreadful trait, we could probably find references where biblical characters experienced assaults similar to ours.

Did Moses feel a tinge of jealously or an attack of pride each time Aaron's way with words forced him to realize his inabilities in that area?

Surely Peter was humiliated. Pride would have had him defend his heroic act when Christ promptly restored the servant's severed ear. Could that have been part of the reason for his subsequent denial of Christ? Pride leads to unseemly behavior, and the writer of the Proverbs expresses it forcefully: "Pride goes before destruction" (Proverbs 16:18).

And so in every age the battle goes on. The enemy will not retreat. He sees our frailties and plays on them with relentless persistence. Not only does pride surface in the hour of failure but more often in the hour of greatest triumph.

Thanks be to God for the armor provided for us in Ephesians 6:11–18 and for His promise given in 1 John 4:4: "The one who is in you is greater than the one who is in the world."   BEVERLY HENDRICKSON

The Comforter

Praise be to the God . . . who comforts us . . . so that we can comfort those in any trouble (2 CORINTHIANS 1:3, 4).

As soon as the telegram through the American Embassy in Quito informed us that our son, John, was critically injured in Bermuda, I hurried to his side.

A young officer in the Navy, he had been struck by a taxi while riding a motorcycle. I did not ask, "Why, Lord?" for I had learned that God never makes a mistake. But I could not say, "Thank You, Lord." In the intensive care unit, I read to John, "Give thanks in all circumstances, for this is God's will for you in Christ Jesus" (1 Thessalonians 5:18). My son nodded his head in assent. He loved the Lord and passed into His presence. I struggled, for I really could not feel thankful.

Throughout my 30 years of missionary service, I had helped cope with the griefs of many people. Now the problem was my own. Finally I allowed God to speak to me. "Vera, how selfish can you be? We have John in heaven with us, away from the sin and sorrow of the world, and you cannot thank me?" It was then that my heart filled with praise, and I could say sincerely, "Thank You, Lord."

Back in Ecuador, my husband and I were delayed by poor weather. The airline arranged for us and three other passengers—the widow and the parents of a young pilot who had been killed in a hijacking attempt—to stay in a hotel. After telling the parents of our loss, we learned that our sons were of the same age and rank, and death had come at almost the same time. We had a marvelous opportunity to share the gracious comfort with which God had comforted us.   VERA C. MILLER

Privacy

I have become all things to all men so that by all possible means I might save some (1 CORINTHIANS 9:22b).

These words were also my words as my husband and I sought to bring the gospel to Muslim people in the southern Philippines.

What does it mean to be all things to all people in order to reach them for Christ? Though we regard missionary life a joy rather than a sacrifice, there are changes in lifestyle that must be made. To be all things to all people, we had to give up something most of us treasure — our privacy.

To be all things to all men means *people*. Yes, people at your door all day long — sick people who want medicine; curious people who walk into your home, look into your closets and want to know what you paid for each item; interested people who want to pull your children's blond hair and pinch their white skin; hungry people who look in your window as you eat your meal; dirty people who sit in your *sala* (living room) in dirty *malongs* (wraparound skirts) and spit on your floor.

Can you refuse when they ask for food? Can you push them out your door and forbid them to touch your children? Can you tell them it is not their business to know what you pay for things? Can you refuse to allow them into your house? Can you control your revulsion as you see them sit, with oozing wounds, on your chairs?

Yes, you can tell them these things; you can keep them outside. But you will have lost them as friends. And you can never win a Muslim to the Lord unless he first sees friendship in you.

So my daily prayer is still that I may be all things to all people — joyfully!   ELIZABETH ABRAMS

Whatever You Do

So whether you eat or drink or whatever you do, do it all for the glory of God (1 CORINTHIANS 10:31).

"Whatever you do" is a phrase that echoes in my mind. It reminds me that God is interested in all aspects of my service for Him. Even minute details come under the "whatevers" in my daily life.

Twice a week my Chilean friend, a fine Christian, comes to clean our house. She tries very hard to please us. She does an excellent job of sweeping, waxing and buffing the tile floors. She carefully cleans the bathroom fixtures and the kitchen. When she has finished her work, I pay her, and we kiss each other goodbye until the next cleaning day comes around.

Although my friend goes home satisfied with her efforts, we often discover some neglected areas. Sometimes we find cobwebs hanging from the ceiling and mirrors that have not been dusted.

How easy it is in our Christian walk to look around and tend to the most obvious and noteworthy tasks that God puts before us. How easy to skip over the details and forget the less conspicuous tasks that God has for us to do.

We must clean the cobwebs and dust the mirrors in our spiritual lives by obeying Him *completely*. What a blessing it will be then to hear our Father say, "Well done" when at last we see Him face to face. JEAN WOEHR

SEPTEMBER 13

God Is Sovereign

According to the plan of him who works out everything in conformity with the purpose of his will (EPHESIANS 1:11).

It was early 1975, and I was on missionary furlough. As I spoke in churches, I told how, while South Vietnam fought for its life against Communist onslaught, God wonderfully sent revival to the missionaries and to the Christians of the South Vietnamese highlands. My favorite theme had been the sovereignty of God who, sometimes by miraculously turning back the enemy, had kept the doors open for the preaching of the gospel.

But soon the newscasts began relating the collapse of the South Vietnamese army. I wept and prayed earnestly that God would again intervene and spare the country. Then as I saw people fleeing their homes, harassed by merciless Communist soldiers, I knew it was over, and I was crushed.

As I cried out, "Lord, why don't you do something?" He reminded me of what I had said about His sovereignty and how He continues to work out His own purposes in spite of man's plans. He brought me to the place where I could say from my heart, "I know You are working out Your own good will even in this."

What peace flooded my heart as I confessed to the Lord. Though I still wept and suffered with my people in their anguish, underneath was the sure knowledge that God was working out His plan.

Not only in the affairs of nations but also in the everyday lives of His children, God is sovereign! What He requires from us is commitment and absolute trust in Him. Do we have the deep peace that results from this kind of trust?

HELEN EVANS

No Fear, No Worry

The Lord himself goes before you and will be with you; he will never leave you nor forsake you. Do not be afraid; do not be discouraged (DEUTERONOMY 31:8).

I watched a bird constructing her nest, amazed at the way she carried each twig to the ledge just below the tree where she was building her future family's home. She would pause, twig in beak, and carefully scan the area. Satisfied that all was clear, she quickly flew into the chosen spot. The foliage stirred briefly, then the bird was off again.

How much our Father's care resembles that of the mother bird. Carefully He prepared our lives even before we came into the picture. He created our innermost parts and knew us before we were born. He knew what each and every day of our lives would hold.

His will and desire is that each specific event in our lives will shape and mold us into the man or woman He wants us to be. Nothing happens to us that has not filtered through the hands of God.

Just as the mother bird will provide for the needs of her young, God carefully watches out for us and will be with us in times of need. "God has said, 'Never will I leave you; never will I forsake you'" (Hebrews 13:5). Truly, we have nothing to fear, nothing to worry about.

PAM BERTOLET

God's Role Model

For this is the way the holy women of the past who put their hope in God used to make themselves beautiful. They were submissive to their own husbands (1 PETER 3:5).

In these days when young women need Christian role models, God gives us mature Christians a formula to follow in Titus 2:3–5.

The role model must display a reverent, quiet spirit. One cannot have such a spirit and be a malicious gossip. The two do not go together. Rather, God's role model is to teach what is good.

What good things should we teach? Our instructions: encourage the young women to (1) love their husbands, (2) love their children, (3) be self-controlled, (4) be pure, (5) be workers at home, (6) be kind and (7) be subject to their husbands. In short, we should teach them how to live at home.

Love is not only an emotion, it is part of our will. We should will to love our husbands and show love in our daily actions. Our children also need to feel and see our love. One of the most important things a woman can do is make a loving home for her husband and children.

A pure heart does not hold grudges or desire to get even. One of the surest tests of a woman's respect and love for her husband is if she willingly submits herself to his being the head of the family.

Let us be women who willingly follow God's role model so that we might lead others, bringing honor to God, to His Word and to the church.   NORA MCGARVEY

SEPTEMBER 16
Spiritual Mosaics

For we are God's workmanship, created in Christ Jesus to do good works, which God prepared in advance for us to do (EPHESIANS 2:10).

I had joined the throngs of Chicago's after-Thanksgiving shoppers, many of whom waited in long lines to admire store windows festively decorated for the holidays. While negotiating my way through the crowded department store, I discovered, quite by accident, the "Tiffany Favrile Glass Mosaic Dome" that hangs suspended over the center of Marshall Fields' sixth floor.

The Tiffany Dome is one of the finest examples of glass mosaics in the country and one of Chicago's most prized architectural treasures. Designed by Louis C. Tiffany and constructed under his direction, the dome is the largest unbroken surface mosaic in the country. It covers an estimated area of 6,000 square feet and contains approximately 1,600,000 pieces. This multi-hued blue dome stands as a modern monument to the creative artistry of its designer.

Paul says that we are God's workmanship, His "artistic production." Far more intricately crafted than Tiffany's dome, His "workmanship" is best reflected in the good works which God prepared for us to do. Note that Paul is careful to distinguish our good works from salvation, which is God's gift to us.

We are co-workers with God as, by piecing together the people, circumstances, struggles and opportunities which impact us, He makes of our lives a spiritual mosaic. Fifty men worked more than a year to create the Tiffany dome. We are investing a lifetime with the Creator of the universe in making of our lives a thing of beauty.   LESLIE ANDREWS

There in Rough Places

When you pass through the waters, I will be with you (ISAIAH 43:2).

While Dave and I were still in language school in Seoul, four-year-old Joel was badly burned in a kitchen accident. Late one evening, he and I were alone in his hospital room. Tears drifted down my cheeks as Joel moaned in pain. "Mommie," he whispered, "when can I have my medicine?" How could I tell him that he had another three hours to endure before his next shot? In my helplessness, I cried out to God.

Just then, a fellow missionary stood hesitantly at the door. Taking in the scene at a glance, he walked softly to Joel's side, and placing his hand on the little blonde head, he prayed simply and earnestly, gave me an encouraging smile and left.

As the door closed, I felt completely empty and alone. There was no sound except the occasional rustle of sheets and Joel's moans. Gradually, however, I became aware of a warm breeze filling the room. I realized with awe that I was in the Lord's presence. Suddenly Joel and I were enfolded in a tender embrace that left me speechless with joy and worship. Joel's groaning ceased, and he fell into a peaceful and uninterrupted sleep.

That memory has sustained me through other trials and remains a source of comfort and encouragement. Though God's path for us may lie through many rough places, He has promised to be with us. We need only believe that He is there and open our hearts and lives to Him. CINDI STRONG

The Watchful Servant

So you also must be ready, because the Son of Man will come at an hour when you do not expect him (MATTHEW 24:44).

A sudden squeal came from the shower room. "Mom, my hair is all sudsy and the water quit running. How am I going to rinse?" asked my daughter Jennifer, home on vacation from boarding school.

Thinking of a quick answer to her predicament, I called to her, "Use the water in the cistern." That is our backup water for when we have no electricity to pump the water into the house. "But Mom," she groaned in exasperation, "the cistern is empty." Someone had used all the water and not refilled it.

Thankfully our Indonesian helper, Ibu, had filled a cistern in her washroom, and Jennifer was able to take advantage of her kindness.

As Jennifer finished her shampoo, I thought about Jesus' words to His children about readiness. A glorious day is coming when we will put aside our work and stand in His presence. There, with myriads of our brothers and sisters in Christ, we will be able to worship Him. There Jesus Christ will receive the glory and praise that all the universe stands poised to give Him.

But for now, He reminds me to do the work He has called me to do — teaching in a Bible college, helping Indonesian men and women to prepare for the gospel ministry. By doing His work faithfully and watching for Him, I will be ready for His coming.

A day with no electricity and no water available is truly a nuisance. But to experience the day of the Lord and not be ready would prove fatal.   ANNE D. HOBBS

A Battle Rages

If you make the Most High your dwelling — even the Lord, who is my refuge — then no harm will befall you, no disaster will come near your tent (PSALM 91:9–10).

My husband held the newspaper open so that I could see the headlines — "58 Men Killed in Hijacked Plane." I wanted to take my family and hide. Was there no place where we could be safe?

There is a battle raging. The fighting intensifies as the enemy advances. Terrorists attack the innocent with little risk of retaliation. Children are kidnapped. There are wars, famine, earthquakes.

If the battle is to be won, soldiers must advance. Yet voices from within and without urge us to "Flee to the mountains! Hold on tightly. Avoid all risks. Stay within the borders of safety." As women of God we cannot, must not, retreat. Secure in His love and faithfulness, we must continue to advance. By our lives we must declare the good news, "Our God reigns." He is in control. He is not only able but willing to care for those who take refuge in Him.

Secure in Him we must seek to share our faith with those who are fearful. Uncertainty over the future has shaken the self-confidence of many and provided an opportune time to introduce men and women to the only One in whom they can find true sanctuary.

The best legacy we can leave to our families is the firm knowledge that those who trust in God are truly safe. Our faith in Him will give them courage to face the future, not with fear, but with excitement, knowing that He cannot fail.   DIANA STIMMEL

Sow, Reap, Break Up

Sow for yourselves righteousness, reap the fruit of unfailing love, and break up your unplowed ground; for it is time to seek the Lord (HOSEA 10:12).

Chapter 10 of Hosea reveals the harsh reality of sin's effect—God's judgment on His people. Yet here we see revealed the purpose of judgment—to bring them to repentance. There is still time to seek the Lord.

God is still the same, and true repentance brings total forgiveness. Sowing . . . reaping . . . breaking up the unplowed ground result in a shower of righteousness.

But would it not be more logical that the breaking up come first, then plowing and reaping? No. There is a definite lesson in this progression. That first sowing of righteousness is not necessarily the whole field; it can begin in one small spot. We begin with one area of our lives—the spot where God leads us first. That plant is allowed to grow, flourish and bear fruit. As this planting matures, we are gaining strength and vision.

Drawn by the Holy Spirit, we look more closely to see the unplowed ground, and the process begins again on a larger scale.

The more we sow and reap and are encouraged by showers of righteousness, the more unplowed ground we will see and begin to turn over.

We must not let the sight of acres of weed-infested fields make us so discouraged that we do not begin by planting in the corner to which God first leads us.   BETH MANGIN

Evaluate Your Spiritual Heart

Above all else, guard your heart, for it is the wellspring of life (PROVERBS 4:23).

Today a dear friend lies in critical condition, the result of heart disease—a condition ranked as the number one killer of adults. As I meditate on God's Word, I consider what He says about my *spiritual* heart—my mind, soul, spirit—the center of my understanding. Inattention to my spiritual center will bring sickness, disease and, quite possibly, death—eternal death.

Heart trouble takes many forms. A "congenital heart problem" is present at birth and will, if not corrected, cause lifelong problems and premature death. Often surgery will restore normal function. Original sin caused my spiritual heart defect. But Jesus Christ gave me a new heart.

"Angina" is recurrent pain caused by a sudden decrease of blood supply. I have experienced spiritual angina when I have failed to seek God's daily cleansing for my sins.

"Arrythmia" is irregularity in the rhythm of the heart's beating. David reminds me to guard my heart, to keep its beat in tune with the beat of God's heart.

"Chronic heart disease" resists all efforts to eradicate the problem. John states clearly that if I continue in sin, I walk in darkness and have not the light (1 John 1:6).

Remind us today, Lord, that You desire to be our pacemaker—Your life implanted deep within, restoring, cleansing and healing—the very wellspring of our hearts.

JOYCE B. SECKINGER

The Night Hours

The Lord gives strength to his people; the Lord blesses his people with peace (PSALM 29:11).

The multitudes had been fed, and in their boat on the Sea of Galilee, the disciples had many things to discuss. Alone on the mountainside, in quiet fellowship with His Father, Jesus prayed. As happens so often when we are rejoicing over an exciting evidence of God at work, a storm arose. The winds howled and lashed the waves into fury. The boat was in danger of being swamped—and it was night, when we are least able to cope with trouble.

That is when the Lord comes! Do we recognize Him as He really is: our Savior, Friend, Comforter? Or are we, like the disciples, too overwhelmed by our fears? He has not changed, but perhaps we have lost sight of Him in all the swift changes and events.

Jesus does not want us to founder in our fears. He speaks, and if we are able to still our inner storm, we can hear His comforting voice assuring us of His presence. "Take courage; it is I. Do not be afraid." He is in the storm with us, not beckoning us to somehow get out of the storm and find our way to Him!

Jesus brings peace with Him—perfect peace. Peter felt that peace when the Lord spoke. He knew Jesus' voice. He may have been frightened and may have forgotten the Lord's ever-present help in time of trouble, but He knew the Lord's voice. That comes only from spending much time in Jesus' presence. Peter called to Him, "Lord," and once again his life was back on an even keel, despite the raging of the storm.   RUTH H. HOOVER

Christ Is Sufficient

I can do everything through him who gives me strength (PHILIPPI-
ANS 4:13).

As a missionary candidate, I was responsible for raising
my financial and prayer support. On the day I left
home to begin contacting churches that might support me,
I felt like Abraham must have felt: Where do I go? How do
I approach anyone about openings in the churches? How
do I minister? The only thing I could do was to rely on
God's promise, and He did the "immeasurably more."

The Lord always seemed to lead me to the right
churches. I remember my experience in one particular denominational church. My sense of unease in the strange
atmosphere turned to horror as I realized I had mislaid my
notes. After prayer and acknowledgement of my predicament, I shared my testimony. Then the Lord brought to
mind the message He had given me. Afterward, people
commented that it was "just what we needed."

Church planting was God's appointment almost from the
day I reached Taiwan. After we had a group of believers, a
man was sent to pastor them. When the day came that I
exhorted the congregation to become self-governing and
self-supporting, he was so upset that he called me a hypo-
crite. As my tears flowed, God the Holy Spirit instantly
comforted me. Four years later, that same pastor came to
help me with another church I had started. Before ministering, he confessed to the congregation that the two of us
had not always seen eye to eye. Then for four days, he not
only preached salvation messages but stressed tithing, total
commitment to the Lord for service at home and abroad
and faithful support of the work.

Truly, with Christ all things are possible!   PEARL FUSTEY

Happiness Is the Lord

I delight greatly in the Lord; my soul rejoices in my God. For he has clothed me with garments of salvation and arrayed me in a robe of righteousness (ISAIAH 61:10).

As God's children, we can know the deep abiding joy that only comes from being in His presence. Even though swirling around me this morning there are situations that would cause me to be anything but happy, I am conscious of Him!

As I read what Isaiah has said, my heart feels a lightness that lifts the burden of present conditions. I can tell you what constitutes true happiness. He has clothed me with His garments of salvation. Upon that truth everything else hangs. Next He has draped about me a beautiful robe, His robe of righteousness, which is a figure of sanctification.

Each day there are happy occasions when, as I spend time with Him, my Lord teaches me to know Him better. Then He will let others know about Himself through my life, and they will praise Him, too.

His righteousness, that robe upon me, will be as a budding tree, bringing forth the fruit of the Spirit. Also, it will be as a garden of new little plants just sprouting up everywhere.

Our Lord wants to clothe, shape and make us His own and reveal Himself to others through us.   DELORES TAYLOR

He Became Sin

God made him who had no sin to be sin for us, so that in him we might become the righteousness of God (2 CORINTHIANS 5:21).

Not long ago I began to wonder just what it meant for Christ to take our sins in His body on the cross. As a child it had seemed simple enough, but now it seemed too simple. When someone challenged me by asking how Christ's death was any more terrible than that of the thousands who have been tortured or who have been burned alive or suffered months of agonizingly painful disease, the explanation I tried to give seemed to fall short.

Then I happened to read an illustration that went something like this: A handsome, well-dressed man comes down the street and approaches a beggar. As he passes the beggar, we notice that the beggar now has the fine clothes and stature of the young man, while the young man, now scruffy in appearance, walks on in the beggar's rags.

Next, the man passes a sickly child, and the child becomes strong and runs home while the benefactor becomes weak and ill. When he meets a cripple, the lame man walks away whole while our friend hobbles painfully along on his journey.

One by one, they cross His path in their frail and sinful condition — prostitutes, addicts, thieves, murderers, the self-righteous, sick, bitter and angry — and all become whole and new.

Our hero continues on to disappear into a horrible wasteland and then emerges on the other side in a state even more glorious than was His originally. He was victorious over death and took our sins away forever. He now offers us abundant, eternal life in exchange for those sins! How can anyone reject such love? MARTIE GAINES

She Did What She Could

Give her the reward she has earned, and let her works bring her praise at the city gate (PROVERBS 31:31).

One evening at our family devotions, six-year-old Heather cuddled her teddy bear. A few minutes later, as we shared prayer requests, she said, "I'm going to pray for the lady who made my bear. She made me very happy." As Heather prayed for "the bear lady," my heart filled with warm remembrances of a brief encounter six years earlier.

It was our first furlough, and the children were little— Jimmy was two and Heather, two months. I had shared about our Indonesian ministry at an area women's missionary gathering. As I greeted ladies at the door, a young woman pressed a teddy bear into my arms. "This is for your son," she said. "I know you have a baby girl, too, so I'll make her a bear and send it to you." Days before we left America to return to Indonesia, a package arrived— Heather's bear!

Bear Lady, I don't know your real name, but I praise the Lord for you. You have given lasting joy to my children.

Often during furlough we hear women say, "I wish I could go to the foreign fields, too. Since I can't, I'll do what I can." We missionaries sleep between sheets and under quilts and blankets given by women's missionary prayer groups. Some make toys for our children or give Tupperware to keep weevils and ants out of our food. Others write encouraging letters. These women are the unsung heroines, and we appreciate their love for us. May God reward them.   SHARON T. KENDALL

Helps for Ministry

Help these women who have contended at my side in the cause of the gospel . . . whose names are in the book of life . . . if anything is excellent or praiseworthy — think on these things (PHILIPPIANS 4:3–8).

The secret of effective ministry is unfolded in the quiet, gentle, winsome characteristics mentioned in Philippians 4 that enhance the life of a woman filled with the Holy Spirit.

Be joyful. A pleasant attitude is more important than perfect performance. Attractive, contagious, it can dispel a husband's gloom, brighten the face of a child and bless an assembly of listeners.

Be prayerful. A disciplined prayer life is basic to inner freedom from the enclosure of self-concern. Having committed our own families to the Lord, our hearts are released to be sensitive to the needs of others.

Be peaceful. Peace is "made," constructed, largely by our words. Words that communicate peace to a husband are loving, loyal, encouraging. Children need happy, affectionate, affirming words. How necessary are fitting words — accepting and gracious — in the larger world of family, friends, church and neighborhood.

Be positive. A nurturing of our thought life with those things that are true, honest, just, pure and lovely will provide a reservoir of materials for response to people in need.

Be a practicer. Excellence in ministry comes from faithfully doing the small tasks; then we are prepared for new and larger things. Faithfulness will be the scale of God's evaluation of a woman's serving, supportive role in the Christian church.   HELEN BAILEY

A Child's Faith

Consider well her ramparts, view her citadels, that you may tell of them to the next generation. For this God is our God for ever and ever; he will be our guide even to the end (PSALM 48:13–14).

My daughter Mara Lea and I both have the dubious privilege of being allergic to anything that has four legs and fur and either barks or meows. Because we love God's creatures, we have adopted, in lieu of a dog or a cat, fantail goldfish, plus the neighborhood flock of wild ducks, and all of them bring us delight and joy.

All of Mara Lea's fish have names and know her. But her very favorite fish, bought with her own money, was named Amen. Much to our dismay, after only a few weeks, Amen took ill and — in spite of our doctoring and praying — died.

Very carefully, I picked up the fish, wrapped it in a tissue, and we went out into the back yard to bury it. As Mara Lea sobbed, we held a little service and thanked God that we had enjoyed His little fish for a brief time.

Later, as I was putting Mara Lea to bed, she again cried over her fish. I took my Bible and read from Ecclesiastes 3:1–4, the familiar passage, "A time to be born, and a time to die . . . a time to weep, and a time to laugh; a time to mourn, and a time to dance." I also explained to her what the fish's name meant. Amen not only means that the prayer is finished, but there is no more to be said or done.

My Bible dictionary states that Jesus used Amen to put His authority on God's promises to us, His children. As His daughters, we can know that when hurts large or small come to our families, we can claim God's promises and know they will be fulfilled.   HELEN M. CRIMM

Cloud-covered, Glory-filled

So the cloud of the Lord was over the tabernacle by day, and fire was in the cloud by night, in the sight of all the house of Israel during all their travels (EXODUS 40:38).

The children of Israel had moved out of Egypt, survived the pursuit of Pharoah's army and passed over the Red Sea without even getting their sandals wet. If they had turned to look back, they could have seen their enemy going under for the third time.

After the Red Sea experience, the Israelites moved along at a fine pace until they came to Mt. Sinai, where Moses received the Ten Commandments. While waiting there, God gave Moses His instructions for a building program — plans for a tabernacle that was to be His dwelling place among His people. In Exodus 40, we read that when the Tabernacle was finished, "The cloud covered the Tent of Meeting, and the glory of the Lord filled the tabernacle . . . whenever the cloud lifted from above the tabernacle, [the children of Israel] would set out" (verse 34, 36).

Sometimes it seems that after a very busy time of ministry, God brings us to a halt. After God has delivered us from Egypt, defeated our enemies, provided manna for our hunger and water for our thirst, we find ourselves in a holding pattern. With God's cloud hovering over us, we wait. During this time, He gives us instructions for a building program. While He hovers over us, we are growing spiritually, and He is preparing us for a job yet to be accomplished. His glory is filling us, and we can rest securely, knowing we are in His care.   DELORES TAYLOR

The Stretched Heart

I now realize how true it is that God does not show favoritism, but accepts men from every nation (ACTS 10:34–35).

We had been asked to leave our mission field and serve on our board's administrative team in the States.

For a year, Ev served as a guest professor at Asbury College in Wilmore, Kentucky. When his teaching assignment ended, he was asked to become vice-president of field ministries. As I suddenly realized that I would not be going back to Korea, I prayed, "Lord, don't take Korea out of my heart, but stretch me to love other countries just as much." God did exactly that. An encounter on a flight from Singapore to Manila serves as an illustration.

A young family sat near me on the crowded plane. The beautiful mother had two small boys. Next to me sat the father, and before we were off the ground, he asked who I was and where I was going. He then told me that he worked for Gillette in the Philippines.

He began to ask questions about Christianity — not just, "Who is Jesus Christ?" but rather, "If God created us, who created God?" We talked at length about cults and Christianity. Before we parted, they invited us to their home.

At dinner around their lovely table, they accepted Christ. Two big tears trickled down the mother's lovely face — a sight I shall never forget. The following day, they met our missionaries, and later they were baptized.

My stretched heart included him, not a Korean but a Chinese from Malaysia who spoke impeccable English, lived in Manila and later emigrated to Australia.

This couple represents our world. Affluent? Yes. But they had the same need to know Jesus. Jesus needs our love to reach others like them. CARROLL F. HUNT

OCTOBER 1

He Was There

He will cover you with his feathers, and under his wings you will find refuge (PSALM 91:4).

After a period of hospitalization, my husband had been advised to rest in some retreat, away from the busy area where we lived. As we reached this quiet spot, we had a sense of peaceful release after the weeks of illness and physical exhaustion.

A couple of days into our vacation, it began to rain—nothing out of the ordinary for a summer day in Minnesota. Suddenly, though, the sky had darkened and a severe storm was upon us. Gale-force winds lifted, twisted and forced our house trailer over on its side, blocking both doors. Windows were broken and glass fragments fell in among food items and hanging light fixtures. As the trailer came to rest, so did the stove, refrigerator, table and chairs—all on top of us. As we cried to God, my husband was able to shift the refrigerator and release us both.

We crawled out through the only window that was not barred by debris, then checked on the car and found it had escaped with only a few scratches. The tornado had taken its toll. Hundreds of trees were lying at odd angles, and the car was completely fenced in. Now what, Lord?

Through the deep gloom, we could see headlights approaching. Rain soaked and scratched, we must have been a rare sight to the neighbor who came to check on us.

Soon, in the home of nearby friends, we shared coffee, lunch and a time of praise with other victims. What could have been fatal resulted only in minor scratches, bruises and some fractured ribs. In our hour of need, *He was there!* And whatever *your* need is today, He is there waiting to meet it.   ELEANOR L. BERRETH

Forget the Failure

But one thing I do: Forgetting what is behind and straining toward what is ahead, I press on toward the goal (PHILIPPIANS 3:13).

The teenage girl was learning to drive. While backing out of a grocery store parking lot, it happened. She scratched another car. Compounding the shock of having an accident in her first month of driving was her father's insistence that she help him find the car's owner. Would you believe it belonged to one of her teachers? After the situation was explained, apologies given and addresses exchanged, the girl vowed she would never drive again.

Both teacher and father disagreed and marched her outside, put her in the driver's seat and told her to drive home. That moment of getting back into the car and continuing her driving practice was the point of victory. She had to forget the failure and go on if she ever expected to learn to drive. That girl loves to drive now, but the story might have been quite different.

We all fail, and some of us fail more dramatically than others. We can become so defeated and discouraged that we waste precious time kicking ourselves and grumbling about our mistakes.

Satan delights in defeating us. Imprisoned by our self-reproach, we become non-productive. Victory comes in forgetting failure and pressing forward. Failure is meant not to bind but to teach. Let us let go of our errors and reach out for His enablement.   JUDY THOMPSON

OCTOBER 3

God's "I Wills"

It is not for your sake, O house of Israel, that I am going to do these things, but for the sake of my holy name (EZEKIEL 36:22).

This portion of Scripture (36:16–38) beautifully declares the sovereign work of God. The Jews' vile conduct earned His wrath, and they were dispersed among the nations. Now we see His redemptive power at work in a series of "I wills."

I will show the holiness of my great name. He promised to gather them from all nations, and this He has done through establishing them as a nation in 1948. In 1967, against all odds, the Jews regained Jerusalem.

I will sprinkle clean water upon you . . . a new heart will I give you. This is yet to be, but the day is coming when their hearts will be not the hearts of stone, but new hearts of flesh.

I will put my Spirit in you. Some day, they will follow His decrees and keep His laws. As Christians, we have this new Spirit that makes us desire to keep His laws; for Israel this is yet to come.

I will call for grain . . . I will increase the fruit of the trees and the crops of the field. This has been partially fulfilled as Israel has begun to irrigate the desert. At present, fruit from Israel is being shipped all over the world.

When will God complete His work? In His time and season. Meanwhile, we must pray for God's chosen people. We must love them. Individual Jews are experiencing these promises of Ezekiel today, and we praise the Lord for each one. But the best is yet to come! Let us not fail to receive the promise that is for those who "pray for the peace of Jerusalem."   DEDE ROBERTSON

One Another

This is my commandment, That you love one another, as I have loved you (JOHN 15:12).

The above and following Scripture passages (taken from the NASB) all contain the term "one another." God's repetition of the words is proof of His concern that we have a proper regard for each other.

"Be subject to one another in the fear of Christ" (Ephesians 5:21). "Do not lie to one another" (Colossians 3:9). "Do not speak against one another. Do not complain . . . against one another" (James 4:11 and 5:9).

"Do nothing from selfishness or empty conceit, but with humility of mind let each of you regard one another as more important than himself" (Philippians 2:3). "There should be no division in the body, but the members should have the same care for one another" (1 Corinthians 12:25). "Bear one another's burdens" (Galatians 6:2). "Be kind to one another, tender-hearted, forgiving each other, just as God in Christ also has forgiven you" (Ephesians 4:32). "Be hospitable to one another without complaint" (1 Peter 4:9).

"Through love serve one another" (Galatians 5:13). "With all humility and gentleness, with patience, showing forbearance to one another in love" (Ephesians 4:2). "So then let us pursue the things which make for peace and the building up of one another" (Romans 14:19). "And may the Lord cause you to increase and abound in love for one another, and for all men, just as we also do for you; so that He may establish your hearts unblamable in holiness before our God and Father at the coming of our Lord Jesus with all His saints" (1 Thessalonians 3:12).   HELEN G. MCGARVEY

His Circle

Many are the woes of the wicked, but the Lord's unfailing love surrounds the man who trusts in him (PSALM 32:10).

What a happy privilege it is to trust One who is completely trustworthy, One who knows exactly what is best for us personally, One whose love surrounds us in all circumstances.

The source of much that comes our way in life may be evil. We cannot say that God causes the unkind acts of others or even natural disasters and sickness. But nothing reaches the person who really trusts the Lord without coming through the surrounding shield of His unfailing love. By the time it reaches the trusting soul, it is God's perfect will for that life. This gives the Christian a calm acceptance and a peace about which the unbeliever knows nothing.

Many years ago at the Missionary Training Institute (now Nyack College), Professor Harold M. Freligh would often draw a circle on the blackboard, then place a dot in the middle and quote this short poem:

> In the center of the circle
>   Of the will of God I stand.
> There can be no second causes,
>   All must come from His dear hand.

It has been interesting to find that many of his students remember this more than any other one thing about his teaching.

How encouraging to know that "all things," not just "some things," work together for good to those who love God. How comforting to know that God's unfailing love surrounds the one who trusts in Him!   HELEN JULIAN

OCTOBER 6

Commit, Trust, Rest

Come to me, all you who are weary and burdened, and I will give you rest (MATTHEW 11:28).

Sometimes it is difficult to make decisions. This was especially true in our recent change in location and ministry. I wanted so much to know clearly God's will concerning whether we should go or stay. In the past, decisions of this magnitude were made after God provided a verse of special assurance. This time, however, no verse came. And peace escaped me.

Finally, totally frustrated, I decided I would stay in God's Word until the answer came. There, in Psalm 37, three words almost shouted at me: *Commit, Trust, Rest*. Not exactly what I had hoped to find. I looked for a promise; He gave commands.

Commit. Rather than committing, I was trying to ignore the whole situation, because I knew I would have to move. I confessed my stubborn and selfish will and did commit my way. He was not finished!

Trust. I wanted to trust Him, but I had so many questions. This was to be a new ministry. Would I have friends? Would I fit in? Would we all adjust? When I had exhausted all my questions, He said, "I am with you, trust Me." I relinquished my struggle and agreed to trust.

Rest. "Be still before the Lord and wait patiently before Him" (verse 7). How did I expect Him to show me His will when I had been talking instead of listening? "Speak to me, for I am ready to listen," was my prayer.

What joy and peace came as I obeyed. I did commit my way. We did move. And He is faithfully working out every detail. Each day I realize more how precious it is to rest, be still and wait in His presence. EDNA MAPSTONE

OCTOBER 7
His Purpose

And we know that in all things God works for the good of those who love him, who have been called according to his purpose (ROMANS 8:28).

The old Westminster Confessions states that God is the Originator and Executor of "Whatsoever comes to pass." We know Him to be Sovereign in that what He purposes He brings to pass.

But what of those circumstances that arise in our lives over which we have no control, such as the loss of a job due to the economy; an accident or death caused by a drunken driver; the tearful announcement that a teenage daughter is pregnant or the shocking revelation that a son has been caught using drugs? How can God work His purpose for our good in these circumstances?

Benjamin Warfield in his *Biblical Doctrines* states: "In the infinite wisdom of the Lord of all the earth, each event falls with exact precision into its proper place in this unfolding of His eternal plan; nothing, however small, however strange, occurs without His ordering, or without its peculiar fitness for its place in the working out of His purposes; and the end of all shall be the manifestation of His glory, and accumulation of His praise."

His divine plan for us is "not because of anything we have done (or our circumstances) but because of His own *purpose* and grace. This grace was given us in Christ Jesus before the beginning of time" (2 Timothy 1:9).

When we seek His divine purpose in all of our circumstances, we can praise Him in the valleys of despair as well as on the pleasant mountaintops.   HELEN YOUNG

Rejoice!

Rejoice in the Lord always. I will say it again: Rejoice! (PHILIPPI-
ANS 4:4).

To feel or express joy at all times seems like a tall order. Before going to India as new missionaries, a group of us were commissioned, prayed for and given a "nerve tonic" which helped me many times in my ministry on the field. It was Philippians 4:4–8. We were told that this rejoicing would keep us on top of strange and difficult circumstances and would be a source of help and strength in everyday living.

Over and over again I remembered these words of admonition. Anxiety would vanish through prayer and rejoicing; hard places would become stepping stones to greater blessing; depression would dissolve as His peace filled my mind; frustration would be exchanged for new ventures of service for Him.

We are all prone to look on the dark side when things go wrong. If we cannot in all honesty rejoice in our circumstances, we are admonished to rejoice in Someone greater than our circumstances. That Someone is the Lord. In the darkest hours we have Him, His care and help. When we remember that He is Savior, Sanctifier, Healer and Coming King; when we consider that He is Almighty God, King of Kings and Lord of Lords; and when we reflect upon what He can do, such reflections will produce within us the promised joy that is the strength of His people.

Yes, to rejoice always *is* a large order! But to rejoice in the Lord, what results this brings!   ANN DROPPA

His Touch

They begged him to let them touch even the edge of his cloak, and all who touched him were healed (MARK 6:56).

Jesus and His disciples had crossed the Lake of Galilee to Gennesaret, and at once the people recognized Him as the One who could perform miracles. They spread the word near and far so that all might come and hear Him.

Presently the marketplace and streets were filled with their sick. How well I remember those marketplaces. Here the merchants buy and sell; children play; beggars sit with sad, upturned faces; friends meet and greet friends. In the jostling crowd are the affluent and the poor, all intent and concerned with their own personal needs and problems.

Today in Israel, much remains the same as it was in Christ's day, with one difference. Now our precious Lord is looking down, hoping that someone in the crowded streets will know Him as his Savior.

What a privilege to serve Him and to pray that those touched today will also be made whole. On my last visit, I met many who touched Him. I remember sitting in our Jerusalem chapel. Tears filled my eyes as I chatted with an old friend. Born into a Muslim family, he touched the Lord by faith in 1930 and found forgiveness for His sins and a new life in Christ. He has been faithful to the Lord all these years, loving Him and witnessing the good news.

I met many others, and my heart rejoiced to see God's faithfulness in keeping His flock together. Wherever the good news is preached, the Holy Spirit is there, and the touch of Christ may be experienced by faith. He is just the same now as then — willing to cleanse, forgive, restore and heal. What a sublime joy to know that we can still *reach out and touch Him*! CAROLYN IRISH

Bind the Sacrifice

Bind the sacrifice with cords, even unto the horns of the altar (PSALM 118:27, KJV).

Have you ever given a sacrifice to God and then taken it back? Have you ever made a vow to God and then did not keep it?

In First Samuel, chapter 2, we are told of a woman named Hannah. She promised God that if He would give her a son, she would give him to the Lord to serve Him all his life. God did just that, and Hannah kept her vow. As soon as Samuel was weaned, she took him to the temple, there to be reared and trained by the priest, Eli.

She could have reneged, and few of us would have blamed her. Eli's evil and undisciplined sons also lived in the temple area, where little Samuel saw their wicked deeds. Hannah no doubt heard all the details from the temple worshipers each year as she came to bring Samuel new clothing. She could have rationalized, as you and I might have done, "I had better take my little boy home with me. I could do a much better job than Eli is doing."

Hannah bound her sacrifice with cords, as did Abraham. And because God overruled, Samuel grew up to be a choice servant of God in spite of his environment. Samuel was the only man recorded in sacred history who became a priest, a prophet and a judge.

God wants His children to trust Him implicitly, present all that we are and own and bind our sacrifice with cords. There is nothing that we can surrender that is not absolutely safe with God. In such a full and utter relinquishment lies the path to perfect peace.   DOROTHY HARVEY

Take Courage

God is our refuge and strength, an ever present help in trouble (PSALM 46:1).

The small boat carrying the followers of Christ across the Sea of Galilee pitched and rolled. Waves crashed over and into the small open craft, and fear gripped the hearts of every man on board. Without warning, they caught sight of a form coming toward them. Fear turned to terror and a feeling of utter helplessness.

The Word tells us that Jesus immediately said to them: "Take courage! It is I. Don't be afraid" (Matthew 14:27). *Immediately*—a beautiful word which indicates the Lord's interest, love and gentleness—He spoke to dispel the fear that had gripped the hearts of His disciples.

That storm provided an opportunity for faith. Peter suddenly cried out, "Lord, if it is you, tell me to come to you on the water." He did not have to wait for circumstances to change, he could step over the side of the boat onto the troubled water because His Lord could do anything.

Unfortunately, that was not the end of the story. Circumstances caught Peter's attention, and doubt shouted in his ear, "You just cannot do what you are doing," and he began to sink. Though Jesus chided Peter's lack of faith, His response to Peter's cry was immediate and positive.

We were never promised smooth, placid seas, but we have been promised victory as we go step by step through life. As surely as Christ tells us to come, He will make it possible for us to do His will in spite of circumstances. Let us not look at the waves or wind but rather at our unchanging Christ.   CAROL NIELSEN

Recognize and Resist

Put on the full armor of God so that you can take your stand against the devil's schemes (EPHESIANS 6:11).

David, my earnest seven-year-old, was at the point of tears as he described his nightmare. The devil had been chasing him and was so close that David could actually see him.

As I comforted him I said, "Remember the verse we learned for Bible quizzing, James 4:7, 'Resist the devil, and he will flee from you!'"

As I reflected on the event, I wondered how good I was at resisting the devil. The trouble is that lots of times when he is close, I am not as smart as David! I do not recognize him! Because, you see, the devil is not wearing his traditional horns-and-pitchfork outfit. He may come as an "angel of light" (2 Corinthians 11:14), or he may simply influence my thinking in such a subtle way that I do not even detect his presence.

For example, my husband was working on a project in the dining room, and he used some spray adhesive that I thought smelled just awful! The smell did not bother him at all, but my concentration on my writing project was ruined.

I had reminded my husband earlier in the day that we had been asked to speak at a couple's seminar and that satan would surely try to drive a wedge between us. But I did not recognize his influence on my thoughts and attitudes. Each time I saw that can of adhesive, I allowed myself to become irritated.

Ephesians 6:12 and 13 is a reminder that each of us needs God's help to *recognize* the source of the problem so that we know how to *resist*.   JOY JACOBS

Expectations

Find rest, O my soul, in God alone; my [expectation] comes from him (PSALM 62:5).

Our daily lives seem to be governed by expectations. We arise each morning expecting a cloudy or sunny day, depending on what the weatherman has forecast. We send our children off to school and ourselves and/or husbands off to work, expecting that we will all have a profitable day. Yet with all our high expectations, we are often disappointed because we are human and prone to failure.

There are many biblical characters who entertained certain expectations concerning their coming Lord and His role in their lives:

• Zechariah, father of John the Baptist, expected God to accomplish redemption for His people (Luke 1:67–79). As the Holy Spirit filled his mind and his mouth, he praised God and prophesied of His goodness to Israel.

• Elizabeth, wife of Zechariah, expected God to bring her great joy and make His presence known to those round about (Luke 1:41–45).

• Simeon, a righteous and devout man, expected the consolation of God's people in the coming of the Lord's Christ (Luke 2:25–35). As he gave over his expectations to the Holy Spirit, God kept His promise.

• Anna, the aged prophetess, expected to see the redemption and salvation of Jerusalem (Luke 2:36–38). As a result of her continual praise and worship, many were blessed.

What can we learn from this? We, like them, can live above and beyond life's hurts and disappointments. If we give ourselves, our hopes, plans, dreams and, yes, *all* our expectations to Jesus, He will take them and turn them into contentment and happiness.　　MARYANN SCHULER

Where Does Your Confidence Lie?

My grace is sufficient for you, for my power is made perfect in weakness (2 CORINTHIANS 12:9).

Can you think of something in your life at which you failed miserably and will most likely never try again? Is there something which you have never had the courage to try?

The reason we do not do these things is because we lack confidence. Our confidence, it seems, lies within our already developed talents and abilities, not in God.

Paul calls this "putting confidence in the flesh." Read through Philippians 3:1–21, and you will see how Paul recognized his inability and acted upon it. When God prompts, we should also act regardless of our apparent inadequacies.

Each time God has said, "Go," He has equipped the individuals. He equipped Moses, Jacob, Abraham, David and some uneducated fishermen, and He, likewise, equips us.

In Second Corinthians 12, Paul says, "When I am weak, then I am strong." If you are weak in an area, great! If you are inexperienced, fantastic! That is when God acts! When we acknowledge our weaknesses, God can act through them.

Do you have a thorn in your flesh as Paul did? Great! God can and will use that, too. Weakness is never a valid reason to lack confidence. It is the world's reason, but it is not the Christian's!   PAM BERTOLET

Sowing the Seed

So is my word that goes out from my mouth: it will not return to me empty, but will accomplish what I desire (ISAIAH 55:11).

God promises that the seed you sow will not be wasted. Have you sown any seed lately? What about the salesperson who calls you on the phone? Do you listen politely, thank that person for his message, and then say to him that you have a message that will make him rich spiritually?

Jesus told the demon-possessed man of Gerasenes, "Tell them how much the Lord has done for you" (Mark 5:19). You can tell others how much the Lord has done for you — the repairman, the paperboy, the meter reader, the person next to you on the bus or plane. Keep a supply of short visualized tracts with you for the person too busy to talk to you. You have the only really "good news." Share it!

Do you know of someone in physical need, a sick neighbor perhaps? Take her a bowl of soup and an encouraging word. Take something you have baked to a new neighbor. Make yourself available to help.

Do you pray each morning, "Lord, send some soul to me today and love that soul through me"? And don't fall off your chair when the Lord answers that request.

Psalm 126:6 tells us that "He who goes out weeping, carrying seed to sow, will return with songs of joy, carrying sheaves with him."

When we come into His presence, how many sheaves will we bring with us?   LOUISE COOLEY

OCTOBER 16

Answers to Prayer

Do not be anxious about anything, but in everything, by prayer and petition, with thanksgiving, present your requests to God (PHILIPPIANS 4:6).

W hen I recall all the marvelous ways in which God has answered our prayers in the past, it makes me ashamed to think how I sometimes worry before I remember to pray.

My husband and I are missionaries in Zaire, Africa. Anticipating the arrival of our third child, we sent home a list of items we would need.

My mother filled two cases with these items to send along as extra baggage with another couple. Mom decided to phone the airline to inquire about the extra charge. The clerk informed her it would cost $30 per case. When she called the second time to verify the price, she was told it would be $100 a case (apparently the first price was an error). A third call discouraged us even further; the clerk told my mother that the actual price was $130 for each case. When we received her note, we knew we could not afford that price, and we could hardly expect our family to pay.

Our first reaction was to worry. Then we were reminded of God's Word not to worry but to pray and thank God for His answers. We began to pray.

My mother went to the airport with our friends, and the baggage clerk allowed ours to go through *free*. He said, "It's the least I can do for missionaries."

God answered our prayer above and beyond what we expected. Everything arrived safely (another answer to prayer) and without charge. God says, "Don't worry; just pray about *everything*." So why worry when you can pray? And do not forget to thank Him!   DIANE FINNEMORE

My Thanks

Always giving thanks to God the Father for everything, in the name of our Lord Jesus Christ (EPHESIANS 5:20).

Thank You, Lord, for a million little things, for parking places in the rain and lost things found and cakes that turn out okay.

"Thank You for lights that work and spare tires that still have air in them.

"Thank You for woolly lambs and for smiles with holes in them. Thank You for the warmth of fire and for friends, for music and for sweet words. How I love words!

"Thank You for letters in the mailbox and for telephone calls that matter. Thank You for a million scenes stored forever in my mind's eye—scenes of sunsets, of ocean beaches sparkling in the sun, of redwood trees and brooks and river banks and a place called home.

"Thank You for people who love and say so and are not afraid to touch and hug.

"But most of all, thank You for being there always and for allowing me to say, like Thomas, 'My Lord and my God.'"

May we *always* give thanks for *everything*, knowing that our Heavenly Father is pleased when we accept each situation as His will.   ROSALIND MCNAIR

Leaning

The eternal God is your refuge, and underneath are the everlasting arms (DEUTERONOMY 33:27).

Our oldest son, Danny, a victim of cystic fibrosis, suffered for four years with frequent episodes of digestive and respiratory crises. I was expecting our second child when Danny's last crisis came. As he struggled to breathe, I left his hospital room and walked the corridor trying to pray. *Where was God? Why wasn't He listening? Why wasn't He healing my little boy? I had given God my whole life to serve Him in the ministry with my husband; now why wasn't God coming to my aid when I most needed Him?*

In spite of the efforts of medical personnel, our son died that morning as my husband and I stood by his bedside.

The funeral of Danny and the birth of our new child came and went in a blur. Though I could not pray, I knew that those "everlasting arms" were beneath me and were holding me up. I realized that God is sovereign, that He was in control and that He "healed" Danny in His own way to completely relieve his suffering. And some day, I shall meet my son again — whole and vital and alive.

Do you know someone who has recently lost a loved one? The very best thing you can do is to pray that he or she will experience the everlasting arms of the Savior.

> Art thou sunk in depths of sorrow
> Where no arm can reach so low?
> There is one whose arms almighty
> Reach beyond thy deepest woe.
> Underneath thy deepest sorrow
> Are the everlasting arms.

(Hymn, "The Everlasting Arms," by A.B. Simpson)

DAROLYN IRVIN

Learning to Pray

When he finished, one of his disciples said to him, "Lord, teach us to pray, just as John taught his disciples" (LUKE 11:1).

At an early age I memorized the model prayer and even learned to repeat it with the right emphasis. Yet, it took some very difficult places in my daily walk to teach me what I was really saying.

Our Father in heaven. This phrase has become more meaningful now that I have been born into His family. Our relationship is truly that of Father and child.

Hallowed be your name. Yes. He is my Father, truly holy, all wise, sovereign, majestic and mighty.

Your kingdom come. Let all the earth hear that word and through that word be brought to accept Christ as Lord.

Your will be done in earth as it is in heaven. When I try to help God answer my prayer, my will gets in the way. I am learning that He knows, even better than I can voice them, the cries and frustrations of my heart.

Give us today our daily bread. No, I have not yet been physically hungry. But when I have needed strength to get through the day, my Heavenly Father has supplied my daily need. I am learning how to trust.

Forgive us our debts as we have forgiven our debtors. My biggest debt was my sin, and that was paid at Calvary. For this I thank Him. I am learning that true repentance and faith produce a disposition to forgive. I can freely forgive others.

Lead us not into temptation. My constant prayer is that I will not listen to the taunts of Satan. Christ paid the price for my redemption, and through His abiding love and grace I may have victory over sin in my life.

When our requests are uttered, answers will come as we learn to give God all glory and honor. VIRGINIA CUTHRIELL

OCTOBER 20

Victory in Jesus

But thanks be to God, who always leads us in triumphal procession in Christ and through us spreads everywhere the fragrance of the knowledge of him (2 CORINTHIANS 2:14).

It was the last morning of our vacation, and I was sitting on the deck having my devotions. The sky was a bit overcast with a nice cool breeze blowing off the ocean. The beach was almost deserted, except for a few seagulls. I felt I was one of the most fortunate women in the world.

I chose to turn to the New Testament rather than my regular place in Deuteronomy, and I began to read in Second Corinthians, chapter 2. I had read verse 14 many times, but it had never struck me in quite the same way.

Paul tells me that I can be triumphant! I can know victory right here and now and from here on out. My victory can and will be in Christ. It does not mean that every concern of mine will be victorious as the world counts victory. My victory is in Him. The singing group in which I am involved may fold, my solo ministry may fade, the dress shop may die from malnutrition and any number of things may go wrong. But I am still on top because of Christ — not a trumped-up, "hip-hip-hooray" type of success but the calm assurance that He is in control.

Next I notice the beautiful thought that He spreads abroad the fragrance of Himself through me in every place. He will so fill "myself" with Himself that if I let Him have total control of my life, He will permeate every place I go with this awareness. We are to be a sweet fragrance to God of Christ. What a high and holy calling!

Though your schedule may be hectic, there will be many opportunities to allow Christ to be a sweet fragrance through you today. Do not miss them!   DELORES TAYLOR

Surrender Your Suffering

Therefore, since Christ suffered in his body, arm yourselves also with the same attitude, because he who has suffered in his body is done with sin (1 PETER 4:1).

While it is natural to associate Christ's suffering solely with His cruel crucifixion and His death on the cross, there were other ways in which He suffered. His own family members often misunderstood Him and withheld credibility until after His death.

Later in His ministry, even after He had gained a following and some measure of popularity, most of the religious leaders treated Him with disdain and suspicion. They even plotted ways to ruin His ministry and to destroy Him. At one point, many of His followers turned away and left Him.

At the most difficult hour of Jesus' life, when hostility and hatred had reached their peak and the cross was before Him, His dearest friends failed Him. He had poured Himself into them for years, but when He most needed their prayer and loving support, they left Him.

Finally, He found Himself numbered among criminals as He came to trial and then was crucified.

As Christians, God has called us to suffer, and it is a high and holy calling. Such suffering binds us to Him.

Are you suffering today? Is it from loneliness, from misunderstanding or rejection? Did someone very dear to you fail you? Do not rail out against the offender? Instead, embrace the suffering as God's will for you this moment. Press close to Him and allow the work of holiness to be perfected in your life. YVONNE SWOPE

Think First

Remind the people . . . to slander no one, to be peaceable and considerate, and to show true humility to all men (TITUS 3:1–2).

Before I left for the mission field, my mother, herself a former missionary, told me, "Make it a point not to say anything critical or negative about your fellow workers, especially behind their backs."

This was excellent advice. I am sorry I did not follow it. In my first few years, there were so many things to comment on.

Then one day after our annual mission conference, one of my missionary friends came to me and said, "I think you should know what someone is saying about you." She went on to repeat the negative comment. While it was true, it was something I could not change. The man who had criticized had not known the whole story or why I could not change, and this hurt me all the more. But after I calmed down, I began thinking of what my mother had said and of how many times I had been guilty of doing this same thing.

How precious to have a friend with whom your reputation is safe, and even more wonderful to be the kind of person who always believes in people and stands her ground in their defense. Since that time, I have tried to think before I speak and to remember the hurt someone might feel if he or she could hear my remark.

Things come full circle. Now my youngest sister is serving as a missionary in Africa. I was not at home to see her off, but I wrote and advised her "Whatever you do, make it a point not to say anything critical or negative about your fellow workers." I urged her to develop the habit of thinking before speaking and told her, from experience, that it would make life much easier.   DEBBIE COWLES

OCTOBER 23

Something to Give

And God is able to make all grace abound to you, so that in all things at all times, having all that you need, you will abound in every good work (2 CORINTHIANS 9:8).

Each of us has something with which we can display God's love to others. It will be something tailor-made to fit our own abilities.

We had just come through the shock of finding that our first child had been stillborn. Though the trauma left us heartbroken, God gave us comfort. What I needed now was something to take my mind off my sorrow.

At about this same time, a neighbor had a nervous breakdown, and our church wanted to show her and her unsaved husband that we cared. We planned a "pounding," and for two days people dropped food items at our house. Our finances were tight at the time, and I found I had no food items to contribute, nor did I have money to buy any.

At the appointed time, several families came by, and we gathered up the food items and took them to our neighbor's home. All the time, my sinking heart reminded me that I had not donated any of the food.

To our surprise, the unsaved husband asked if one of us could fry some of the chicken that was brought and prepare the noon meal the following day. Before anyone else had an opportunity to react, I said, "I'll do it!"

The next day as I busied myself in my neighbor's kitchen, my heart literally sang, for I sensed that God was using me for this made-to-order occasion. My joy was complete when my neighbor invited my husband and me to share the meal.

Let us be eager and available so that God may give us a tailor-made opportunity to serve someone today.

LOIS T. GLUCK

OCTOBER 24

Life's Garden

But I will restore you to health and heal your wounds, declares the Lord (JEREMIAH 30:17).

When we returned from New Jersey one July, we found our garden at the peak of production. Each day offered baskets of beans and enormous tomatoes. Then quite suddenly, it dwindled to a handful of beans and a few half-spoiled tomatoes. The border of marigolds that only a few weeks before had been bright and beautiful was now droopy and faded. Cornstalks lay in an unsightly heap. *Guess that's it*, I thought, and tended it less and less. We dusted for bugs one last time and left the garden to expire on its own.

Then came a few good late-summer rains. Straggly tomato plants leaned against the bean fence. Equally pathetic bean vines clung to the struggling tomatoes in a tangled embrace, each gathering support from the other. Later I was able to gather a basketful of beans and discovered many young tomatoes on their vines. Though the beans were not as crisp and the tomatoes not as boastful in size, we were grateful for the added harvest.

This can happen in the garden of life. Weeds and lack of rain stifle productivity. On its own and without water, the garden becomes a place where weeds alone can thrive, and we tend to give up. But God often moves in the midst of plants and people at their lowest points. They lose their independent spirit and lean on one another for support. He applies the Water of the Word to root and vine and, sometimes without the help of those who should care, He restores. He is the divine gardener who desires that the garden of our lives produce good fruit. PAULINE SUTTON

Holding Up Our Corner

Now the body is not made up of one part but of many (1 CORINTHIANS 12:14).

According to the account of the paralytic man in Mark 2:2–5, it took four men to make sure that he was brought to where Jesus could help him. Each man was necessary for this undertaking. Each one had his corner to hold, plus other responsibilities for getting him through the roof and down to Jesus.

In First Corinthians 13, Paul indicates that this kind of involvement in another's need is love in action. In verse 7 we learn that love "always protects, always trusts, always hopes, always perseveres."

God has equipped each of us with gifts and talents that fit into His plan of service to those around us. When we do not allow ourselves to be used according to our own unique blend of spiritual graces, one corner of someone's "need" is left to rest on the shoulders of another who is already carrying his share.

As the responsibility for the paralytic man's healing was shared by each of the four, the burden became lighter and easier to bear. Let us not be found guilty of letting down our corner when God has called us to "bear one another's burdens."

> I shall pass through this world but once. Any good, therefore, that I can do, or any kindness that I can show, let me do it now; let me not defer or neglect it, for I shall not pass this way again. (Stephen Gellett)

JUDY LAWRENCE

Wonderful Counselor

Who, then, is the man that fears the Lord? He will instruct him in the way chosen for him (PSALM 25:12).

Our world seems to abound with people, young and old, who lack confidence and direction in their lives. If we fear (reverence) the Lord, He promises to instruct us in making the choices of life.

This Scripture came alive when, as a young person, I was seeking God's will concerning a husband. I had been dating a young man for a short time when the Lord pointed out the difference in our callings. He made it clear that, though the man was a fine Christian, He had other plans for me. When my friend did not accept this but insisted that it was God's will for us to marry, I began to wonder if perhaps I was mistaken.

So I asked friends to pray about the problem. Many volunteered their advice, but I did not have peace. I agreed with their reasoning that my friend and I could serve the Lord together, but I kept searching the Word.

When I read Matthew 6:23, I saw that I had been disregarding the light He had already given, and it had become darkness to me. I saw that I had turned off His path for my life. When I took the final step of obedience, peace flooded my heart and all my confusion was gone.

I served the Lord as a single person for years, sometimes lonely, but never regretting that choice. At last the Lord led a God-fearing widower to invite me to share his home and family.

The only truly happy, confident people are those who wait in God's presence until they receive His instruction and guidance. Wonderful Counselor, mighty God is He! ELLA MAE DODGE

Not Made for Defeat

Weeping may remain for a night, but rejoicing comes in the morning (PSALM 30:5).

When I reached the place where the Lord wanted me to serve, I learned that another single lady and I would be left on our own. If we were successful, we would be allowed to continue the work; if we were not, it would be our own funeral!

A friend's suggestion that I return to Canada drove me to my knees for the Lord's direction. His message to me was "do not consult with any man" (Galatians 1:16). I believed God was in control and, with renewed courage, continued waiting for His instruction. Another missionary whom I had just met insisted that I visit a retired missionary with whom I later lived, studied the language and began teaching Sunday school.

For a missionary without a national helper, church planting is a slow, rigorous process. Several times after we had seen souls saved and come to be fed and built up, the enemy made inroads, and soon the congregation dwindled. In addition, recurring, severe headaches made it difficult to study, meditate and pray. I finally decided just to wait in the Lord's presence for His answer to all of our problems.

Turning toward my bookcase, I asked the Lord what I should read. Suddenly, the title on Oswald Smith's book loomed up before me, *Not Made for Defeat*. Like a bolt from the sky it hit me, and I responded, "Yes, Lord, You made me for Your pleasure, Your honor, glory and praise, and in Christ's name I refuse defeat." I declared Satan beaten, bid him leave and rejoiced in the victory.   PEARL FUSTEY

OCTOBER 28

The Language of Love

If I speak in the tongues of men and of angels, but have not love, I am only a resounding gong or a clanging cymbal (1 CORINTHIANS 13:1).

After three terms Africa, a missionary friend was going home, broken in body and confused in mind. Many difficulties had taken their toll—the peril of war, the death of an infant son and the heartache of separation as her children went off to school. Underlying everything was the gnawing sense of failure because she had never mastered the intricacies of the native language.

Before she left, she had confided in me. "I work so hard, but I cannot seem to learn the language. And if I cannot speak their language, how can I convey to the people that God loves them—that I love them?"

I watched as the cot, which served as a stretcher for her, was lifted onto the truck bed. The entire village followed the slow-moving truck to the boat landing on the Nile River for a final farewell. As I stood among the hushed group that watched the steamer Nasir disappear around a bend in the river, I was lost in my own thoughts. The abrupt questioning of an old woman jarred me into the present:

"Where is the 'satta sitt' (noble lady) going?"

"To her father's village in a far country," I replied.

"Will she walk again to the villages of the Dinkas and sit by their cooking fires?"

"Do I know?" I countered. "Why do you ask?"

With simplicity and discernment the old lady replied, "It is the desire of our hearts that she return to our cooking fires. She loves us. *Her heart speaks our language!*"

Inwardly I cried, "Oh, God, may such a love for others be seen in me." MARJORIE REIDHEAD

OCTOBER 29

A Way of Escape

When I said, "This far you may come and no farther; here is where your proud waves halt" (JOB 38:11).
And God is faithful; he will not let you be tempted beyond what you can bear. But when you are tempted, he will also provide a way out so that you can stand up under it (1 CORINTHIANS 10:13).

Have you had the thrill of lying awake at night in a cottage by the seashore listening to the waves crashing on the rocks nearby? The night may be dark, with no stars showing, and all you can see is the froth of the whitecaps as they break and recede. When you think of the tremendous power involved, the thunder of the waves can be awesome and a little frightening.

There can come hours of dark despair when the breakers of depression, sorrow and pain seem to wash over us and we fear that we shall be carried out to sea. We may feel the cold of the ocean on our feet, and we do not know which way to turn.

But God, the God who made and controls the universe, who says to the waves, "This far you may come, and no farther," will not let the evil one overwhelm us. We do not need to turn either way. All we need to do is just look up to Him. He "will provide a way out." RUBY WATROUS

Arise, Go Thy Way!

Though I walk in the midst of trouble, you preserve my life (PSALM 138:7).

It was St. Valentine's Day, 1975. As I opened my eyes and became aware of my husband's presence by my bed, I searched his face for the answer to my question. Yes, the surgeon had removed the cancerous breast.

In the days that followed, friends were there to comfort and support. Pastors and their wives visited and prayed. Later, the office staff brought cake, ice cream and gifts to celebrate my birthday. Cards, letters and plants arrived in abundance. I felt that I was being carried on a blanket of prayer and love. Two weeks later, recovery was going well and I looked forward to returning home.

One day I was alone for the first time during the afternoon visiting hours. A nurse came in with some pills and a glass of milk, the beginning of an oral chemotherapy I was to eventually take for the next six years. When she left after kindly and carefully explaining the procedure to me, I lay back on the pillow. Suddenly I was overwhelmed with the reality of it — *I was a cancer patient!*

All those notes and cards had contained Scripture verses and I remembered one from Psalm 138. "When I called, you answered me; you made me bold and stouthearted" (verse 3).

Then I understood. The paralyzed man of Mark, chapter 2, needed to have four friends carry him to Jesus, but after prayer was answered, Jesus' message to him was, "Get up, take your mat and go home."

At this writing, I have been "going" for almost 10 years, grateful for God's touch of healing.   RUTH E. CLARK

God's Time Clock

All the days ordained for me were written in your book before one of them came to be (PSALM 139:16).

It is a source of great joy to me to realize that God has taken the time and gone to the trouble to plan each one of my days, even before one of them had come into being. He chose the day I would be born, the family into which I would come, the husband whom I would marry. He even has written on His divine calendar the day of my death and everything that will happen in my life between now and then. What a delight to know that God cares so much for me!

There is one small problem, though. I cannot see God's calendar on which all of these appointments are recorded. Consequently, there are times when I am impatient — impatient for the salvation of a loved one, impatient for the ending of a trial, impatient for that good thing that God has promised will come to fruition in my life.

Lately, the Holy Spirit has prompted me to notice what the Scripture has to say about time. In various books and several versions I have noted these phrases: in due season, in the fullness of time, at the proper time, in due time, in His times, at the appointed time, at the set time of which God had spoken and in His own time. My desire is that the appointments God has set on my calendar be met in His own time. I am learning to say as the psalmist did, "I trust in you, O Lord; I say, 'You are my God.' My times are in your hands" (Psalm 31:14–15).

It is safest and most rewarding to trust God's methods and to go by His clock.   JOYCE CARNEFF

Christ and Teenagers

We have this hope as an anchor for the soul, firm and secure (HE-BREWS 6:19).

The Lord created a special place in my heart for teenagers. I have taught them and ministered to them.

During my children's teen years, Christ was my Handkerchief and my Hope. I use the word handkerchief because if you have had teenagers—and if you are perfectly honest—then you remember times when you cried with them or for them. The Scriptures tell us that Christ cried, and I knew that if, with my small amount of human love, I could cry for my teenager, Christ would know how I felt. But more than that, He was my Handkerchief and dried my tears. I could take any problem to Him.

Christ was my help when grades were bad. He was there when we wondered where our children were, why they had not come home as they had been instructed, what they were doing and if they were all right.

Christ was and is my Hope. I learned something as a mother of teenagers. I could love them and still want them even when they were so rebellious that I thought, *I cannot tolerate you right now; I wish you didn't live here.* But I never ever reached the point where I did not love my children or not want them, and I still feel the same way. My hopes for them never died, even through the rebellious times.

If, in my small way of loving, I could hold onto hope for my teenagers and love them no matter what they did, imagine how Christ can love me. Just as teenagers who are trying hard to grow up make many mistakes and struggle with authority, we as Christians also rebel and sometimes fail. But Christ never ever quits loving us. He will be our Hope in this life and our Eternal Joy.   SANDRA MINTER

NOVEMBER 2

A Priceless Heritage

One generation will commend your works to another; they will tell of your mighty acts (PSALM 145:4).

At the close of missionary furlough in 1969, word came that we would not be allowed to return to Guinea, West Africa. The government had decided to curtail foreign missionary activity and was not granting visas. At the request of the remaining Guinea missionaries, we were stationed across the border in Sierra Leone for Fula language study.

During our Sierra Leone sojourn, I learned that my great-great-grandfather, Anson Carter, had been one of the first American missionaries to Sierra Leone. He died of malaria a few months after his arrival in the country. His wife, still in America, died soon afterward, leaving a 12-year-old daughter, Adelia. I discovered that Adelia's grave was in the same cemetery in Athens, Pennsylvania, as her daughter, Rachel (my grandmother), and her grandson (my father).

I know nothing more about Adelia, but can speculate from the fact that her daughter was one of the charter members of The Christian and Missionary Alliance Church in Waverly, New York, that Adelia had held no grudge against God for the loss of both her parents. It seemed rather that she had continued in the faith of her parents and had instilled in her children that same love for God and a deep concern for the lost of this world.

News came that we would be allowed to return to Guinea, but before we left, we were able to visit Anson Carter's grave in Komende.

What a wonderful heritage I have been given. It both challenges and encourages me to be faithful in passing on this priceless inheritance to my children. NORMA D. GARDNER

Little Reminders

Sons are a heritage from the Lord, children a reward from him (PSALM 127:3).

As I watch our children grow, I look at them with wonder. I remember when they first learned to say mommy and daddy, to empty the lower cupboards and to spill their plates on the floor.

Being a mother makes for many interesting and trying times. I am first delighted, for instance, when at the doctor's office, the nurse talks about what good children I have. But no sooner has she spoken than they are fighting over who will sit in the red chair. There goes my delight!

Grocery shopping with the three is another experience! The baby has just learned that she can reach over and pull things off the shelf. The other two run up and down the aisle singing, "We're off to see the Wizard." I have to round them up, bring them back and get them quiet, then try to finish my shopping. In the meantime, the baby is eating the grocery list. Finally one of them looks up and says, "Mommy, aren't you glad that you have such good children like us?" Then I thank the Lord for the reminder.

Occasionally we venture an outing to McDonalds. Without waiting for their food, the children run out to the playground. I grab baby, food and highchair and head outside. Of course, by the time I get set up at a table, the sandwiches are soggy, and the drinks are half spilled.

But then, there are those special times as when I listen to the children praying so earnestly for their friends or their pets. They know their prayer is going to be answered. Their simple faith makes me stop and say, "Thank you, Lord, for reminding me."   DIANA NILES

I'm a Grandmother

I was young and now I am old, yet I have never seen the righteous forsaken (PSALM 37:25).

Now that I am old enough to be a grandmother, I can recall how Christ met my every need. Trouble came, and He was very present. Sorrow came, and I was comforted. There were failures, but I was not utterly cast down, and my feet were turned again in the right direction. There were needs, and I found His grace sufficient.

During my children's growing years, I had a keen sense of responsibility for their physical and spiritual welfare. I remember wishing I could pray profound prayers that would be doubly effective in their lives. I soon learned, however, that God hears and honors sincere prayer whether profound or simple.

Sometimes in a busy day, there was time only for a short prayer, and I found it to be enough. For my children I prayed: "Lord, save them. Help them to make the right decisions in life. Help them to have the strength in life to resist temptation, and may they always be aware of Your presence." I even prayed that they would be good marriage partners, and I prayed for the ones they would marry.

You see, the same spiritual foundation we build for our children continues in our grandchildren. My children and grandchildren are very special to me. We have been blessed with a very close relationship.

Now that I realize how much influence parents and grandparents have on the lives of the young, I am so glad that my husband and I chose to follow God. My prayer as a grandmother is that all of my family will love and serve Him. PAULINE BEALE

I'm a Working Mother

I was pushed back and about to fall, but the Lord helped me. The Lord is my strength and my song; he has become my salvation (PSALM 118:13–14).

When, after 12 years as a housewife, I went back to work, our family did not adjust well.

Every working mother, I decided, could work for a circus as a juggler. We juggle husbands, children, ball games, grocery shopping, housework, PTA, medical appointments, babysitters, devotions, church activities — the list goes on and on. But we cannot possibly juggle all those things.

When things get out of balance — and they often do — we fall and everything comes flying down on top of us. And we fall with people watching us, because our families see us as we are, unlovely and unlovable!

But Christ is the net that catches us and the entire situation. He comes to us in our need, and He loves us.

It is possible to get so busy at work that you forget about your children until the phone rings. At 2:15 every afternoon Maralee calls, "Mother, what is there to eat in the house? I'm hungry. What are we having for supper?"

Maybe all working mothers face that. But I was going through a hard time, recently, and it seemed as though it was just too much. I sat down one morning before I went to work and had a good cry. After I had cried to the Lord and told Him I could not handle things, I opened my Bible and in Psalm 26:12 I read, "My feet stand on level ground." He would be my sufficiency.

Christ cares about me. He loves me. He loves my child. He loves my husband. He will perfect that which concerns me. HELEN CRIMM

A Lesson from the Potter

So I went down to the potter's house, and I saw him working at the wheel. But the pot he was shaping from the clay was marred in his hands; so the potter formed it into another pot, shaping it as seemed best to him (JEREMIAH 18:3–4).

Several years ago our family traveled across the United States. Along the way we stopped at a pottery factory and saw a skilled potter shaping a beautiful vessel at his wheel.

Suppose the vessel had been marred in the process. He would not have thrown away the clay but would have reshaped it and made it into another piece of pottery, possibly even lovelier than the first.

Many lives have been marred by sin, mistakes and wrong decisions. Satan would have us believe that all is lost and nothing can be done about our past failures.

It is true that we often reap what we sow, that there are scars that will last a lifetime, but God can use these things to perfect us and make each one of us into the person He wants us to be. He can use the same clay that has brought us shame to make a second vessel, beautiful in His sight and useful for His service.

If you think your past is irreparable or that you have failed in your responsibility to your children or in your influence on others, remember, if you will only yield to God, He can touch you right where you are and make you anew.

The lesson that Jeremiah learned at the potter's house can be just as meaningful today! HELEN JULIAN

Hurry Up—and Wait!

Those who [wait on] the Lord will renew their strength. They will soar on wings like eagles; they will run and not grow weary, they will walk and not be faint (ISAIAH 40:31).

Americans spend a great deal of their time waiting. Where have you waited lately? Have you been stalled in the doctor's office, in rush-hour traffic, in line at the grocery store or are you *still* waiting for your son or daughter to clean up his or her room?

The Lord allows us to wait on Him, and such waiting is not only beautiful but productive, as we see the development of our Christian walk. This Scripture became special to us when my husband fell deathly ill.

A kidney transplant was performed, and we began the long wait for the kidney to begin to function. Because he was in a hospital 80 miles away, the waiting was intensified.

The Lord showed us many things as we waited, cried and prayed. He first revealed that waiting is synonymous with hoping, and hope denotes a confidence in something or Someone outside oneself.

We learned that in waiting we gain new strength—new spiritual strength—and new insights into the very person of Christ and His death for us. While my husband lay in the hospital, waiting, I waited at home. I confess I could not always pray, but each night as I listened to our little daughter pray for her daddy, those beautiful, simplistic petitions would bring new hope, peace and joy.

While we are waiting, we are growing in Christ and continuing in the process of becoming conformed to His image (Romans 8:29). And the waiting goes on. Yet our hope, our confidence, our strength and our growth is in Him who will not, cannot fail.   MARYANN SCHULER

Our Omniscient Lord

Trust in the Lord with all your heart and lean not on your own understanding (PROVERBS 3:5).

Did I hear what I thought I heard? Yes, I did hear correctly. My husband had just told me that I would have to apply for secular employment once again. His pastoral ministry had always been to rebuild small congregations. During the five years of our first pastorate, we both worked. The six years in our second pastorate were ideal, because we were both able to give full time to the church ministry, and I was a happy wife, mother and homemaker.

We were now in the second year of a totally new extension work. Subsidy had been reduced and funds were needed. My life had been an extension of my husband's ministry for over seven years, and the Lord had blessed in the growth of the church. Now the Lord was leading me to use my individual talents and abilities outside the home.

When I started work at Penn State University, it was not easy. Jesus knew, however, why He was allowing me to return to secular employment. As I review my career, I can say, "Thank You, Lord. You knew all the time that I would one day appreciate having a position after our two daughters had their own homes. You also knew my husband would be traveling a great deal in his administrative ministry, and there would be lonely days. You knew I needed all those years of office experience to serve You now."

Jesus not only knows our present, He knows our future. When we learn the spiritual lesson of committing ourselves to Jesus and rejoicing in His plan for us, His presence can be just as real in the office as it is in the home. The secret is in being faithful to His purpose and witnessing for Him.   GLADYS J. DIBBLE

The Lord, My Friend

(a paraphrase of Psalm 23)

I have come that they may have life, and have it to the full. I am the good shepherd. The good shepherd lays down his life for the sheep (JOHN 10:10–11).

The Lord is my friend. He remains closer to me than a brother.

He never leaves me to struggle alone;
He is always there, watching over me to prevent me from stumbling.

He writes love letters to me. They strengthen me, uplift me, encourage me and give nourishment to my soul.

He provides love for me when I am lonely and discouraged. He gives wisdom when I need it most.

As I go through life, He is my best friend, and some day I shall go to where He is. There I shall spend eternity with Him where I can forever be by His side.   MELBA STUMBO

NOVEMBER **10**

Success in Failure

Now for a little while you may have had to suffer grief in all kinds of trials. These have come so that your faith — of greater worth than gold, which perishes even though refined by fire — may be proved genuine (1 PETER 1:6–7).

O urs is a success-oriented world, where one's value is often measured by wealth, social position or profession. Failure in such a world is frowned upon.

Thankfully, that is not the way of God's kingdom. The Lord has a different way of measuring, for He "does not look at the things man looks at. Man looks at the outward appearance, but the Lord looks at the heart" (1 Samuel 16:7).

But Christians still fall prey to the world's standard for success. Struggles, unmet goals and unrealized expectations can lead to despair, a sense of failure and a feeling of worthlessness. The Scriptures, however, present a different outlook. God's Word says struggle and failure can become sources of strength and a means to personal growth. They can be stepping stones to heavenly success (Psalm 37:23–24).

The supreme human example is our Lord. His crucifixion was, by all worldly standards, a failure — a failure to justify His three years of ministry, a failure to overcome the might of Rome and a failure to keep the promises He made to His followers. But their verdict of failure was only an illusion. His death and resurrection raised Him into glory and broke sin's hold over us.

Our struggles and apparent failures can raise us up to a new maturity in Christ which will sustain us and give us a ministry to others. This is God's promise to us, and His promises never fail (Joshua 23:14).   CAROL NAZARETIAN

Friendship

A man of many companions may come to ruin, but there is a friend who sticks closer than a brother (PROVERBS 18:24).

Recently a new acquaintance related to me an experience she was going through with a close friend. Her friend, a non-Christian, was considering leaving her husband. Mary expressed her regrets, both in light of social values and of scriptural injunction. She encouraged her friend to remain with her husband, but assured her that she would be praying for her and that their friendship would remain intact whatever she decided.

As Mary talked on about her friend's problems, I thought to myself that here was the kind of friend I would like to have—one who may not agree with my decisions or like all my quirks and eccentricities but would always stand by me.

Most of us have had such friends, but we may have had the other kind as well—those who turn against us when they disagree with us.

We would all like to have a friend like Mary. Are we determined, then, to *be* that kind of friend? Are you grieving over a broken friendship? Reach out, mend fences and perhaps that relationship can be restored.

Wise Solomon once said, "A friend loveth at all times." How many true friends do we have? How true a friend are we?   BEVERLY HENDRICKSON

Spared for the Master's Use

I lift my eyes to the hills — where does my help come from? My help comes from the Lord, the Maker of heaven and earth (PSALM 121:1–2).

This Scripture became very real to me a few years ago when I had to have surgery. I was depressed, although I knew that as God's child, He would take care of me. The night before surgery, I could not seem to touch the hem of His garment as I wanted to; the peace of mind I sought eluded me. Later that night, a nurse came in, picked up my Bible and read Psalm 121. It was just what my soul needed, and peace flooded my heart.

The next morning I went into the operating room, and what was to have been a minor surgical procedure became a critical one. When they brought me down five hours later, the doctor told my husband, "Rev. Humbard, we did all we could do to save your wife, and we might have lost her except that a Higher Power stepped in." That day as my life hung in the balance, the Lord reached down His hand and said that my work on this earth was not finished.

Since that time, the songs that I have sung have become more real. I believe with all of my heart that is why I am here today — because of that portion of Scripture, "I lift up my eyes to the hills — where does my help come from? My help comes from the Lord." God does not slumber nor does He sleep. If He takes note of the little sparrow that falls, how much more does He look after His children?

MAUDE AIMEE HUMBARD

Experiencing God's Love

Not only so, but we also rejoice in our sufferings, because we know that suffering produces perseverance; perseverance, character; and character, hope. (ROMANS 5:3–4).

Suffering. It is easy to rejoice in our precious salvation or in God's call to a special ministry. But to rejoice when we are ridiculed is a different story. Is a smile of joy possible when a Muslim woman slaps your face as you witness to her of the true meaning of Christmas? Can you rejoice when a Muslim religious man has, to his mind, just torn apart your story of the work of Christ in salvation?

Perseverance. It takes years to develop perseverance when it involves taking sarcasm from Muslims and not being able to freely give the truth you so earnestly want to give. It takes perseverance as you listen an hour to a Muslim telling what he believes, and he allows you only five minutes to tell him what you believe.

Character. The longer and more patiently you endure in difficult situations, the more Christian character is being developed in you. Such character is absolutely necessary in order to approach a people whose very teaching of life is against everything you know to be true.

Hope. Our hope is to see Muslims who will someday stand before the Lord with us. The first step in reaching them is to show forth the love of God.   ELIZABETH ABRAMS

Do We Really See?

When he saw the crowds, he had compassion on them, because they were harassed and helpless (MATTHEW 9:36).

Nearing hysteria, I stood frozen in the aisle. With my energetic two-year-old and newborn, I was walking through the large department store when my two-year-old slipped away without a word and vanished.

At first I was irritated and had my disapproval speech planned for when she came running back, but she was nowhere to be seen. Irritation quickly became panic as I stood there, not knowing what to do. This store had many doors leading into the large shopping mall and parking lot. "What if . . .?" brought me to tears as I strained to see a bright red coat with my blonde pigtailed daughter in it. But I saw nothing except adults who were all going about their business. Can they not see what is going on? How can they be so close and so unaware of my great despair? I wanted to scream. Instead, I began searching in other areas.

Relief almost overwhelmed me as I spotted her in the jeans section, quietly pulling off sizing labels. Our reunion and familiar speech over, I clutched her hand. We walked back through the store, past clerks who had been close enough to reach out but who were blind to my need.

I could not blame these women. Indeed, I wondered how many of the people who stood near me that day might have been experiencing great trauma and despair. Am I too busy counting out pennies and wishing a "Good day" to be aware of the great needs of those near me?

If we could only see the world through the Lord's eyes! May He help us to see the distressed and downcast around us and, seeing, offer the loving compassion of the Lord Jesus. DENISE S. HAMMER

NOVEMBER 15

Share My Roses

I am the true vine and my Father is the gardener. . . . No branch can bear fruit by itself; it must remain in the vine (JOHN 15:1, 4).

The home in which I am now living has *two* rose gardens. The owners grew roses for competition, so they are not your average garden variety. Actually, they are exquisite!

Before we rented this house, I knew nothing about the growing and tending of roses, but I am learning. And as I learn, the Holy Spirit is teaching me spiritual truths.

One day I accidentally clipped partway through a stem. The next day the stem had turned brown, and the leaves were dry and curling. It was no longer "remaining in the vine" and had begun to wither, so I removed it completely and threw it on the trash pile to be burned.

In learning how to prune roses, I found that I should not simply cut the canes haphazardly. Just the opposite. I had to carefully study the bush and locate the "bud eyes" (the beginning of new branches). I had to make the cuts precisely in order to shape the plant. I dared not take off too much, because it takes 25 to 35 leaves to support one bloom.

When the grower desires a perfect blossom, he must first disbud the bloom and remove all the secondary flower buds from the stem. There is really nothing wrong with the secondary buds, but they must be sacrificed so that they will not take the strength and nourishment needed to bring the primary bloom to its excellence.

And that is how the Lord works with us. "He cuts off every branch in me that bears no fruit, while every branch that does bear fruit he trims clean so that it will be even more fruitful" (15:2).   JOYCE CARNEFF

Watching over Me

I am with you and will watch over you wherever you go (GENESIS 28:15).

I was traveling between Peru's modern capital city of Lima and the high Andean metropolis of Huancayo. About half an hour outside Lima, at the first ID checkpoint, I was ordered out of my car.

In a small windowless room, the customs inspector questioned me. Seeing that I had no visa, he began threatening to jail me in Lima. At the time, my papers were in the hands of government officials for renewal, but I carried with me a letter authorizing me to travel without a visa. Because it was dated seven months earlier, the inspector rejected its validity. For 25 minutes we argued back and forth. He stubbornly insisted I was to be jailed. He would not permit me to phone either my husband in Huancayo or our field chairman in Lima.

The tiny room quickly filled with men as other buses and cars stopped for their ID inspection. All the men began yelling at the inspector, "Let this gringo woman go." "Oh, God," my heart cried out, "where are you? Don't you see that I am in trouble?" Large teardrops began silently rolling down my cheeks. At this, the inspector became visibly flustered. "Leave," he angrily sputtered at me.

An hour later, up the twisting highway, I understood the *why* of God's delay. A large vegetable truck had overturned, demolishing several cars. The accident had occurred approximately 25 minutes before we arrived at the scene. All the while, God had been quietly watching over me.

We are never alone, for His Word promises that He is always with us. Under His watchful eye, His children can walk without fear. MARILYN SMITH

The Way to Peace

Great peace have they who love your law, and nothing can make them stumble (PSALM 119:165).

Perhaps you thought that with the passing of the years would come the diminishing of problems. Think again! The Lord has admonished us to bear fruit in old age; but remember, in order to bear fruit, trees have to be pruned and sprayed, as well as watered and nurtured. It is not only in the nurturing and watering, but also in the fighting of adverse elements and in the submission to the pruning knife that the fruit comes.

As we grow older and more set in our ways, it is easy to become frustrated, defeated and soured by the little things that we allow to fester. We need to learn to cast them upon the Lord and to say, "Lord, that is *your* problem." The solution rests with Him, not in our chafing attempts at righting the wrong.

Someone has said, "We cannot be hurt by things; we can only be hurt by our reaction to them." How often we have to remind ourselves of this when someone unjustly (we feel) criticizes us, when we see others at our places of employment "get by" with wasted time, when someone else receives the praise for what we have done, when situations arise which disturb our neat little schedule, when fellow church members fail to pull their share of the load and when friends and family do things that wear our patience thin.

David expresses this so beautifully when he says, "Great peace have they who love your law." If we abide in God's Word and live in obedience to it, we can trust the Lord to help us not to stumble over the little things.   RUTH MARTIN

Have Faith in God

"Have faith in God," Jesus answered (MARK 11:22).

During World War 2, my missionary husband and I were working in French territory in West Africa. Walter carried a British passport and was detained under house arrest. An American, I was allowed to leave the country — alone.

One night as I prayed, I sensed that the Lord would enable both Walter and me to leave via the Gold Coast. I was so happy that as I packed my suitcase, I begged Walter to pack his. He refused, knowing that he would be arrested for trying to leave. He was, however, permitted to accompany the children and me to the border.

As we traveled to the border town by truck, it began to rain. I held the baby in the cab, but the others were in the back of the truck with no covering but a tarpaulin.

Cold and wet, we spent that night in an inn. Worse than the physical discomfort was the ache in my heart. I had not received permission for Walter to leave with us, and I felt my Lord had let me down. The following morning the children and I got into a small boat and were taken into English territory.

A short time later, I was taken to a hospital. One night I felt sure I was dying, and I cried out to God. His message to me was, "Have faith in God." The next day, the children rushed into my room saying, "Daddy is coming tomorrow!" I was so weak I began to cry, and my son, David, said, "I thought you would be happy, but here you are crying!"

The Lord had enabled Walter to escape and to join me and the children. Eventually we were able to come back to America via the Gold Coast, just as the Lord had promised me.   FLORENCE ARNOLD

NOVEMBER **19**

His Presence

Then the Lord said, "There is a place near me where you may stand on a rock. When my glory passes by, I will put you in a cleft in the rock and cover you (EXODUS 33:21–22).

D o you ever feel that God has placed you in a cold, hard rock cleft? Many times as we look around at our circumstances, we see only the hardships—financial problems, physical ailments and even spiritual struggles in our relationship with God and with others.

Much of our prayer time is spent pleading for God to change our problems. Instead, we need to acknowledge that He has placed us in our present circumstances. He is covering us with His hand (verse 22). When we realize that even in the cleft of the rock we are in His presence, we will be able to look up and see His glory (verse 23).

When my children were infants, I would sometimes sit by their cribs if they were sick. Often, they would wake up from a restless nap and begin to cry. They had not opened their eyes to see me sitting there, and in their loneliness they cried. When they noticed me, their tears immediately stopped as they smiled and reached out their arms to me.

We are so often like children. I picture our Father, God, waiting patiently for us to acknowledge that He is right beside us all the time.

He does not demand our thanks for His protecting hand, but He deserves our praise. Today, may we look up and out of our daily routine to see God's love and plan for our lives. Let us thank Him that His hand of protection is always over us—even when we do not see it.   NANCY W. WONG

Willing to Receive

Each one should use whatever gift he has received to serve others, . . . so that in all things God may be praised through Jesus Christ (1 PETER 4:10–11).

How often have you read this passage or heard a sermon on the topic of spiritual gifts? It is one thing to discover our gift and use it to minister to others. It is quite another thing to allow someone to use his gift in ministering to us.

As young newlyweds we wanted to be independent of our parents' help. So when our water heater had to be replaced and my father-in-law offered his financial aid, we quickly refused. I did not understand at that time that he had a real gift of giving. As the years have gone by, I have seen that in order for a person to exercise the gift of giving, I may have to humble myself and receive the gift.

This is the beauty of the body of Christ as it is described in 1 Corinthians 12. Each of us has special gifts and also great weaknesses. It is not a sign of immaturity to admit that we do not "have it all together." Indeed, a strong person is one who admits she is weak in certain areas and needs the body of Christ to help her.

Jesus used people to accomplish His work. Not that He could not do it without us, but that He chooses to work through us. The question is: Are we willing to allow others to minister to us?   DORI MITCHELL

Reach Out

I thank my God every time I remember you . . . I always pray with joy because of your partnership in the gospel (PHILIPPIANS 1:3–5).

It was mail day, the highlight of a missionary's week. Excited, I flipped through the letters we had received. Noting one from a good friend, I tore it open first. Her letter was bound to cheer me up this lonely Thanksgiving week. My thoughts had turned to our families in the States and to our children who were still in boarding school awaiting the Christmas vacation.

But this time, instead of the usual chuckles and smiles, her words brought tears. I cried, but nevertheless I was left with a warm feeling.

She understands me! God gave her to me to be a partner in my ministry. She is the one who unfailingly offers encouragement when I am tired, lonely or depressed.

To whom can you be a partner? Do you know someone with whom you could share the burden of reaching those overseas who need to hear about Christ's offer of salvation?

FRAN CORBY

A Special Promise

So do not fear, for I am with you; do not be dismayed, for I am your God. I will strengthen you and help you; I will uphold you with my righteous right hand (ISAIAH 41:10).

God's Word can bring new strength and courage as we read and meditate upon it each day. Many years ago, when we were about to enter a new kind of ministry, the Lord gave me this special promise.

Do not fear. "Fear not, for I have redeemed you; I have called you by name; you are mine" (Isaiah 43:1).

I am with you. "When you pass through the waters, I will be with you; and when you pass through the rivers, they will not sweep over you" (Isaiah 43:2).

Do not be dismayed. "Lift your eyes and look to the heavens: Who created all these? He who brings out the starry host one by one, and calls them each by name" (Isaiah 40:26).

I am your God. "For I am the Lord, your God, the Holy One of Israel, your Savior" (Isaiah 43:3).

I will strengthen you. "He gives strength to the weary and increases the power of the weak. . . . But those who hope in the Lord will renew their strength" (Isaiah 40:29, 31).

And help you. "This is what the Lord says—he who made you, who formed you in the womb, and who will help you" (Isaiah 44:2). "Do not fear; I will help you" (Isaiah 41:13b).

I will uphold you. "You whom I have upheld since you were conceived and have carried since your birth" (Isaiah 46:3).

With my righteous right hand. "You stretch out your hand against the anger of my foes, with your right hand you save me" (Psalm 138:7).

How can we doubt or despair when we have His "very great and precious promises"?   HELEN G. MCGARVEY

His Stubborn Love

Because he loves me . . . . I will rescue him; I will protect him, for he acknowledges my name. He will call upon me, . . . and I will deliver him and honor him (PSALM 91:14–15).

From early childhood I was aware of the love of God drawing me to Himself. I can recall looking up into the sky and saying, "God, I can't see You, but I know You are there, and I wish I could know You." Reading the book, *In His Steps*, by H.M. Sheldon, only deepened my longing. I cried out, "If I am of any value to you, if you can use me, lead me to where I will find what my heart longs for."

His love drew me to the very church to which I determined I would never go, because I believed they were "holy rollers." On my third visit, I received Christ.

After being rejected for missionary service on three occasions, I told the Lord I would never apply again. When God spoke from Isaiah 52:12, I said that if He wanted me on the field, He would have to push me out. When He began to do that, I was full of excuses—I was too old to learn the language, I was in poor health, etc. etc. Convinced that the Lord was leading, I began to follow, but with reservations. "Lord, unless You give me my boat fare all in one lump sum, I still will not go."

I was speaking at a midweek service in a small-town church. I was not acquainted with any of its members. There were only a few people in attendance, among them a young lady who had saved money to go to Bible school but felt moved by God to give it to me. How I wept that night, not tears of joy but of sorrow. His stubborn love had won.

I went to the land of His choosing, and the land became my home. The only place where we can know complete fulfillment is in the center of God's will.   PEARL FUSTEY

Those in the Boat

Immediately Jesus reached out his hand and caught him. "You of little faith," he said, "why did you doubt?" (MATTHEW 14:31).

If there was ever a point in Peter's life when he wanted to do nothing more than to enjoy the presence of the Lord, this was it! But Jesus had other plans. In essence Jesus was telling Peter that though he felt that the test was over, one vital question still remained. He wanted Peter to face up to the problem of "Why did you doubt?" Peter had to answer that question, even if only in his heart. He had to realize that doubt had gained a foothold when his eyes had strayed from Jesus to conditions around him.

The wind on which Peter had focused was a very real problem. It continued throughout the whole exchange between Jesus and Peter. But when they were back in the boat, it ceased. The Lord could have stopped the wind at any point. He chose, however, to allow that wind to continue until the whole issue of faith versus doubt was settled.

Those in the boat saw it all. They knew Peter—and his doubts. They also knew the Lord. They had the opportunity to be spectators as the Lord Jesus did a mighty work in a very human man. Perhaps they needed to know that God honors our individual differences by answering prayers specifically in a way that will strengthen our faith. Or maybe they were having doubts, deep within their hearts, that they had been ashamed to admit. Whatever their condition, they all came to the same response: worship!

We are not placed on this earth to be hermit Christians. We benefit each other when we walk, sink, rise and worship together. Even in his sinking moments, Peter's experience helped those on the boat to come to a deeper understanding of the power of God.   RUTH H. HOOVER

Follow an Example

My heart says of you, "Seek his face!" Your face, Lord, I will seek (PSALM 27:8).

Mother's life was characterized by deliberate and quick obedience to the voice of the Lord. Her total commitment to that One greater than herself caused her to be expendable in His service. It never occurred to her to "fulfill herself." In her giving, God filled her full. As her daughters, Caroll and I saw the peace and joy produced by that kind of self-denial and self-sacrifice.

The message of Mother's life had an even greater impact in her later years after the accident which took our father's life and left her a dependent invalid. Though we would not have chosen the particular path we walked then, together we proved continuously that "Every path he guides us on is fragrant with his loving kindness and his truth" (Psalm 25:10, TLB). Loving kindness was expressed often through the prayers and concerns of our denominational family. Truth was increasingly confirmed and affirmed in Mother's life and experience. He is worthy to be trusted. Her response to the tragedy that radically changed her life was expressed often: "God has been good to me all my life — except for this one thing — and I have decided not to hold this against Him. There is nothing but goodness in Him."

In a notebook of thoughts and gleanings she was completing for me, she wrote on the first page, "Our children too shall serve him, for they shall hear from us about the wonders of the Lord" (Psalm 22:30, TLB).

This indeed has been our heritage. Mother was a woman who lived in His presence and shared His wonders with us. As a result, we love Him!   JOYCE BAILEY SECKINGER

He Promises Peace

You will keep in perfect peace him whose mind is steadfast, because he trusts in you (ISAIAH 26:3).

As my husband wheeled me into the so-called maternity building of an African hospital to await delivery of our third child, I prayed, "Oh, Lord, give me peace." We had been told the hospital was the best in the area, and we were thankful for the experienced Canadian missionary doctor and also for the British pediatrician who would be on hand if needed.

Everything around me shouted, "Is this real? Is this really happening to me? Are those walls and floors as dirty as they look? *Sterile* is a lost word here. Surely the delivery room must be cleaner."

The ground level windows, some of which had screens, wore dirty tan-colored curtains and were open to the world outside. Not only did the surroundings scream of filth and germs, but I seemed to be the central attraction of the morning. Our African sisters were inquisitive to see if we actually have babies just as they do, and people were treating our room like Grand Central Station.

Through all this confusion, God filled me with His peace. The doctor arrived on time and put a stop to all the extra traffic. Our daughter, Rachel, was born within the hour—lovely, pink and squalling.

Later when they wrapped all 6 pounds, 4 ounces of little Rachel in a type of old dropcloth, I just had to laugh. The Lord protected her, and today we are back at our mission station and she is doing well.

God gave us peace in the circumstances that were filled with confusion. He promises it, if we keep our minds on Him. DIANE FINNEMORE

Giving Thanks

T   *Thankful* — "Thanks be to God for his indescribable gift" (2 Corinthians 9:15).

H   *Helping* — "As you help us by your prayers. Then many will give thanks on our behalf" (2 Corinthians 1:11).

A   *All things* — "Always giving thanks to God the Father for everything" (Ephesians 5:20).

N   *Noised abroad* — "Proclaiming aloud your praise and telling of all your wonderful deeds" (Psalm 26:7).

K   *Knowledge* — "But thanks be to God, who always leads us in triumphal procession in Christ and through us spreads everywhere the fragance of the knowledge of him" (2 Corinthians 2:14).

S   *Sacrifice* — "I will sacrifice a thank offering to you" (Psalm 116:17).

G   *Grace* — "All this is for your benefit, so that the grace that is reaching more and more people may cause thanksgiving to overflow" (2 Corinthians 4:15).

I   *Individuals* — "I always thank God for you because of his grace given you in Christ Jesus" (1 Corinthians 1:4).

V   *Victory* — "But thanks be to God! He gives us the victory through our Lord Jesus Christ" (1 Corinthians 15:57).

I   *I* (personal pronoun) — "I thank Christ Jesus our Lord, who has given *me* strength, . . . appointing *me* to his service" (1 Timothy 1:12).

N   *No anxiety* — "Do not be anxious about anything, but in everything, by prayer and petition, with thanksgiving, present your requests to God" (Philippians 4:6).

G   *Gladness* — "Joy and gladness will be found in her, thanksgiving and the sound of singing" (Isaiah 51:3).

JANET C. JONES

Free to Forgive

*Now instead, you ought to forgive and comfort him . . . I urge you,
therefore, to reaffirm your love for him* (2 CORINTHIANS 2:7–8).

The man was proud of his children. For years he and his
wife had worked hard, even sacrificed, to give them a
good life. Now the children were all grown, and one by one
they were being married. His oldest son and his wife were
expecting their first child, the first grandchild. The old
man was so excited that he could hardly wait. He thought,
Surely, this child will be a boy, and they will name him after me.
This had become a family tradition. The oldest grandson
was always named after his grandfather.

When the first grandchild was born, it was a boy—but
the child was not named after his grandfather. The old man
was deeply hurt. His disappointment became anger and
festered in him until finally, he confronted his son. There
was a bitter argument. Harsh words flew back and forth
between the two men, and then they parted. For 15 years
the grandfather did not speak to his son or see his grandson.

We say, "How sad. How tragic that a hurt could go so
deep or have such damaging results."

Forgiveness has two inseparable sides—the forgiveness
each of us needs from God and the forgiveness we owe to
others.

With God's help, we can forgive the worst offense. Jesus
is the supreme example of the ability to forgive. He drew
from God the power to excuse his murderers. This same
resource is available to us, and it will make the difference.
When we are hurt to the point of becoming bitter, we need
only ask God for His help. At the very point where our
strength fails, God's power takes over.   JOYCE STRECKER

Unquenchable Joy!

I am coming to you now, but I say these things while I am still in the world, so that they may have the full measure of my joy within them (JOHN 17:13).

What produced that inner, unquenchable joy in the "man of sorrows, and familiar with suffering"? Just prior to His crucifixion, Jesus prayed that His disciples might experience that same fullness of joy.

Exhorting His followers to produce the fruit of love and of obedience to His commandments, He added, "I have told you this so that my joy may be in you and that your joy may be complete" (John 15:11). Jesus' statement reveals that understanding the principles involved in spiritual fruit bearing is absolutely essential to our joy. To view fruit-bearing from God's perspective—His will, His purpose, His ways—will produce the kind of joy Jesus experienced.

Proverbs 3:13–20 graphically depicts the joy derived from wisdom and understanding. Learning spiritual truths is exciting. The disciples on the road to Emmaus testified: "Were not our hearts burning within us while he talked with us on the road and opened the Scriptures to us?" (Luke 24:32).

Personal knowledge of God and His ways is the prerequisite to experiencing Jesus' joy! Once we know that joy does not depend on what happens to us, but rather on what we know about God, we are released from our circumstances, and His joy is channeled to us through the Word.

HALEE SPRIGGINS

NOVEMBER **30**

Their Works Follow Them

And as for you, brothers, never tire of doing what is right (2 THES-SALONIANS 3:13).

We live in the wake of good deeds done by Christians who lived before us. Our good deeds and acts of kindness, too, are not done in a vacuum but in a world of interaction where their effects will go on and on.

On the mission field we live and minister in the wake of Christians who never tired of doing good. The harvests we reap, the hospitals where we receive care and the understanding attitude of government officials are ours because of a few who served God with small and, to them, inconsequential deeds.

The Bible tells us our good works not only benefit others, they also follow us. Recently I had a very vivid reminder of this truth. At Christmas, the Christian dry cleaner who provides door-to-door service on his motorbike, was severely burned in a fire that also cost him his daughter and his business. As a community of believers, we responded with prayer, money and clothing.

The first day he was back at work, I slipped a canned chicken into his backpack along with the clothes so that his wife, who was also injured, would not have to cook dinner.

Some time later we noticed that he had tagged our returned clothing with a strange I.D. — "chicken meat." He could not remember our name, but he remembered that one act of kindness and marked us by it.

As we have opportunities to show kindness to others, let us use them joyfully, as gifts of ministry to the Lord that will follow us into eternity. CINDI STRONG

DECEMBER 1

God's Promises

God is not a man, that he should lie, nor a son of man, that he should change his mind. Does he speak and then not act? Does he promise and not fulfill? (NUMBERS 23:19–20).

Life has many changing seasons to which we must make adjustments; yet, no matter in what season we find ourselves, God's Word remains steadfast, unchangeable and true. He does not promise and then not fulfill. Sarah laughed when the angel of the Lord promised her a son in her advanced years. *Will I really have a child, now that I am old?* she thought. Nevertheless, we read in Genesis 21:1 that "The Lord did for Sarah what he had promised."

The Bible is full of God's promises to us as Christians. We have the promise of the comfort of God's divine presence in trials (Isaiah 43:2). He gives courage in life's battles (Deuteronomy 20:1), sufficiency of divine grace (2 Corinthians 12:9), answers to prayer (Mark 11:24), power for service (John 14:12) and removal of obstacles (Luke 17:6). The list is long. What has God promised you today?

Are you laughing with unbelief, as Sarah did, at the promise God has given you? Though it may seem at times that God is slow in keeping His promise, Second Peter 3:9 gives us assurance that this is not so. He is faithful to *all* His promises (Psalm 145:13). If He has given you His promise, then stand boldly in His presence. Believe God that by faith you *will* receive as He promised even when you cannot perceive Him! MARILYN SMITH

Wet Feet

Immediately Jesus reached out his hand and caught him. "You of little faith," he said, "why did you doubt?" (Matthew 14:31).

Do you wish to overcome your fear of life's storms? The order of the action in Matthew 14:29 teaches us the pattern to follow. *"Come,"* He said. This first step we take in the midst of our storms is only to be taken at Christ's word. We often get the order backward, and begin on our own. Only when in the throes of drowning do we try desperately to hear the Lord's voice of direction.

Some may criticize Peter for his dramatic request. God knows the heart, and He allows us to have different ways of experiencing His power. Peter, being Peter, was impetuous. Sometimes this attribute got him into trouble, but this time the Lord knew that he was asking the big, the unusual, as a test of his faith. It was an issue of faith versus doubt. He gave no voice to the doubt, but in faith said, "Lord, if it is you, tell me to come to you on the water."

And Jesus said, "Come." He always welcomes those who come in faith! Peter put feet to his faith; God supplied the missing ingredients, and Peter walked toward his Lord.

Faith was winning, but doubt was only dormant, not dead. Peter began to have "eye trouble." Because he took his eyes off Jesus, he saw the boistrous waves. He then did the best thing he could have done. He admitted his doubts. "Lord, save me!" Peter was not a stranger to the Lord. It was not as though he was in trouble and decided to call on the name of the "Miracle Worker." No, this was friend calling friend. Immediately Jesus' hand was there, and comfort was in the touch of the only One who could help Peter at that point — the One who was walking on the same water with him!   RUTH H. HOOVER

DECEMBER 3

In His Image

Then God said, "Let us make man in our image, in our likeness,"
... in the image of God he created him; male and female he created
them (GENESIS 1:26–27).

We are blessed, are we not, to be created in God's image? Sometimes, though, when we look into a mirror, we might wonder! My nine-year-old daughter spends more time than I care to relate in front of the mirror, curling iron and brush in hand. This bathroom clog-up usually takes place on Sunday morning when we are all scrambling to get ready for Sunday school and church. What will it be like when she is a teenager!

This crazy world in which we live overemphasizes the outward beauty of face and figure. We are trying to teach our children to give God His rightful glory as the Creator of all things. In Psalm 139:13 and 14 we are told, "For you created my inmost being; you knit me together in my mother's womb. I praise you because I am fearfully and wonderfully made; your works are wonderful, I know that full well." Our precious little girl who gazes into that mirror is one of those fearfully and wonderfully made works of God!

Imagine, before he or she is born, each tiny infant has been shaped and molded by the mighty hand of God. "For we [notice the personal pronoun] are God's workmanship, created in Christ Jesus to do good works" (Ephesians 2:10). I do not know about you, but that makes me want to love, worship and adore a Savior who does all things well.

He deserves all our praise today, for we are His children, His image, His likeness! MARYANN SCHULER

DECEMBER 4

Our Loving God

Jesus replied: "Love the Lord your God with all your heart and with all your soul and with all your mind" (MATTHEW 22:37).

Sometimes we may think we are acting out of love for God, when in reality we may have an entirely different motive. I was made keenly aware of this as I prepared to return to Africa. After an exciting furlough in the States, I found it embarrassing when people asked if I was eager to return. They obviously expected an affirmative response. My conscience would not permit me to lie, and I tried to analyze why I was not looking forward to returning.

My imagination came up with the analogy of an experienced soldier who has been on the front lines; he has no illusions about what it is like out there. Having experienced the sting of defeat as well as the thrill of victory, he is not anxious to get back, but he knows that is where his job is. He would have no peace if he was to stay at home. This is how I felt. It is my job out there.

That explanation was satisfactory until God spoke to me through the words of Paul: "Endure hardship with us like a good soldier of Christ Jesus. No one serving as a soldier gets involved in civilian affairs — he wants to please his commanding officer" (2 Timothy 2:3–4).

It was the verb "to please" that stood out to me. God said, "Your return should be an expression of your love to Me and not of your sense of duty. Endure hardship because you love Me more than home, family, friends and ease." I repented of my coldness and hardness of heart.

One can be in the geographical center of God's will and yet not be in the proper relationship with Him. To seek to please God with heart, soul and mind — this should be our greatest motive in all that we do.   HALEE SPRIGGINS

The Hard Way

Give thanks in all circumstances, for this is God's will for you in Christ Jesus (1 THESSALONIANS 5:18).

Our Lord teaches us many valuable lessons through our everyday situations and circumstances. We should thank Him for each situation, even an unpleasant one, for that is His command.

The instruction to "Give thanks" is an important one. In this way we say, "OK, Lord. Even though I don't really understand it, I thank You for this situation, for You have a lesson to teach me, and I am ready to learn." We are allowing God freedom to work His will *in* us so that He can work *through* us. "For it is God who works in you to will and to act according to his good purpose" (Philippians 2:13).

God teaches us at the most unexpected times — unexpected to us but not to Him. One evening, while I was driving to school to pick up our boys from basketball practice, it began snowing rather hard. The scenery was very beautiful, and as I looked about, I was fascinated with the tire tracks that were being left behind in the snow. I did not think I had looked that long; however, when I glanced forward again I was headed for the soft snow at the side of the road. At that point I felt like such a "dodo." I asked the Lord's forgiveness for being so careless. Immediately I thought of Philippians 3:13–14, "But one thing I do: Forgetting what is behind . . . I press on toward the goal." So I continued toward my goal of picking up our sons and no longer checked behind to see where I had been.

I am amazed, yet so thankful, that the Lord is *always* ready to teach us lessons. My desire is to be teachable. Is that your desire also?   YVONNE DAVEY

DECEMBER 6

With You Always

Teaching them to obey everything I have commanded you. And surely I will be with you always, to the very end of the age (MATTHEW 28:20).

My husband and I were serving as missionaries in the jungle interior of Kalimantan (formerly Borneo), Indonesia. I was alone at home with our four-month-old daughter. I had left her lying in the playpen in the bedroom and went to check on her. As I brushed the side of the bassinet ruffle I suddenly heard a hiss. Startled, I saw a large black cobra dart out and slither down to the floor. It came toward me. I backed up—the snake followed. I took another step backward—he followed.

Just like a flash came the words, "I will be with you always." I did not want that deadly serpent to go near the baby, so I kept backing up, all the while staring at it. The cobra reared its head and prepared to strike at me. Quickly I backed out of the doorway into the next room but kept my eyes fixed on it. Finally the snake disappeared under a wardrobe. Then, with flashlight in one hand and a dyak machete in the other, I got down to search for it.

I could not locate the cobra. In the somewhat crudely built house in which we lived, he could have escaped through any one of the holes in the wall or floor. But I could not know for sure.

One thing I did know for sure was Christ's glorious promise of His continual presence, and upon that promise I stood. It was not *my* feeling that made His promise sure; it was *His* infinite faithfulness.   MARY POST

Rejoice!

Rejoice in the Lord always. I will say it again: Rejoice! (PHILIPPI-
ANS 4:4).

Is it not fun to be with people who are happy? What a contrast they are to those who are continually fretting about this, that or the other thing.

I wonder how the Lord feels when He sees His children fussing about all sorts of things, especially the trivial circumstances that seem to grow out of proportion in our minds. Do you sometimes find yourself "under the circumstances"? It is hard to be happy when it is raining and you were hoping for sunshine, or when your washing machine breaks down midway through a large laundry, and all the towels are sopping wet. Or what about when you had planned to accomplish so much, and interruptions—one after another—eat away your time? Perhaps your anxieties are brought on by bigger, more threatening situations. Perhaps it is a financial problem, health difficulties or anxiety about safety for one reason or another.

Our Heavenly Father made us, and He knows us. He knows we are subject to weakness and worry. Does He let us just struggle with them? No, He tells us, "Do not be anxious about anything, but in everything, by prayer and petition, with thanksgiving, present your requests to God" (Philippians 4:6).

Like Peter (Matthew 14:25–32), we can learn to "be on top" of our problems by keeping our eyes on the Lord, or we can sink into them by focusing on the waves of trouble that threaten to overwhelm us. When anxiety threatens to inundate us, if we turn our eyes to our Heavenly Father and pray with thanksgiving and praise, He gives peace that passes all understanding.   MARIAN KEIDEL

Always Alert

The Sovereign Lord has given me an instructed tongue, to know the word that sustains the weary. He wakens me morning by morning, wakens my ear to listen like one being taught. (ISAIAH 50:4).

It is a humbling thought that the God of the universe would condescend to speak His wisdom "morning by morning" into our ears. For what purpose? That we will know how to speak the word that will sustain those who are weary.

How vital it is to have an attentive ear to hear God's instruction. We have no way of knowing each day who will cross our path needing the word of encouragement that will help to banish weariness. People are weary of the battle with sin, either in their own lives or the life of someone close to them; they are weary of the cares and perplexities of life. Problems and worries abound! It is important that we have an "instructed tongue" and a special word from God.

David said, "Morning by morning, O Lord, you hear my voice; morning by morning I lay my requests before you and wait in expectation" (Psalm 5:3). We should meet the Lord each morning, listen to Him and receive His counsel and wisdom for the day.

Just think! We may be God's instrument to ease another's load, not because we are so wise or have all the right answers, but because day by day we have heard directly from the One who is the "wisdom of God" (1 Corinthians 1:24). When we listen, we can be sure that we will have that "instructed tongue," and we shall know the "word that sustains."

MARIAN E. PAYNE

DECEMBER 9

Priorities

Then I said, "Here I am — it is written about me in the scroll — I have come to do your will, O God" (HEBREWS 10:7).

Jesus gave Himself freely in ministry to people. Whether in the synagogue or private homes, He met people's needs. He was not a recluse, but He did spend much time alone with His Father. Although He worked late, He arose early in order to pray.

Because He did this, Jesus was able to keep His priorities straight. Instead of being pressured by the crowd, He knew why He was here and stuck to that purpose. He purposely avoided the acclaim of the crowds much of the time, because His eyes were focused on His Father. He came to do His Father's will, and He ascertained the details of that will in prayer. Because He was careful to put fellowship with His Father first, the other details of His life were kept in proper perspective. He knew God's will and had the power to carry it out.

Are we ever unsure of God's specific will in our circumstances? Does the pressure from others dictate our decisions and our ministry? Are we sometimes so busy serving that we do not have time to communicate with God as we should? Do we sometimes get sidetracked from His purpose for us by people who press us into doing the things that seem needful to them?

Jesus got up very early and prayed in a solitary place. Even his closest companions were left behind. We, too, need to be alone with God, to hear His voice above the noise of the crowd, so that we can know the details of His specific will for us. Then our priorities will be kept straight, and we will have the time and energy to do the things He wants us to do.   LINDA MCKELVEY

Joy, Real Joy

With joy you will draw water from the wells of salvation (ISAIAH 12:3).

During the rainy season in Thailand, weary people, bucket in hand, would crowd around a well just outside our town and wait for the water to seep into the well a cupful at a time. What a contrast we found when we visited in Lebanon. We drove up into the mountains above Beirut, where cool, clear water constantly gushed from a spring. I drank and felt so alive! The water reminded me that Jesus, our salvation, is the water of life. He who drinks of His water shall never thirst. So with joy we may draw water!

Why is this joy so important? Joy is a gift from God. To be healthy spiritually and physically, we need this joy. It is not dependent on circumstances. We cannot always be extremely pleased with our circumstances, but we are responsible to be committed to God's will in all things. It is the will, not the emotions, that determines whether or not we have joy. It was when Jesus was facing death that He passed on to His disciples His legacy of joy.

What is required of us in order to draw water from the well of salvation? Naturally we must have a place to put it. Our Lord will not pour water into a dirty cup. Worry, stubbornness, bitterness, resentment and a critical nature can fill our lives so that the living water cannot be poured in. We have to *want* to draw water! We have to be thirsty and bring our need to the One who can supply this water.

The surest way to find joy is not to seek it just for our own satisfaction. We will find the joy we are looking for when we forget ourselves. Yet for us to possess this joy is most important both to us and to those who observe us. It is a compelling evidence that we are His!   MARION KERR

Just Ask!

Pray continually (1 THESSALONIANS 5:17).

Pray continually? Every second, every minute? But we have work to do. We have to get on with the business of the day. Is it not true that if our hearts are in tune with God's heart it is possible to maintain a prayerful spirit throughout the day? Then, when a need arises, our hearts can quickly respond to the need with a prayer for God's help. How many of us have heard news broadcasts which could mean danger for our missionaries and have immediately prayed and asked God for His divine protection?

When we pray continually, we are obeying the scriptural injunction to "[make] the most of every opportunity" (Ephesians 5:16). We take advantage of every chance to pray, to worship, to serve and to witness. The days are evil, and we need to surround our families with a hedge of prayer.

As part of our continual prayer, we are told to "Ask and it will be given to you" (Matthew 7:7). Just ask! We have a Heavenly Father who is more than willing to give us the desires of our hearts. If we really do believe His promises, we will ask.

The time we have left to pray may be shorter than we think. In Hebrews 10:37 we read, "For in just a very little while, He who is coming will come and will not delay." We are now over 1,900 years closer to His return than when the writer to the Hebrews made this statement under the inspiration of God's Holy Spirit. We have that much *less* time to pray. May we truly pray "continually."   BETTY PEACE

DECEMBER 12

Life's Book

So then, each of us will give an account of himself to God (ROMANS 14:12).

Carl F. Fischbach penned the following verses in tribute to my father upon his homegoing. What kind of book are *you* writing? Will it please our Master?

> Perhaps you are writing a diary,
>   A history of days going by,
> An aid and a help to your memory:
>   So swiftly the days seem to fly.
>
> To each a white book is given
>   On which we may write, as we will,
> The thoughts of our hearts and its victories,
>   With something each page we must fill.
>
> We know not how long we'll be writing,
>   How large is the size of our book,
> How soon the last page will be written,
>   Handed in for the Master to look.
>
> How precious should be the last pages,
>   Let life's story be bright as the sun
> That the Master, when closing the cover,
>   May say to the writer, "Well done!"

SUZANNE RICH

Occupy Till I Come

And he called his ten servants, and delivered them ten pounds, and said unto them, Occupy till I come (LUKE 19:13, KJV).

In South China there is a certain hilltop that holds special memories for a host of Chinese Christians as well as former missionaries to the area. It was there that the Alliance Bible School was located, through whose halls strode a succession of such teachers and leaders as Robert Jaffray, Silas Wong, Walter Oldfield and William Newbern.

From the foot of the hill, a winding path and a series of 100 steps led to the top where for many years the Alliance Guest Home welcomed visitors to this inland province.

During our early years in China, we lived in the guest home. There we learned the language. There, even though we often had to take refuge from Japanese air raids, our children enjoyed security. From that vantage point we observed the increasing threat of communism.

When we finally left, we were grieved by the message of a large motto on the living room wall, "Occupy Till I Come." Here we were, running away. The answer to my "Why, Lord?" seemed to be that one can "occupy" anywhere — not just on this Wuchow hilltop.

Not long ago, my daughter and her family returned to that hillside and to that house. Things had changed; rooms had shrunk. The motto was gone, but in the city a congregation of Christians was still meeting. The travelers met several active pastors who had known her as a little girl. At one place they surprised a group of 30 Christians being taught by a martyred pastor's aged widow.

Praise God. The Word is still going out and "occupying" will continue *"till He comes."*   FLORENCE B. HOLTON

New Garments

The oil of gladness instead of mourning, and a garment of praise instead of a spirit of despair (ISAIAH 61:3).

The heated discussion with my husband had left me irritable and weary. Feeling guilty about always wanting to be right, I found it hard to pray. As I closed my eyes, a scene began to develop.

Our large walk-in closet became the stage. The articles of clothing seemed to represent my life: the dresses represented my surface appearance — no one could see my inner pride, jealousy, hate; the shoes evidenced my tendency to walk in the flesh; the hats said that my mind was not always in submission to the Holy Spirit; scarves and other accessories represented all the extra things that clutter my life.

As I looked at the clothes, I saw my life with absolute clarity. Then an amazing thing happened. Jesus Himself walked into that closet. Unseen hands began to pack the entire contents into boxes and to carry them away.

Finished, Jesus looked at me. Though I did not speak audibly, He understood that I accepted the removal of the clothes. But now I needed something to wear. He seemed pleased and began to fill the closet with garments of His own choosing — garments of righteousness.

The scene over, I was at peace. The next morning as I tried to relate the experience to my husband, tears came in torrents.

Only a dream? I am not sure, but my life has been different since that night. Jesus is still teaching me that I do not have to wear the old garments of the flesh, but daily in my prayer closet I may put on the garments of righteousness that He has provided for me.   JOAN S. COFFEY

The Safest Place

Uphold me, and I will be delivered; I will always have regard for your decrees (PSALM 119:117).

Remember how thankful you were the last time you came through a hair-raising experience unscathed? Safety is something that most of us take for granted, that is, until it is tested.

Trust, like everything else, is learned through practical experience. Recently, I had a very productive "practice" session. My husband was scheduled to fly to Chicago. We awoke at 5:00 a.m. to a howling, icy snowstorm. Limousine service had been suspended, which meant that we had to drive the 30 miles to New York's LaGuardia Airport.

Normally I am not afraid of icy roads, but that morning I felt uneasy. My unrest intensified when, a few miles from the airport, the windshield wiper on the driver's side broke from the weight of the ice.

As I left Richard at the passenger departure section, I knew he was praying for my safety. I drove cautiously out of the airport, unable to see if I was even on the right road. Another attempt to encourage the broken wiper was futile. Slipping back into the driver's seat, I wailed aloud, "I'm never going to make it home!" Then came the quiet voice from within. "Can't you trust Me for this?"

Yes, I decided that I would trust, and the feeling of panic left me. Even though it was a difficult two-hour journey through flooded, icy roads with limited visibility, I was able to remain calm. By the time I reached my doorstep I was singing and shouting my thankfulness.

When the Lord upholds and delivers us in our times of emergency, it is not only so that we will be safe but that we will learn more and more about how trustworthy He is!

CAROLYN BUSH

Discipleship

Then Jesus said to his disciples, "If anyone would come after me, he must deny himself and take up his cross and follow me" (MATTHEW 16:24).

What does it mean to be a real disciple? The quest for answers led me through the Scriptures.

John 10:14–15. We are known by Christ. We are not lost in the crowd; we are important. So we should not allow Christ to become lost in the clutter of our lives.

Matthew 16:24–25. Being a disciple means denying ourselves and putting Christ first. This is a difficult task and takes continual effort.

John 10:27. Jesus said that His sheep listen to His voice and follow Him. Do we? If we truly love Him, we will want to follow His leading and direction.

Luke 14:26. Discipleship means putting Christ before husband, parents, friends.

1 Peter 2:21. Discipleship involves suffering. In this we are to follow Christ's example.

Colossians 3:10. As disciples, we are to fashion our lives according to the plan of God. As our knowledge of God increases, we strive to make our actions conform to His Word.

1 John 2:6. Discipleship means walking, talking and acting like Jesus.

As Christians, we desire to obey all the instructions that pertain to discipleship, but at times they seem very difficult. We surely cannot do it in our own strength, but the Holy Spirit will come alongside us to help us as we yield to His leading.   REBECCA STEINER

A New Song

I will sing for the one I love (ISAIAH 5:1).

Beginning back when I was a small girl, music has played an important part in my life. My earliest memories include hearing the sound of singing that came from the room where my grandmother lay dying. They were singing words that went something like this: "One more day, Lord, only one more day; then I will see Your face, Lord, then I will see Your face." I can remember that I was not afraid. I sensed that what was happening in that room could not be so bad if they were singing about it.

Later, with an older cousin, I attended Sunday school for the first time. I remember singing, "Have you ever been lonely, have you ever been blue?" Apparently no one had cautioned me that you were supposed to sing "Jesus Loves Me." I recall hearing my mother sing "What a Friend We Have in Jesus" as she built a fire in the woodstove to prepare breakfast for the family. This gave me a real sense of security.

Then one day I met the One my grandmother went home to meet and the Friend my mother sang about as she did her work. He became my Friend, my Savior and my Lord. From that day, 40 years ago, my songs have been sung to Him and about Him. Many beautiful and wonderful experiences have been mine as I sang my song to Him.

Now, 40 years and 35 or more songs later, I still enjoy speaking, singing and writing of the "one I love."

DELORES TAYLOR

Why We Fail

But I have prayed for you, Simon, that your faith may not fail. And when you have turned back, strengthen your brothers (LUKE 22:32).

We can easily identify with Peter in his failure. His trembling denial that he knew Jesus reminds us of some of our failures. Have we noted the similarity in the cause of his failure and our own? When he should have been praying for strength, he was sleeping.

Luke tells us that Jesus went often to the Mount of Olives to pray. His disciples were not disturbed by this but by some of the things He had been telling them. Exhausted by sorrow, they slept while He prayed. He came from the experience strengthened; they remained weak.

Most of us have felt the exhaustion of sorrow or of frustration. We tend to take a sleeping pill and try to rest. We do not hear Jesus' words of warning any more than the disciples did. The enemy knows when we are weak. He chooses that particular time to try us. Like Peter, we are not aware of our vulnerability, and we trust that rest will do what only prayer can really accomplish. Then we wonder why we fail the test.

There is comfort in knowing that Peter's failure was not the end of his ministry. During those dark days of self-reproach and remorse, how he must have clung to his Master's words, "I have prayed for you that your faith may not fail."

When we fail, we have the assurance that Jesus is praying for us. Our sincere confession of failure brings restoration, renewed fellowship and opportunity for service. He wants to turn us back from those failures and use us to strengthen others.   LINDA MCKELVEY

DECEMBER 19

Something or All?

He poured out his life unto death, and was numbered with the transgressors (ISAIAH 53:12).

I have a friend who is very active in the Lord's work. He is the president of a Christian organization, pastor of a local church, leader of a youth group and, at the same time, is quite involved in social work.

One day as we talked, I asked him why he was involved in so many things. His answer was, "Many years ago, a pastor said to me, 'Young man, should we just do *something* for the One who has done it *all* for us?' That question struck deeply in my heart, and from that time on I have committed my life completely to Christ."

Isaiah 53 gives us a small glimpse of what Christ has done for us.

- He was despised and rejected.
- A man of sorrows, He was familiar with suffering.
- He took up our infirmities and sorrows.
- He was pierced for *our* transgressions and crushed for our iniquities.
- His punishment was the price of our peace; His wounds provided our healing.
- Our iniquity was laid upon Him.
- He was cut off from the land of the living for the world's sin.

Since Christ has done *all* so that we "may have life, and have it to the full" (John 10:10), should we then use that life, which was bought at such a price, to please ourselves? Should we not show our gratitude by doing something for Him? Surely we can do nothing less than give our *all* to Him. Even then, it is too little when compared to what He has done for us.

MINH THI

I Believe It

Everything is possible for him who believes (MARK 9:23).

A friend of mine died today. It had been some time since we talked and laughed over a hot fudge sundae or went shopping. I had not seen her for several days, and on that last occasion I had done all the talking. Whitney had been in a coma. But now she was gone—freed from her silent prison. I had honestly believed that she knew when I was there. I believed she was aware of things that were said and done. Most of all, I guess, I believed that Whit was putting forth every effort she could.

Now I am not sure. Had she really received the extensive brain damage they said she had? Did she just plain give up? But I want to believe that Jesus said, "Let's go home. You've had enough." And I do believe it, and believing it, I have peace.

When a dream dies or a relationship ends or a close friend passes on, we like to think there was a purpose. We want to know all the reasons. We would like to have all our questions answered. Sometimes we strive and struggle and bend every effort. Maybe we give up. Maybe Jesus intervenes and says, "Let's move on." I want to believe that God miraculously works in our lives. And I do believe it. And believing it, I am at peace.   PAM BERTOLET

DECEMBER 21

Does He Care?

Cast all your anxiety on him because he cares for you (1 PETER 5:7).

Does Jesus care?" The refrain of that old hymn has filtered through my mind and heart, and over the years, I have laid claim to its message many times.

The Scripture tells us of several occasions when Jesus wept over things that were dear to Him. When He came to the tomb of Lazarus, we are told that Jesus wept. (John 11:35).

At another time, Jesus looked out over Jerusalem and wept because of the people's sin and failure to receive Him, God's remedy.

Hebrews tells us that we have a loving and tender high priest. "For we do not have a high priest who is unable to sympathize with our weaknesses" (4:15). When our children hurt, we hurt. Would Jesus, who loves us more than we could ever love our children, then be unmoved by our cares and sorrows?

Each verse of this lovely old hymn, written over 50 years ago by Frank Graeff, has served the church well in reminding us that the sympathizing Jesus offers strength and comfort.

> Does Jesus care when my heart is pained
>> Too deeply for mirth or song.
> As the burdens press, and the cares distress,
>> And the way grows weary and long?
>
> Oh, yes, He cares, I know He cares,
>> His heart is touched with my grief;
> When the days are weary, the long night dreary
>> I know my Savior cares.

VIRGINIA CUTHRIELL

God's Love

We love because he first loved us (1 JOHN 4:19).

Some time ago I read a story about a widow who, when taking her infant son across a mountain to visit relatives, was caught in a sudden fierce storm. The next day her body was found. Most of her clothing had been removed and wrapped about her baby, who was sheltered quite safely in a nook.

Years later, the son of the minister who had conducted the mother's funeral went to Glasgow to preach. Somehow he felt led to repeat the story he had so often heard his father tell.

A few days later, the minister was called to the bedside of a dying man. "You do not know me," said the man. "I have never attended a church, but the other day I happened to pass your door as it began to snow. When I heard singing, I slipped into a back seat, and there I heard the story of the widow and her baby son." The man paused, and weeping he said, "I am that son. I never forgot my mother's love, but I never saw the love of God in giving Himself for me until now. My mother did not die in vain. Her prayer is answered."

If we as Christians would continually focus our minds on the love of God and realize what that love really means, it would put an end to our selfish living. The old gospel song by F.M. Lehman says it so well:

> The love of God is greater far,
> > Than tongue or pen can ever tell;
> It goes beyond the highest star,
> > And reaches to the lowest hell.

HAZEL HIERS

Christmas Gems

I am the Root and the Offspring of David, and the bright Morning Star (REVELATION 22:16).

Someone once said to me, "You should not have a Christmas tree in your home, for it does not honor Jesus Christ." I began to think about why we did (and still do) have a beautifully decorated and lighted tree in our home and why it was so much a part of our holiday celebration.

The treetop *star* reminds me of the star that guided the wisemen to Jesus (Matthew 2:2), and of Jesus Christ Himself who is the "bright and Morning Star" (Revelation 22:16). Thank You, Lord, for the Star!

The *lights* tell me that Jesus Christ is the "true light" (John 1:9), who came into the world to shine in our hearts to "give us the light of the knowledge of the glory of God" (2 Corinthians 4:6). Thank you, Lord, for the Light of the world who lives in my heart!

The different *ornaments* remind me of the ornaments with which Jesus Christ desires me, His child, to be adorned—a meek and quiet spirit (1 Peter 3:4); good works that glorify my Heavenly Father (Matthew 5:16); love, joy, peace, patience and gentleness (Galatians 5:22–23). The ornaments are prettiest when they reflect the lights that shine on them. So, too, only as I live my Christian life controlled by the Holy Spirit who lives within me, can I reflect Jesus Christ to those with whom I come in contact.

As we decorate our tree this year, I will again be reminded of the faithfulness of the *star* who lives within my heart, and no matter what the situation or circumstance in which I find myself, His promise in Second Corinthians 12:9 is forever true: "My grace is sufficient for you."

YVONNE DAVEY

God with Us

The virgin will be with child and will give birth to a son, and they will call him Immanuel — which means, God with us (MATTHEW 1:23).

Why did Jesus leave heaven to come to earth? Such love defies reason or logic. Only God could have thought of such a plan, and only God's Son could have carried it out.

We cannot even guess what it involved for Jesus to put on humanity with all its temptations, problems and weaknesses. His willingness to come to earth to save sinful humanity is inconceivable.

There are many times when the trials and sorrows of this life are overwhelming. Loved ones fall prey to disease and pain and death. Friends turn against each other. Those who once followed the Lord now have no desire for the Word or for the house of God. Life's painful burdens cause us to cry out, "O Lord, when are You coming to take us out of all of this? How could You have left heaven for this?"

The Word tells us, "For your sakes he became poor, so that you through his poverty might become rich" (2 Corinthians 8:9). Jesus left heaven and became a man. He suffered pain in His body, shed tears at the loss of a loved one, knew the hurt of being forsaken by friends and died in shame on a cross. Why did He agree to do this? Not only so that we might have forgiveness from sin but that in time of need His loving presence would be our comfort. "His name shall be called Immanuel — God with us."   JUDY FREELAND

Advent Light

In the beginning was the Word, and the Word was with God, and the Word was God. . . . The Word became flesh and lived for a while among us (JOHN 1:1, 14).

When I felt the plodding
rhythm of a depressed mood
that a minor musical key often
creates, I realized that an
old hymn, originally recorded
in Latin during the ninth
century, was pacing through
my head at a plod of a 4/4
beat. The song:

"O Come, O Come, Emmanuel!"

Outside my window, repetitive
rain drips . . . . and
I know that the miracle of the
son is trying to renew His joy
and love of re-creation in me
and in *you*. "Rejoice! rejoice! Emmanuel
shall come to thee, O Israel!

ERNESTINE M. SCHINDLER

Wherever You Lead

He will cover you with his feathers, and under his wings you will find refuge; his faithfulness will be your shield and rampart (PSALM 91:4).

Hot tears of pain and soul anguish escaped from tightly closed eyes as I recalled the doctor's words to the nurse that morning. Thinking I was not able to hear, he had said, "Has anyone notified her husband? There is nothing more we can do." I thought of my husband and four children, each suffering my pain in his or her own private way. "Oh, God, they need me to be well even more than I do!"

I had taken seriously the responsibility of being a good mother to the children God gave us and a worthy wife to God's man. "How can You now ask me to leave these whom You have given me to care for, my Father?"

My reverie was interrupted by the shrill ring of the phone. A woman from our congregation had been praying for me and felt impressed to call. She shared a Scripture verse, "Can a mother forget the baby at her breast and have no compassion on the child she has borne? Though she may forget, I will not forget you! See, I have engraved you on the palms of my hands" (Isaiah 49:15–16).

Sobbing now, I hung up the phone. Contrite, I approached the Lord and reaffirmed my faith in Him and my love for Him. I seemed to sense the still small voice of the Lord. "Dear one, do you not yet know that it is you that I want. I know that you have given your loved ones to Me, but you have kept back yourself. As you long for them, I long for you." In the stillness I bowed my heart in the presence of Almighty God and, for the first time in my 30 years of Christian living, made a *full* and complete surrender. *Whether in life or in death, He is Lord!*　　SUSAN BLISS

DECEMBER 27
Daily Strength

It is God who arms me with strength and makes my way perfect (2 SAMUEL 22:33).

Each new day dawns with its own problems, vitality-sapping duties, upsetting emergencies and unexpected encounters. The question is, how to get through it victoriously and still be able to stand. The answer is found in over 237 places in God's Word.

Peter says that it is the God of grace who will make us *strong*, firm and steadfast (1 Peter 5:10). Our gracious Father says over and over, "I will strengthen you," (Isaiah 41:10). He further adds, "I will strengthen them in the Lord and in his name they will walk" (Zechariah 10:12). When the battle is fierce and our enemy seems to be getting the upper hand, He reminds us, "My grace is sufficient for you, for my power is made perfect in weakness" (2 Corinthians 12:9), and "your strength will equal your days" (Deuteronomy 33:25).

If we are still not convinced, we find that "The God of Israel gives power and strength to his people" (Psalm 68:35). He will be the "stronghold" of our life (Psalm 27:1).

Is it any wonder that the psalmist cried out, "Sing for joy to God our strength" (Psalm 81:1). "Trust ye in the Lord for ever: for in the Lord Jehovah is everlasting strength" (Isaiah 26:4, KJV). Because we have this assurance, we are able to go "from strength to strength" (Psalm 84:7).

As we face each day, we may put on His strength and join David as he sings, "The Lord is my strength and my shield" (Psalm 28:7). Moreover, we are ready to face with confidence whatever the day may bring, for we have this assurance: "I can do everything through him who gives me strength" (Philippians 4:13). MARJORIE E. JONES

Lost People

And even if our gospel is veiled, it is veiled to those who are perishing. The god of this age has blinded the minds of unbelievers, so that they cannot see the light of the gospel of the glory of Christ, who is the image of God (2 CORINTHIANS 4:3–4).

While we were missionaries in Japan, we were having a series of evangelistic meetings in a large tent and had felt the oppression of the powers of darkness. After the service one evening, the Lord laid the following thoughts on my heart:

I stood before lost souls today,
Souls bound by sin, held in Satan's power—
No hope within.

I looked from face to face to seek
Some trace of joy or peace—
But none could find.

My heart was crushed,
For these were souls whom Jesus died to save!
My heart cried out—
"Oh, God, if only I could believe for these,
That they might live!"

The answer came: "It cannot be—
But I can live my life through thee.
Prevailing prayer in Jesus' name
Will set these captives free;
I have no other plan!"

HELEN G. MCGARVEY

My Tribute

How can we sing the songs of the Lord while in a foreign land?
(PSALM 137:4).

The captive Hebrew singers sat beside the rivers of Babylon and wept as they remembered how life had been in their homeland. Their enemies tormented them, demanding that they sing happy songs of Zion. But the Hebrews were so discouraged that they ceased singing and hung their harps on a willow tree.

I awakened on a Sunday morning eagerly looking forward to being in the house of the Lord. Instead I was taken to the local hospital. My good health was shattered overnight. A CAT scan had revealed a brain tumor, and I became a captive in a strange land. I ceased singing my songs of praise and "hung up my harp."

Early the next morning, a young couple visited me. Joseph anointed me and prayed for my healing. Janet read a letter of praise and encouragement that I had written to her six years earlier when she faced the decision of whether or not to have an abortion to save her life. (She chose to trust God and delivered a perfect baby boy!)

I was sent home for 30 days and then went back for more tests to determine the prognosis. The CAT scan indicated that the tumor was half the original size and was no longer a problem. The new diagnosis was multiple sclerosis.

Once again I was tempted to stifle my song, that is, until I discovered El Shaddai, the All-sufficient One, who is always with us.

You will not find my harp on any willow tree. It is accompanying my songs of praise — *I will praise you, O Lord, with all my heart; . . . When I called, you answered me; you made me bold and stouthearted* (Psalm 138:1, 3).　　　RUTH LUCAS

DECEMBER 30
Sufficient Grace

My grace is sufficient for you, for my power is made perfect in weakness (2 CORINTHIANS 12:9).

One of my favorite people was a tiny, energetic missionary in the southern Philippines — Annetta Holsted, our language supervisor. But more than that, she was an excellent role model because of her love for the Filipinos and her devotion to prayer and the reading and memorization of Scripture.

After we had completed our two years of language study, Annetta returned to the United States for a year of furlough and, in God's providence, was near enough to New York City to be on hand when we were evacuated from the Philippines for a medical emergency. Both our two-year-old daughter, Debbie, and my husband, Bob, (in the same year the Salk vaccine was released) had contracted polio.

After the ambulance ride from the airport to the hospital, I was driven to the missionary guest house. Completely exhausted from the 36-hour trip, I turned our two other children over to my parents and started down the hall to the bedroom to get some rest. Down that hallway came Annetta. She put out her arms to me and said these words, "The Lord has given me a message for you: 'Grace is better than healing.'"

At the time, I did not realize the importance of the message and even wondered what it meant. But years later when Debbie returned to the Philippines as a missionary, Annetta's words came back to me with full force. In the midst of the most difficult circumstances, it is possible to experience the full measure of God's grace and peace in our lives, trusting Him to use our weakness to further His kingdom.   MARJORIE COWLES

Only a Guest

For I am thy passing guest, a sojourner, like all my fathers. (PSALM 39:12b RSV, Harper's Study Bible).

Three months after the moving van had carried our furniture and other posssessions to another house, I had not finished unpacking. Leaving "Bethesda," the large home traditionally occupied by the college president's family, and moving across town was unsettling. And 14 weeks later, even waiting for new carpet could not hide the stacks of boxes. I was grateful to have the packing behind me but longing to build a new nest.

As I was reading in the Psalms, one phrase caught my attention — a phrase that accurately expressed my state. It took on new meaning to view myself as a guest. "I'm cared for as I stop over in this world," I mused. With conviction I reminded myself that this is a transitory existence.

Carpet is now laid and boxes are unpacked. Yet that moment of truth has corrected some natural tendencies. Though provision has been made by the Creator and Sustainer of the whole universe for the "guest stay" of His creatures, He counsels me to remember that I am "passing."

Our natural desire for permanence is always evident as we resist change. It is quite evident in the popular trend toward owning one's home and putting down roots. Unlike the majority who are very much at home in this world, we know that our place and our home is in heaven. As Paul expressed it, "As long as we are at home in the body, we are away from the Lord" (2 Corinthians 5:6).

When I become encumbered with the baggage of life, I hope to repeat with gratitude my true state of being — I am but a "passing guest."   RUTH RAMBO

INDEX

Abrams, Elizabeth 9/11, 11/13
Albrecht, Beverly 8/10, 9/5
Albright, Donna 7/30
Allen, Arliss 6/21, 7/13, 8/14
Ammerman, Lillie 6/1
Andrews, Leslie 9/16
Andrianoff, Jean 5/5
Anonymous 3/11
Arnold, Elizabeth 4/13
Arnold, Florence 11/18
Bailey, Helen 9/27
Baker, Janet 2/13
Banks, Jeanne 2/5
Barker, Barbara 5/30
Barkman, Merlyn 1/3
Barr, Arbutus 6/7
Beale, Pauline 11/4
Becktel, Donna 5/27
Bedford, Curtiss 5/29
Berkner, Maurine 3/22
Berreth, Eleanor 10/1
Bertolet, Pam 9/14, 10/14, 12/20
Blight, Shelva 1/16
Bliss, Susan 5/31, 7/23, 12/26
Block, Mary 4/16
Bollback, Evelyn 3/1
Boon, Beverly 1/13
Bowman, Ruth 4/1, 7/5
Bozeman, Fran 1/28
Brodeen, Judi 3/20
Brown, Audrey 6/19
Brown, May 6/24, 7/10
Brown, Myra 8/15
Bubna, Deloris 5/25
Bubna, Jean 7/1
Burns, Delores 2/10
Bush, Carolyn 7/21, 12/15
Buss, Martha 4/15
Carneff, Joyce 10/31, 11/15
Carter, Gloria 3/28
Cartmel, Beatrice 4/3
Cathey, Astrid 2/6, 3/7
Catto, Mary 3/30, 4/29

Chapman, Judy 3/25
Clark, Ruth 10/30
Coffey, Joan 12/14
Coggins, Jane 5/13
Collmus, Melinda 5/24
Constance, Helen 5/18
Cooley, Louise 10/15
Corby, Fran 11/21
Cowles, Debbie 4/5, 6/28, 7/6, 10/22
Cowles, Marjorie 12/30
Crimm, Helen 8/3, 9/28, 11/5
Cummings, Margaret 7/9
Cuthriell, Virginia 8/16, 10/19, 12/21
Cutrer, Evelyn 7/4, 8/11, 8/29
Cutts, Gracie 2/19
Damron, Eleanor 6/5
Davey, Yvonne 7/17, 8/9, 12/5, 12/23
Davidson, Evangeline 2/22
Davis, Ruth 6/10, 9/3
Dibble, Gladys 11/8
Dirks, Donna 4/14
Dittmar, Sally 6/8
Dodge, Ella Mae 10/26
Droppa, Ann 10/8
Dummer, Beth 1/12, 3/17, 4/9
Dunlap, Mary 4/12
Eagen, Phyllis 5/26
Entz, Muriel 3/27, 4/22
Epperson, Anne 1/22
Esparza, Kate 2/16
Evans, Helen 9/13
Ferrell, Dona 2/14, 3/15
Field, Elois 8/28
Field, Faith 4/10
Finnemore, Diane 10/16, 11/26
Fitzstevens, Esther 1/26
Fraser, Lucille 1/7
Freeland, Judy 5/22, 6/30, 8/4, 12/24
Fustey, Pearl 8/7, 9/8, 9/23, 10/27, 11/23

Gaines, Martie 9/25
Gaither, Gloria 2/9
Gangel, Betty 7/11
Gardner, Elaine 1/31
Gardner, Norma 11/2
Garrick, Helena 4/27
Gluck, Lois 10/23
Groeneweg, Wanetta 4/18
Hadley, Doris 7/12
Hall, Penelope 3/21
Hammer, Denise 6/9, 8/17, 11/14
Hampton, Barbara 2/3
Hancock, Maxine 2/4, 3/5
Havener, Kitty 6/4
Hart, Norma 4/28
Hartley, Sherry 7/15
Harvey, Dorothy 10/10
Hazlett, Vernice 6/2
Hendrickson, Beverly 9/9, 11/11
Henley, Jeanette 7/14
Henry, Svea 3/8
Hiers, Hazel 6/27, 12/22
Hineman, Marie 7/7
Hixson, Mary 4/21
Hobbs, Anne 9/18
Holton, Florence 12/13
Hoover, Ruth 9/22, 11/24, 12/2
Hotalen, Jean 1/2
Humbard, Maude Aimee 11/12
Hunt, Betty 5/7
Hunt, Carroll 9/30
Huttar, Ethel 4/6, 7/3, 8/30
Irish, Carolyn 10/9
Irvin, Darolyn 10/18
Jackson, Elizabeth 1/11
Jacobs, Joy 10/12
Jacobson, Dana 1/8
Jacox, Sue 6/20
Johnson, Ida 1/21
Jones, Janet 6/23, 11/27
Jones, Marjorie 12/27
Julian, Helen 10/5, 11/6
Kadle, Mary 5/10
Kaiser, Alia 6/13

Keidel, Marian 12/7
Kelly, Muriel 5/1
Kendall, Sharon 4/4, 9/26
Kerr, Marion 12/10
King, Esther 1/1
Klinepeter, Ruth 2/21
Knipe, Sally 7/29, 8/5
Kropp, Janice 3/24
LaFlamme, Aline 6/14
Lawrence, Judy 10/25
Lemon, JoAnn 4/24
Leonard, Charlotte 6/26
LeTourneau, Evelyn 5/17
LeTourneau, Louise 1/23
Lewellen, Ruth 3/14
Livingston, Claire 4/25, 5/4
Loh, Dorcas 7/2
Long, Lois 9/4
Lucas, Ruth 12/29
MacIntrye, Phyllis 2/24
Mains, Karen 8/19
Mangham, Evelyn 1/15
Mangham, Martha 1/25
Mangin, Beth 9/20
Mapstone, Edna 10/6
Marshall, Laura 6/29, 7/22, 8/22
Martin, Ruth 11/17
Martinez, Nancy 5/6
Mathison, Nancy 1/9
McDonald, Carol 5/14, 9/7
McGarvey, Helen 3/19, 4/20, 10/4, 11/22, 12/28
McGarvey, Irene 2/20
McGarvey, Mary 1/19
McGarvey, Nora 9/15
McGee, Virginia 1/24
McIlrath, Elsie 6/6, 7/19
McKelvey, Linda 7/20, 8/31, 12/9, 12/18
McKinney, Jeanne 6/25
McMaster, Connie 4/8
McNair, Rosalind 8/12, 10/17
McSpadden, Carol 8/20
Measell, Dorothy 3/3
Miller, Vera 9/10
Minter, Sandra 5/2, 11/1
Mitchell, Dori 11/20
Morris, Pauline 1/18, 5/9
Morrow, Diane 3/10

Multanen, Sue 2/2
Nabors, Lois 1/5
Nazeretian, Carol 11/10
Nehlsen, Jessie 8/25, 9/2
Nelson, Grace 2/27
Nguyen, Hoang 7/24
Nicholson, Wilda 2/15
Nielsen, Carol 10/11
Niles, Diana 11/3
Oster, Lois 8/18
Payne, Marian 12/8
Peace, Betty 7/25, 8/2, 12/11
Pease, Eleanor 1/27
Peterson, Elaine 2/1
Phillips, Betsy 7/16
Polding, Helen 2/18
Posey, Erma 8/26
Post, Mary 12/6
Raffloer, Jane 3/31
Rambo, Ruth 12/31
Reese, Pauline 1/17, 5/12
Reidhead, Marjorie 10/28
Renicks, Joyce 5/19
Rich, Suzanne 12/12
Roberts, Carol 6/12
Robertson, Dede 10/3
Rowett, Jean 5/28
Rupp, Margaret 3/23
Rychner, Evelyn 9/1
Sahlberg, Corrine 1/20
Sandell, Margaret 1/30
Schaefer, Barbara 4/26
Schaeffer, Edith 4/19
Schepens, Dona 4/11, 8/23
Schindler, Ernestine 8/6, 12/25
Schleh, Mildred 6/3
Schuler, Maryann 10/13, 11/7, 12/3
Schuller, Arvella 1/6, 2/8, 3/9, 4/7
Schwalm, Priscilla 6/15
Seckinger, Joyce 9/21, 11/25
Seller, Mary 3/2
Shamburger, Jean 8/13
Shepson, Dorothy 3/13
Short, Lee 3/6
Simpson, Vivian 2/29, 6/18
Smith, Connie 4/2

Smith, Marilyn 11/16, 12/1
Snyder, Esther 3/4
Solvig, Kathleen 3/29, 4/23, 6/16
Sorenson, Barbara 6/22
Speece, Harriet 6/11
Speer, Faye 2/25
Spier, Corabelle 8/24, 9/6
Spriggins, Halee 11/29, 12/4
Staub, Cora 7/31
Steiner, Rebecca 12/16
Stemple, Charlotte 1/4
Strecker, Joyce 5/21, 8/21, 11/28
Stimmel, Diana 9/19
Stringer, Betsy 5/8
Strong, Cindi 9/17, 11/30
Stumbo, Melba 1/10, 2/11, 11/9
Stirzaker, Irene 1/14
Sutton, Pauline 10/24
Swope, Yvonne 10/21
Sylvester, Marion 3/16, 4/17
Taylor, Delores 4/30, 5/3, 5/11, 5/16, 5/20, 6/17, 7/8, 7/18, 8/1, 8/8, 9/24, 9/29, 10/20, 12/17
Taylor, Laverne 2/17
Taylor, Miriam 2/12
Tewinkel, Rae 2/26
Thi, Minh 12/19
Thomas, Ruth 8/27
Thompson, Judy 10/2
Tompkins, Margaret 3/18
Timyan, Janis 3/12
Watrous, Ruby 7/28, 10/29
Weldon, Glenda 3/26
Westover, Phyllis 5/23
Wisley, Sandi 2/28
Woehr, Jean 9/12
Wolfe, Judy 5/15
Wolters, Jean 7/27
Wong, Nancy 11/19
Wood, Linda 2/7
Wyatt, Vivian 7/26
Young, Helen 10/7
Zacharias, Margaret 2/23
Zondervan, Mary 1/29